survey

DOCUMENTATION STANDARDS

Among other books by the same author:

Introduction to Computers
Decision Tables
Techniques for Direct Access
Computer Survival Handbook (with Susan Wooldridge)

DOCUMENTATION STANDARDS

—REVISED EDITION

Keith R. London

 New York 1974

Copyright © Mason & Lipscomb Publishers, Inc. 1974

Published simultaneously in the United Kingdom by Mason & Lipscomb Publishers, Inc. London, England.

All rights reserved. No part of this work covered by the copyrights hereon may be reproduced or used in any form or by any means—graphic, electronic, or mechanical, including photocopying, recording, or taping, or information storage and retrieval systems—without written permission of the publisher.

First Printing

Printed in the United States of America

Library of Congress Cataloging in Publication Data

```
London, Keith R
   Documentation standards.

   Edition of 1969 by M. Gray and K. London.
   Includes bibliographical references.
   1. Electronic data processing documentation.
I. Gray, Max. Documentation standards.  II. Title.
QA76.L574  1973          029.7           73-12155
ISBN 0-88405-052-1
```

Contents

Preface to Revised Edition · vii
Preface to Original Edition · ix

PART I: INTRODUCTION

1. Background to Data Processing Documentation · 1
2. Documentation in a Working Environment · 10

PART II: COMPONENTS OF DEVELOPMENT DOCUMENTATION

3. Analytical Documentation · 19
4. System Documentation · 32
5. Program Documentation · 94
6. Operations Documentation · 105
7. User and Management Aids · 114

PART III: SPECIAL TECHNIQUES

8. Recording Complex Logic · 121
9. Software Documentation Aids · 148
10. Documentation of Software Packages · 183

PART IV: CONTROL OF DOCUMENTATION

11. Development Documentation and Project Control · 193
12. The Documentation Library and Documentation Maintenance · 198
13. Development of Documentation Standards · 209

APPENDIXES

A. Indexed Glossary of Forms · 229
B. System Documentation Example—Composite Descriptive Forms · 233

Useful References · 249
Index

Preface to Revised Edition

Since the publication of the original edition of *Documentation Standards* in 1969, the general climate of data processing has changed and new techniques have come into prominence. Working with institutions, both academic and commercial, who have used the first edition, I have extended the scope of the book and reorganized the material. The task of revision has thus been one of building on top of the first edition while leaving the base unchanged.

One complete new part of three chapters has been added. One chapter deals with the documentation of conditional, complex logic (flowcharts and decision tables), which was treated in a rather fragmented way in the original edition. Another new chapter discusses the documentation requirements of packaged software. The third new chapter deals with automatic documentation aids, which are an increasingly used tool in systems development.

Some more general changes have been made to the content of the remainder of the book. These are principally the reorganization of some of the form descriptions (by placing them as appendixes rather than in the body of text), and incorporating more practical examples to support the general checklists.

The original preface has been retained because it still sums up the objectives and approach of this new edition.

Finally, I would like to acknowledge the help given by the many computer users, colleagues, and software companies, too numerous to list individually, who have participated in the research for this new edition.

Preface to Original Edition

The purpose of this book is to provide to data processing managers, supervisors, and analysts a practical guide for the design and implementation of a standard system of documentation for data processing.

The rate at which computerized information handling systems are being installed is overwhelming. Computers are now the rule rather than the exception in business organizations. As with any popular modern technology, a new thriving industry has been created, with its own terminology, its own job titles—and its own mystique. From the small beginnings of a computerized unit record installation, we have progressed to installations abounding in a multiplicity of job titles such as analyst—job/procedures/methods; systems—analyst/designer/engineer; programmer—coder/utility/maintenance/applications, and so on, with a proportionate abundance of controllers, supervisors, and managers.

With the greater degree of job specialization, the increase in complexity of hardware, the proliferation of programming languages, and the wider range of applications, the industry is facing a crucial communication problem: A greater volume of information of higher complexity passes among growing numbers of people of dissimilar backgrounds. In such a working environment, some attempt must be made to rationalize the information flow in the development of a data processing system. A state of anarchy (or near anarchy) would exist if each individual had to decide

- If he would record anything at all
- What information he would record at any one time in a development project
- What information he would supply to the next person in the development process
- The content, form, and level of detail of the information recorded

Obviously, there must be some agreed level of communication; essentially this must be a definition of who prepares what document, when, and how.

The primary objectives of this book are

- To define the purposes and types of documentation, and to assign responsibilities for preparatory review and approval of documentation
- To describe the role and content of documentation within systems development
- To show the importance of documentation in project control
- To emphasize the importance of documentation standards and to outline methods of developing these standards
- To outline a model documentation system

DOCUMENTATION STANDARDS

PART ONE

INTRODUCTION

CHAPTER 1

Background to Data Processing Documentation

This chapter presents a general background to the topic of data processing documentation by providing basic definitions and a discussion on the purposes and types of documentation that are commonly recognized. Based on the background framework presented in this chapter, a detailed presentation of various document types will be given. The chapter concludes with a general summary and a description of the layout of the book.

DEFINITIONS

For the purposes of this book, data processing documentation can be defined as an organized series of descriptive documents relating to all aspects of systems development and operation. A document is further defined as a written record of the completion of a phase of work. Within the broad definition of documentation as given above, a further breakdown of types of documentation may be made. Basically documentation may be categorized into *development documentation* and *control documentation.* Development documentation is descriptive of a system itself, i.e., a system's operating performance characteristics, tools, and materials. Development documentation is therefore the means of communicating information *about the system.*

Control documentation, on the other hand, is concerned with communicating information *about resources used to develop the system*; it is therefore primarily concerned with project development organization, with personnel, time, materials, and money.

PURPOSES OF DOCUMENTATION

The purposes of documentation may be categorized into

- Inter-task/phase communication

- Quality control and project control
- Historical reference
- Instructional reference

Inter-Task/Phase Communication

It has long been recognized that poor or inadequate communication among personnel is a major problem area. For example, a user (i.e., the service or operating department) advocating a new system or a change to a system has an idea he must communicate to a systems analyst. The systems analyst will communicate with many user personnel during the investigation and analysis of the problem area. The systems analyst must in turn communicate the program requirements to the programmer, who must specify how the computer operators must run the program, and so on. Invariably, without adequate documentation, as in the old "telephone game," the initial idea from the user becomes distorted, the final product bearing little relation to the original intention. Planned standard documentation intends to eliminate this element of distortion by permitting the orderly communication of ideas from one project phase to another.

At a lower level, standard documentation facilitates good communication between project personnel engaged in the same phase of activity. The assignment of personnel can be a great problem area. First there is the perennial data processing employee turnover syndrome. Various estimates have given the average length of stay for programmers as being in the order of 14 to 16 months. In this environment, planned standard documentation would reduce the impact of staff turnover. The changing business climate and a temporary "data processing recession" may reduce the turnover of staff in the short term. However, there is some evidence to show that system development projects, wider in scope than in the early days of data processing, are taking longer to complete. Coping with staff turnover to insure continuity on a project thus still presents a problem.

A more pressing problem in some companies is flexibility of personnel assignment whereby staff may be reassigned to another project before completion of their own (to make use of special skills and requirements). This can only be achieved effectively if there is the minimum of disruption in task turnover. In one company which had used computers for over 12 years, for example, an analyst or programmer who worked on the initial development of a system would be permanently assigned to the maintenance of that system. This was because the original documentation was so poor (nonexistent in many cases) and was never maintained as systems changes were effected anyway. By the time the company was changing to a new, third-generation computer the data processing department was almost collapsing. The management were unhappy because new staff had to be recruited to deal with new development work, with the result that the installation was grossly overstaffed. The majority of the technicians were unhappy because they were grossly underutilized and bored with working with the same system for so long.

A major function of documentation is thus to insure that requirements are adequately communicated from phase to phase, and to insure project continuity despite staff changes.

Quality Control and Project Control

As in the manufacture or creation of any other product, the product of data processing development—the system—must be reviewed not only at implementation but also throughout its development. The only viable method of quality control review in development is to study and assess the product through its documentation as it proceeds from concept to general design and ultimately into operational form.

A good system of documentation specifies not only how information is to be recorded, but also when it is to be recorded. If the system of documentation specifies that documents are to be completed concurrently with tasks, the completion of a task is signified by the availability of the finalized documents. A review of completed documentation thus provides a means for assessing progress and points out inconsistencies between scheduled dates and actual dates. It will also provide for a current assessment of the amount of development work in progress.

A further aspect of standard documentation in this field is in the area of project control. Often data processing management is unable or finds it not feasible to provide regular supervision for the development of a particular system. Documentation describing a system at each step becomes almost indispensable, because it establishes design and performance criteria to be met during subsequent phases of project work. Using standard documentation, the programming or systems analysis supervisory function can constantly review work to insure that it meets all the requirements specified. Management can then limit its review to certain specific delineated project control points. Project control thus becomes a built-in function of documentation and provides a medium for the verification of the satisfactory completion of work performed.

This frees management from the "policing"-type role and also makes increased organizational control and discipline an inherent characteristic of the system development process.

Historical Reference

Documentation functions as a source for historical reference and the provision of a permanent record of work performed. Thus reference can be made for:

- Modifications and improvements to an existing system
- Drawing on past experience in the development of jobs similar to work that has been done before

A system or program is a dynamic entity—as businesses grow and strive to improve their operations, systems must be enhanced. Because of the various combinations and permutations of conditions in a program, one cannot always assume that a program has been adequately tested and is totally free from error. Therefore, it is evident that changes may be required after a system or program is in operation to insure that it continues to meet the needs of the business. Government legislation may require that a system, satisfactory in meeting the business needs of the company, be changed to meet new statutory requirements. The degree to which this happens depends both on the country and type of business. For example, in the United Kingdom there have been or will be changes for decimalization, metrication, value-added tax, income tax credits, and so on.

One of the most time-consuming activities for a programmer can be trying to understand a program that he coded sometime in the past or that another programmer coded. Nothing can be more frustrating to a programmer than to study the documentation of a program, to undertake to make changes on the basis of the information given in the documentation, and then to find that some prior changes have not been documented, thus invalidating the new changes. Adequate documentation, properly maintained, is a necessity for efficient system and program updates. Similarly, adequate documentation of programs previously developed is a necessity for the conversion of a system to new machines. Often, the logical flow of a system is independent of machine type. Common logical functions can be found on different machines or machine configurations; the differences lie in the manner in which the coded instructions cause machines to perform these functions. Therefore, the bulk of the work in a machine conversion is often in the recoding of the programs with a minimum of new systems analysis and of new program logic design.

The historical record provided by adequate documentation can serve as a valuable pool of experience in the development of future systems. Examination of the documentation of systems developed previously can prove valuable in the development of similar systems or systems which are expansions of existing processing. The main areas in which such a review could prove useful are system methodology, project control, and progress.

A common characteristic of initiating a systems development job is that a seemingly urgent need for a system turns it into a "rush job." The general result is that the actual design work for a job is begun too quickly, without adequate analysis and review of previous development work. A review of available information may reveal that previously developed data files can be used in the proposed system; the techniques and methodology used in one

Background to Data Processing Documentation 5

system may be suitable for application to a new system, thereby obviating the development of new techniques. The time criterion for early delivery takes precedence over the development of special, dedicated techniques. In the long run, therefore, the development of systems without adequate planning and review can be more costly and time consuming than if more time and resources were spent on the initial planning phase.

Obviously, where a proposed system interfaces with a previously developed system, it is vital to review the interaction between the two systems. This can only be satisfactorily achieved if the previously designed system is adequately documented.

In the area of project control and review, reference to progress records of similar completed projects can be useful for evaluating schedules and deadlines for a new project. Special problem areas discovered in previous development projects will enable special provision of time and resources to be made in anticipating similar situations on a new project.

During actual project work, comparisons can be made between the developmental stages of the present project and the comparable phases of previous projects as a form of assessing achievement and improvement. If the historical control documentation is adequate and has been sensibly reviewed, the setting and meeting of schedules and dates of past projects should certainly be improved in subsequent projects. This improvement should be especially significant if methodology and information used in existing systems is applied to new projects. Thus, the degree of efficient development of the new system over the previous system will be measured by the degree of improvement.

Instructional Reference

The last of the purposes of documentation is the use of documentation as an instructional device. We have seen that adequate documentation is essential if good communication is to be maintained between data processing personnel. It can also serve a general instruction function for communication between the data processing specialists and the nonspecialists, principally the users. In the modern environment of data processing, there is certainly no case for perpetuating the "closed circle" mystique of data processing. It is vital that users have a clear understanding of their system for only in such cases is it possible to establish good user relations and to enable the user to apply a system intelligently. This is best achieved by evaluating a minimum level of adequate documentation needed to inform the user about the application of his system.

Within the scope of the above discussion it is difficult to conceive of a data processing environment which does not recognize that the four purposes of documentation are axiomatic to its existence. Or that the six fundamental categories below are basic to the operation of any data processing department.

Yet such organizations do exist. Perhaps they exist in their present form because of the "rush-job" concept—do now, document later . . . but later never comes. Alternatively, perhaps such organizations exist because of the false economics of achieving short-term objectives. Experienced project personnel are constantly assigned to projects, the data processing manager is permanently tied down with budgetary problems or as arbitrator between users and thus no one can be spared for the task of reviewing documentation.

As observed in this chapter, documentation is the means to communicate; but how can any organization, data processing or otherwise, exist without a commonly agreed level of communication? Thus, adequate documentation is probably the primary contributing factor toward maximizing efficiency in a data processing installation. Similarly, the converse case of poor, uncoordinated documentation limiting efficiency also holds true.

TYPES OF DOCUMENTATION

Thus far, we have established some basic definitions and examined the primary purposes and objectives of establishing a planned system of adequate documentation. It is now possible to define the elementary types of documentation in relation to the various data processing tasks. Data processing documentation, as has been shown, serves many distinct functions; in addition, it can be categorized into six distinct applicational areas.

- Analytical
- System
- Program
- Operations
- User aids
- Management aids

A general summary illustrating the sequence of document preparation related to development workflow is given in Figure 2.1. Each of the types of documentation listed above is defined below. The relationship between these documents and the working environment is discussed in Chapter 2.

Analytical

Analytical documentation can be defined as that recording and reporting which must precede any systems design or programming work. Principally, it consists of a written and approved statement of the nature and objectives of the project. It may include:

- A user request stating the problem
- An evaluation of the feasibility of the requested system

- An estimate of development time and resources required
- A statement of the objectives and parameters of the proposed system

Simply, then, analytical documentation specifies *what* a system is to do and how it is to be developed.

System

System documentation encompasses all information needed to define the proposed data processing system to a level that it can be programmed, tested, and implemented. The major document is a system specification which acts as the permanent record of the structure, functions, flow, and control of the system. It is the basic medium of communication of information about the proposed system between the systems design, programming, and user functions. System documentation thus specifies *how* a system will operate.

Program

Program documentation comprises the records of the detailed logic and coding of the constituent programs of a system. It is prepared by the programmer and aids

- Program development and acceptance
- Trouble-shooting
- Program maintenance
- Machine conversion
- Programmer change-over

Program documentation covers both specific application programs and general purpose or in-house developed software. Documentation for the latter may require a special level of detail, but in principle, all program types would be covered by the same general rules of documentation.

Operations

Operations documentation specifies those procedures required for the running of the system by data processing operations personnel. It gives the general sequence of events for performing the job and defines precise procedures for

- Data control and security
- Data preparation
- Program running
- Output dispersal
- Ancillary operations

User Aids

User aids comprise all descriptive and instructive material necessary for the user to participate in the running of the operational system. They principally include instructions and schedules for the collection and preparation of data prior to submission to data processing operations, and explanatory notes on the content, review, and distribution of output material.

Management Aids

Management aids are that type of documentation which provides management with nontechnical instructive information. They enable management to evaluate the applicability of a system to a requirement and provide sufficient information to enable management to participate in the operational systems.

SUMMARY

1. Documentation is defined as the collection of reports relating to a complete system.

2. Two categories of documentation are recognized: development documentation, which records information *about a system*, and control documentation, which records information *about a system development project*. In this book, we are primarily concerned with development documentation.

3. Documentation has four main purposes:

- Inter-task/phase communication
- Quality control and project control
- Historical reference
- Instructional reference

4. The six basic classifications of documentation are

- Analytical
- System
- Program
- Operations
- User aids
- Management aids

ORGANIZATION OF THE BOOK

The next chapter in Part I of the book relates the classification of types of documents to the structure and general environment of the development

Background to Data Processing Documentation 9

organization. Part II presents a detailed analysis of the six types of development documentation as defined above, and relates them to a model documentation system. Part III describes special documentation situations: recording complex logic, using automatic (software) documentation aids, and documenting packaged software. Part IV describes the application of documentation in terms of establishing project control points, a documentation library, and methods of documentation maintenance.

CHAPTER 2

Documentation in a Working Environment

FACTORS DETERMINING DOCUMENTATION USAGE

Documentation is concerned with communication. The paths of communication in a data processing department depend on many factors, namely

- Management commitment
- Project characteristics (number, duration, and complexity) and the age of the installation
- The organization structure of the company as a whole, and of the data processing department within it
- The technical environment

Since all the above factors vary from data processing department to data processing department, it is obvious that there is no ideal universal set of documentation standards. The type and level of complexity of documentation for one location may be totally invalid in another environment. Each data processing department must therefore implement a documentation system which suits its own environment. Since it is often possible to adapt documentation from various sources, the impact of the above factors on documentation is discussed below.

Management Commitment

Management commitment is the degree to which management realizes the necessity for good documentation. It includes the time and resources that management is prepared to expend on developing and enforcing documentation standards. In general, therefore, the quality and completeness of documentation is directly affected by the extent to which management is commited to documentation.

Before embarking on a documentation standards program, it may well be necessary to first convince management of the importance of documentation. In some industries, particularly the service industries, projects are undertaken

Documentation in a Working Environment

on a "random" basis, subject only to client standards and approval. In these circumstances, management may find it difficult to understand why rigid standards of documentation are necessary. Other types of businesses may be more accustomed to good record keeping. In such cases, proper documentation standards in data processing would be more readily accepted.

The management commitment will of course influence the attitude of project personnel. Often, in the course of implementing a system, data processing management itself can often influence user management against documentation standards. The classic example of this is the two-choice approach: "We can implement the system in six months with documentation or four months without." The prospect of implementing rigid documentation requirements can raise cries of longer project times, as if adequate documentation were an expensive luxury. Management must thus be presented with the simple argument, "Can we afford *not* to document effectively?"

Project Characteristics and Installation Age

The amount and complexity of documentation is a function of the characteristics of the projects handled. The most influential characteristics are length of project development time and the size of project teams. In Chapter 1, one of the stated purposes of development documentation was that it could be used as a guide in assessing project progress. For projects of long duration, documentation must be created at all crucial stages of development. Thus, the greater the required level of documentation, the better the control over a lengthy project. Similarly, the larger the project team, the greater the need for an adequate level of documentation to facilitate ease of communication.

Projects of long duration or requiring large numbers of personnel therefore require more documentation than projects of shorter duration in order to maintain adequate control and good communication.

The importance, frequency of use, and life expectancy of a system are also influential factors in determining documentation requirements. A system which will be used only once or for a very limited period would not normally require the same level of documentation as a system intended for much longer use. In how many cases, however, does the "temporary" or "one-time" system become "permanent" or "many-time?" Will the "temporary" or "one-time" system form the basis for a more permanent solution? For example, if a program is developed on the assumption that its life would be limited, say, by the very nature of the application, extensive documentation would be unnecessary. Moreover, if the short life was based on organizational functions, such as equipment changes, then other aspects of the program documentation would need to be stressed. Emphasis would be placed on the development documentation showing program logic and methodology so that the program for the new equipment could be based on the techniques and logic in the temporary program.

As discussed in Chapter 1, computer systems are dynamic. Changes become necessary as users revise their requirements, new software or hardware techniques become available, and errors in the original system are discovered. These changes often begin to originate early in the development phase and continue throughout the life of the system. The area most susceptible to such changes is programming. The age of the installation will directly affect the type of systems development work. The older the installation, the greater the maintenance load. The younger the installation, the greater the emphasis will be on developing the basic record-keeping systems.

It is a reasonably safe assumption that changes to long-life programs are assured. These changes, whether they be for error correction or program enhancement, can only be properly implemented if there is adequate and well-maintained program documentation.

Not only is the number of data processing personnel on a project important; the number of users is also an influencing factor. If many people are to have access to a system, it would be of great importance to have very complete documentation. A system catering to few users would probably require a lesser degree of documentation detail.

Corporate Environment and Structure

At its simplest level, one of the most active influences on the level and type of documentation is the general working environment of the company and its organizational structure. A military installation with the general requirements for exact and complete documentation in minute detail would automatically require the same approach to data processing documentation. The requirements for documentation would also reflect the rigid, complex organization of command. On the same principle, a small general service industry with a loose system of documentation and/or reporting structure would have, without strong management, a loose system of data processing documentation.

Thus, a data processing organization with precisely defined job functions and a large number of personnel will require a greater level of documentation than a small, rather loosely organized unit.

Large companies with a number of decentralized data processing organizations, each with its own development capability, generally have an interchange of ideas among the organizations. Similar types of projects may be developed at various locations. Adequate documentation is invaluable if there is not to be a duplication of effort in developing like applications independently.

Finally, there is the internal organization of the data processing department itself. One of the major purposes of documentation is inter-task/phase com-

Documentation in a Working Environment

munication as described previously. The job functions and their assignment among personnel will thus be a major influence on the documentation system used.

A small company may use the programmer/analyst ("progalyst") approach in which one man does both systems and programming work. Some large companies have created five major positions (ignoring the management structure and grades within job):

- *Business Analyst:* an internal business/management consultant who works closely with the users on user requests and feasibility studies, etc.
- *Systems Analyst:* investigates user area in detail, analyzes system problems, produces system outline, aids system implementation, etc.
- *System Designer:* designs the new system (both computer and manual procedures) in detail.
- *Development Programmers:* responsible for all programming work during initial development work.
- *Maintenance Programmers:* responsible for all program changes after original system acceptance and implementation.

Although the basic documentation flow will probably be the same in these two installations, the actual detail (level, when prepared, etc.) will vary considerably.

Technical Environment

The technical environment is taken to be those factors which influence the manner in which project personnel work. Such factors are:

- Software and hardware available
- Level of technical competence
- Communication problems due to geographical distances

To a large extent, hardware is not a major influence on the type of level of documentation. Obviously, an installation using data transmission links or with a large ancillary support to the computer(s) will require more documentation than an installation with only one small computer configuration. The difference is thus in terms of volume rather than document types.

Similarly, the software environment does have some influence on documentation. Because of their similarity to the English language, high-level languages require less-detailed technical program documentation than low-level languages. Further, the form of the system documentation may be dependent on langauge used. For example, files may be specified at system design time in terms of the data-defining method of a specific langauge.

An installation using manufacturer-supplied application packages should be provided with at least outline documentation, which will include the specification of system parameters. Users will generally augment the manufacturer-supplied subroutines by specialized operational subroutines for their particular needs. These subroutines for general use must be described in detail if they are to be available to all programmers in an installation and possibly other installations.

DOCUMENTATION PREPARATION

It is necessary to establish a very generalized organizational structure and project development scheme on which the subsequent documentation types may be based. The first phase in a development project can be considered as Project Initiation comprising such tasks as these:

- Project selection
- Project authorization
- Planning
- Personnel assignment
- Estimating
- Scheduling
- Budgeting

This phase may be said to produce all or most of the analytical documentation. The next phase is Project Fulfillment, covering systems design work and programming.

The systems design tasks will produce systems documentation, some data processing operations documentation, and user and management aids. The programming work results in the preparation of programming documentation and some operations documentation (i.e., computer operating instructions). The final phase, Project Conclusion, includes conversion and a postimplementation audit; in effect, no development documentation is produced, but the validity of the current documentation is checked. The overall sequence of documentation preparation in terms of a systems development project is shown in Figure 2.1.

SUMMARY

1. There are no universal documentation standards which are directly applicable to all installations.
2. Documentation must thus be developed for individual installations.

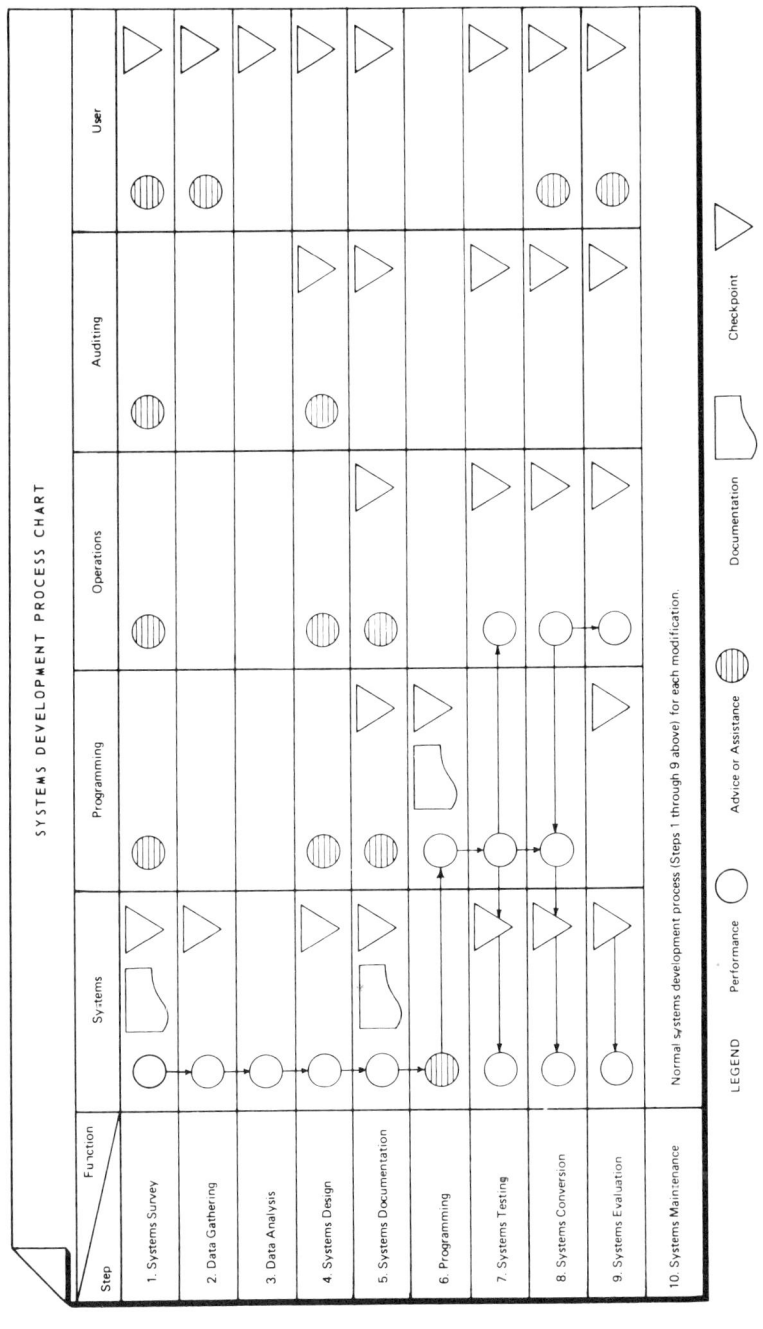

FIGURE 2.1 Sequence of Document Preparation in a Systems Development Project

This can be done by adopting general documentation systems, such as the one presented in this book, to local conditions.

3. The development of a documentation system for a particular data processing organization must take account of the major influencing factors, which are

- Management commitment
- Project characteristics and the age of the installation
- Corporate environment and structure
- Technical environment

PART TWO

COMPONENTS OF DEVELOPMENT DOCUMENTATION

CHAPTER **3**

Analytical Documentation

At the beginning of a development project, prior to the commencement of actual development work, a written and approved statement defining the proposed project should be prepared. Analytical documentation serves this function by stating the nature, objectives, and evaluation of the requested work.

The suggested analytical documentation presented in this chapter is composed of these documents:

- User Request
- Systems Proposal
- Analytical Report
- Design Requirements Statement

although, as explained below, the Systems Proposal, Analytical Report, and Design Requirements Statement present three different approaches. Before considering each of these documents in detail, it is first necessary to define the general relationship between them.

The User Request defines the problem area in outline and presents a formal notification that data processing assistance is required. The Systems Proposal is a preliminary description of the problem, the problem environment, and a proposed approach to a problem solution. It thus includes a feasibility analysis. The Analytical Report is a detailed description of the project, i.e., responsibility allocation, resource requirements and project schedules. The Design Requirements Statement is a detailed description of the objectives and parameters of the proposed system for the subsequent system development work.

To summarize the purposes of the four documents:

1. User Request
   - initial problem definition and request for data processing assistance
2. Systems Proposal
   - further problem definition and solution feasibility analysis

3. Analytical Report • definition of project work required to implement selected solution
4. Design Requirements Statement • detailed specification of the selected solution for subsequent development work (i.e., systems design et al.)

Thus the User Request and Systems Proposal are used to establish a project and as such form an agreed method for communication between user and data processing personnel. The Analytical Report and Design Requirements Statement perform a similar function, but by defining what is to be done and how it is to be done, they additionally form an agreed method for communication between the system analysis and project planning functions, and between the system design and subsequent functions.

In practice, the User Request and at least an outline Analytical Report are almost always required. Generally, the Systems Proposal and Design Requirements Statement are only produced for major development projects or for extensive system modifications.

The degree of detail presented in these documents will depend on the complexity of the problem and the amount of new development work required. For example, most one-time reports produced from existing data sources in previously implemented systems may require the production of a full User Request and limited Analytical Report only. On the other hand, the design and creation of a complete new system or major new file in an existing system may require the production of all four reports in detail.

The remainder of this chapter describes the purpose, contents, and use of the four analytical documents. Note, however, that the types of documents prepared and the actual sequence of preparations depend on the organization structure and assignment of responsibilities in a particular installation. To show the use of the documents in relation to a working environment, the following is a brief description of the "traditional" process flow.

1. Informal discussion between user management and data processing management.

2. Submission of User Request by the user, probably prepared with systems analysis assistance to ensure completeness.

3. Initial review of User Request and assignment of analyst effort to prepare Systems Proposal, *if required*. Note that the Systems Proposal may be a major task, requiring a thorough investigation of a major applicational area. The Systems Proposal is thus *problem* oriented and will form the basis for the subsequent project-oriented Analytical Report.

4. Submission of Systems Proposal and evaluation of project feasibility.

5. Analytical Report prepared by systems analysis function covering the area specified in the User Request or, if prepared, Systems Proposal. Note

Analytical Documentation

that the Analytical Report may be prepared directly after the discussion of the User Request, (3) above. This would take place if the problem area is essentially local, noncomplex, and previously well defined. In effect, therefore, a brief Systems Proposal would be incorporated in the Analytical Report.

    6. If the project is to be undertaken, approve the outline specification in the Systems Proposal and Analytical Report and agree on outline schedules and costs.

    7. Prepare, *if necessary,* a Design Requirements Statement for the subsequent development work. Note that the description of a system approach given in the Systems Proposal may form a basis for the subsequent design work.

    8. Commence detailed project planning, e.g., schedules, resource allocation, budget controls forming the Project Plan.

USER REQUEST

The first formal approach to initiate a project is made by the submission of a *User Request*. This is prepared by the user, although for complex problems, assistance may be given by the systems analysis function to insure completeness. A list of standard items that should appear in the report is given below. To insure that all the required information is provided, consideration should be given to devising a standard form to guide nontechnical users. The provision of standard forms, however, is usually only necessary when significant volumes of requests are anticipated.

The start of a systems development project is an area which is sometimes too nebulous to formalize. In essence it is a review carried out by user management, possibly with business or systems analyst support. This can be viewed as a comparison of the corporate/divisional/department objectives with the existing environment. Environment in this case can mean the people, their jobs, the organization structure, plant, materials, information, systems and procedures, money, and so on. If the existing environment will not meet the objectives, then there is a problem; if that part of the environment which prevents the division or department from meeting its objectives can be identified, then the problem is defined. This is, of course, a very simplified view of project initiation. Continual pressure will be applied to user management to change and refine the objectives. The review may take place across department/divisional boundaries. The actual review procedure can rarely be formalized but it is very important to standardize the output from this task—the User Request.

The User Request may contain the following information:

- *Identification and Authority*—This is a clear identification of the proponent and states the authority for the request.
- *Problem Definition*—The Problem Definition contains a succinct statement of the problem. This generally includes:
  1. Objectives, Boundaries, and Constraints—a statement of the objectives of the work requested: what it will do, whom it will serve, how it is related to the current method (e.g., the report or process to be replaced or supported)
  2. Data Sources—the anticipated source of data
  3. Data Output—brief description of the output desired
  4. Timescale—the date by which the request is to be satisfied, together with other significant dates
- *References*—The content of this section will depend on local conditions; it may contain, for example, the persons to be contacted for further information or a list of attached or available studies or backup material of known or potential value to the systems analyst.

The degree of detail given in the problem definition will depend on the degree of familiarity of the user with data processing in general, with his applications in particular, and the amount of assistance provided by the systems analyst. For the production of a report on an existing system, for example, the user should be able to specify

- Report title
- Frequency, date of production, and effective date of content
- Title or headings desired
- Number of copies and distribution
- Sequence of items, and intermediate and final totals desired

For a new system or application, the report will probably be prepared largely by the systems analyst working in conjunction with the user because many major projects are initiated by the incentive data processing staff rather than the user.

SYSTEMS PROPOSAL

The *Systems Proposal* is a preliminary description of a proposed approach to the project. It is generally prepared by the systems analyst. The Systems Proposal is primarily a study of the problem environment; it is thus a review of current system philosophy and methods and requirements for the new system.

A document of this nature must be an optional document, since it will only be produced for a major project. The review of a total application area, for

Analytical Documentation

example, may represent a major project phase, especially if the system under consideration covers many areas of a company's operations. This review phase may be called the "systems survey." Obviously, the systems survey phase as such would not be required for projects of limited scope. In this case, the outline problem definition in the User Request would be adequate as a basis for future development work.

The content of the Systems Proposal may be summarized as follows. It contains

- The design approach
- Brief analysis of the present environment
- Plan and schedule for implementation

A sample list of contents is given below. This example shows the Systems Proposal at the highest level of detail, i.e., for a major development project as described above.

This example is based on a six-part document comprising

1.0 Introduction
2.0 Management Summary
3.0 Design Alternatives
4.0 Proposed System Description
5.0 Outline Implementation Plan and Schedule
6.0 Graphics and Appendixes

Essentially, the Introduction is a purely housekeeping section while the Management Summary summarizes the detail of the remainder of the report. Section 3, Design Alternatives, briefly describes all the possible approaches to "solving the problem." The Proposed System Description defines, in reasonable detail, the selected or, at this stage, the *recommended* approach to the solution. Section 5, Outline Implementation Plan and Schedule, describes how the recommended approach described in Section 3 may be implemented. The last section contains diagrams and supplementary information.

The Systems Proposal therefore presents a detailed system feasibility study.

Introduction

The *Introduction* consists of a summary of the conditions under which the systems survey was performed.

Scope of Study—the purpose, objectives, background and limitations of the study taken from the initial User Request.

Methods—the methods used in the systems survey and preparation of the Systems Proposal.

Premises and Assumptions—the basic ground rules or actions under which the study is conducted.

Management Summary

The *Management Summary* contains three categories of information

(a) Findings
(b) Recommendations
(c) Plan of Action

The *Findings* describes the current environment. A suggested breakdown is as follows:

Summary—a list of the strengths and weaknesses of the organization and procedures as related to the project.

Organization and Functions—present organizational and functional flowchart.

Present Systems—data processing systems: evaluation of their cost and effectiveness.

Present Systems—nondata processing systems: are they efficient, accurate, and meeting their requirements?

Information Requirements—definition of present and future information requirements.

Personnel—evaluation of the capability of staff to handle new system(s).

The *Recommendations* presents such information as

Information Requirements—system approach in terms of the criteria for purpose, e.g., short-range, intermediate-range, and long-range plans. The recommended information requirements are compared to the original requirements (e.g., as defined in the User Request).

Advantages and Disadvantages—the advantages and disadvantages of the proposed system are listed and compared to the existing or alternative systems in terms of

- Services
- Equipment and facilities
- Organization

Costs—a cost comparison, in the form of tables showing the following items for at least a five-year period

- Development cost of new system by kind of personnel, equipment used, and capital investments
- Operational costs of new system
- Costs of the present system (if applicable); for equipment and person-

nel per unit time, including anticipated system and program maintenance costs.

The rule for the presentation of any cost figures is "divide and rule." This means that summary figures are shown on the main table, with supporting tables (possibly to a number of different levels of detail) showing the derivation of the major entries.

The *Plan of Action* describes the recommended course of action based on the Recommendations given previously. It should include the following.

Management Action—the required management action in terms of

- Organizational and policy decisions
- Procedural changes
- Approval and starting date

Systems Development—a description of the tasks, with approximate schedule, for the system development process.

Equipment Consideration—any special comments on the loading of existing equipment or acquisition of new equipment.

Personnel and Training—a summary of personnel resources and deployment and the required training program.

Design Alternatives

A brief description of all solutions considered should be shown, and the advantages and disadvantages of each discussed.

Proposed System Description

The *System Description* is a narrative definition of the proposed system. There are many ways in which such a definition may be presented. In terms of the model system presented in the book, it is suggested that an overall summary be given showing the major functional activities. These major activities are then split down into a number of Systems Abstracts. Each abstract contains the following:

- Purpose
- Functions
- Data requirements
- Products
- Users

In conclusion, a summary of critical factors affecting the development of the overall system should be presented.

Outline Implementation Plan and Schedule

The *Outline Implementation Plan and Schedule* defines the tasks necessary to accomplish the recommended development work. Both data processing tasks and user participation should be listed, together with the estimated time. The anticipated elapsed time should be shown against significant project milestones. The task/time definitions should also be related to a summary resource schedule.

To establish efficient project control, a negotiated "freeze date" must be specified for system design work. Beyond this date, further changes requested by the proponent should be accepted *only with an accompanying revision in the implementation date.*

In a report of this complexity it should at least be possible to define an outline project task plan and schedule to the level of

- Data gathering and analysis: by major functional areas or by major files
- System design: by major function areas
- Programming: by review of system specifications
    1. software selection and design
    2. logic design
    3. coding
    4. testing
- Training, conversion, and implementation

In addition, a skeleton project review plan should be presented listing major project checkpoints and foreseeable management decisions.

Graphics and Appendixes

The appended materials contain any additional information that may be required.

We may at this point summarize the usage of the Systems Proposal. If it is known from information given in the User Request that the request can be met by minor program modifications and requires little or no systems design work, the Introduction, Management Summary, Proposed System Description, and Outline Implementation Plan and Schedule will usually be sufficient, the others being present in a limited form. However, care should be taken in assigning a request as a "routine local" amendment without prior investigation to establish the impact of the change (possibly unknown to the user) on the system as a whole.

The basic guiding factor in the preparation of the Systems Proposal is that it need only be as long as necessary to meet its purpose. That is, to present a complete and objective statement of problems and requirements upon which decisions can be based. It may be only one or two pages long or it may be a

Analytical Documentation

hundred. In some cases, major sections may be omitted or the sections may be further broken down into chapters and subsections. Further, as we shall see, the Analytical Report and Design Requirements Statement form alternatives to the Systems Proposal as a whole.

ANALYTICAL REPORT

The *Analytical Report* is primarily an alternative to a full Systems Proposal; it may be used, however, to supplement or replace part of a Systems Proposal. It defines the tasks, responsibilities, implementing instructions, and priorities for subsequent development work. It also includes schedules of resources (personnel and equipment) developed to provide the user with the requested support. As such, the Analytical Report in conjunction with the User Request may form all the necessary analytical documentation. Alternatively, local standards may require that an Analytical Report be produced to replace or supplement the Outline Implementation Plan and Schedule in the Systems Proposal.

A sample table of contents is shown in Figure 3.1. Note that it also contains (in Section 7—Background) some information on the evaluation of the system, subsystem, or modification. Where no extensive systems survey or feasibility analysis is made, i.e., no Systems Proposal is prepared, the section should contain sufficient information on project evaluation.

The degree of detail presented in the Analytical Report will depend on the characteristics of each project.

DESIGN REQUIREMENTS STATEMENT

The *Design Requirements Statement* states the objectives and parameters for the project; that is, for the system, subsystem, modification, file, report or file abstract, or additional computations. It serves two purposes, namely:

- To enable the user to agree to and approve the proposed changes
- To provide a positive specification for the subsequent development work

The Design Requirements Statement is prepared

- when no Systems Proposal is prepared, *and*
- the User Request and Analytical Report do not provide enough scope to describe the requirements in systems terms, *or*
- when it is required to supplement or replace Section 4, Proposed System Description, in the Systems Proposal

ANALYTICAL REPORT

Table of Contents

1.0 General Information

    1.1 Cover Page
    1.2 Table of Contents
    1.3 Glossary of Terms
    1.4 Glossary of Symbols
    1.5 Purpose

2.0 Administrative

    2.1 Project Team Structure
    2.2 Personnel Assignments
    2.3 D.P. Dept. Responsibilities
    2.4 Contractor Responsibilities

3.0 Principal Tasks

    3.1 Subject Matter Analysis
    3.2 DP Systems Analysis
    3.3 Data Management Analysis
    3.4 Programming
    3.5 Training
    3.6 Documenting

4.0 Staff Coordinating Instructions

    4.1 Customer Liaison
    4.2 Administrative Coordination
    4.3 D.P. Dept. Project Personnel coordination
    4.4 Contractor Project Personnel Coordination

FIGURE 3.1 Sample Table of Contents—Analytical Report

5.0 Priority

    5.1 Authority
    5.2 Definition
    5.3 Impact on Project
    5.4 Impact on Resources
    5.5 Recommendations

6.0 Schedules

    6.1 Development Tasks
    6.2 Administrative Reporting
    6.3 Documentation
    6.4 Training

7.0 Background

    7.1 Project/Task Library Search
    7.2 Technical Library Search
    7.3 Study and Development Recommendations
    7.4 Experience Requirements

FIGURE 3.1 Continued

DESIGN REQUIREMENTS STATEMENT

Table of Contents

1.0 General Information

    1.1 Cover Page
    1.2 Table of Contents
    1.3 Revision Page
    1.4 References (administrative, correspondence, etc.)

2.0 Objectives

3.0 System Criteria

    3.1 Problem Approach
    3.2 Method of Problem Solution
    3.3 System Capabilities
    3.4 Assumptions
    3.5 Limitations and Restrictions

4.0 Data

    4.1 Definitions
    4.2 Input Sources
    4.3 Output Distributions

5.0 Glossaries

    5.1 Terms
    5.2 Symbols

6.0 Bibliography

FIGURE 3.2 Sample Table of Contents—Design Requirements Statement

Analytical Documentation 31

A sample table of contents for the Design Requirements Statement is shown in Figure 3.2. The degree of detail shown in the Design Requirements Statement will depend on the characteristics of the project.

SUMMARY

1. Analytical documentation is that documentation resulting from the initial phase of a project which establishes the project prior to subsequent development work.

2. Four documents have been described

- User Request
- Systems Proposal
- Analytical Report
- Design Requirements Statement

3. The User Request is the initial approach from the proponent (i.e. the user) for data processing assistance. It contains a brief problem description.

4. The Systems Proposal is essentially a major report resulting from a systems survey. It may be considered as a feasibility report, including a detailed specification of the recommended approach and project plan.

5. The Analytical Report is essentially a project plan, supplemented as necessary with evaluation information.

6. The Design Requirements Statement is essentially a specification of requirements in systems terms.

7. One method of employing these documents is to prepare a User Request and a Systems Proposal. This would be necessary for a major project which required an exhaustive survey and feasibility analysis.

8. An alternative method is to use the User Request and an Analytical Report and/or a Design Requirements Statement.

CHAPTER 4

System Documentation

Detailed systems development begins after the project has been accepted as feasible and resources are allocated. That is, after the analytical documentation has been reviewed and agreed upon.

The scope of detailed systems development and the resources required for the work depends very much on the nature of the project. For example, developing a new computer-based system for an area of the company which has only manual procedures that have been in operation for many years will require considerable investigation and analysis before design can begin. Where the system to be developed is based on an existing relatively new (and well-documented) computer-based system, on the other hand, investigation and analysis will probably form only a small part of the project. The next major document produced will be the System Specification. This will be required for every project and is described later in this chapter. However, a considerable amount of *interim documentation* will be produced during systems development before the final Systems Specification. How much it is practical or even desirable to standardize such interim documentation depends on the installation and on project types within it.

SUMMARY OF INTERIM DOCUMENTATION

The steps in an example project are shown in Figure 4.1. This is typical of a major development project, going from an old manual (or semiautomated) system to a new computer-based system. The tasks are summarized below.

Planning: The prime inputs in this case are the System Proposal and Analytical Report. Together with background information (e.g., information gathered to support the System Proposal), these are used to plan the detailed investigation. The investigation, also known as data gathering or fact finding, will be an in-depth review of the existing environment and management's statements of their future information requirements. The output from this task is a series of

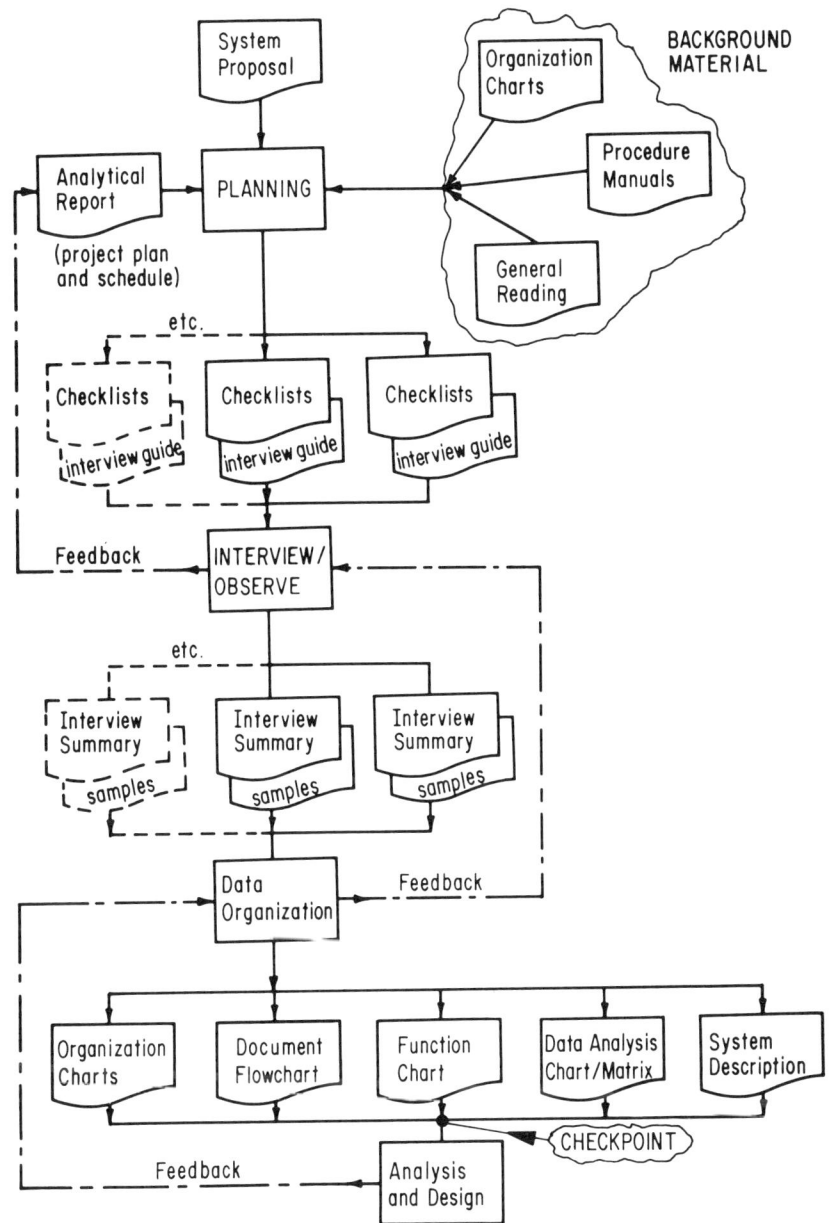

FIGURE 4.1 Example Approach to Investigation and Analysis

checklists and interview guides. A checklist details the *type* of information required. An interview guide is developed from a checklist for a particular user to be interviewed. (It can be thought of as a type of questionnaire for the personal use of an analyst.)

Data Gathering: The analyst goes out into the user environment to interview and observe; he collects and catalogs samples of all relevant documents. The output from this task is a series of interview summaries (the results of applying interview guides), supported by annotated document samples.

Data Organization: This is the organization of the data gathered in the previous phase. (For example, in one project managed by the author, the investigation step generated over 900 interview summaries and approximately 2,000 document samples. This mass of information from many interviews had to be pieced together rather like assembling a jigsaw puzzle.) There are three reasons for organizing the data:

1. As a prerequisite to analysis and design, i.e., understanding the data characteristics and usage, job functions, identifying problems which the new system must solve, etc.
2. To check that the investigation is complete and to check the analysts' understanding of the existing system.
3. To enable a user checkpoint to be set up. This can be very important on a study of a large, complex manual system which has evolved over a long period of time and has never been formally documented. The objective of this checkpoint can be summed up as follows: "Do you, the users, agree that this is the current situation? If you agree, then we can go on to the analysis and design. So let us agree on the development step by step so that we don't have to backtrack."

The agreed description of the existing environment and management's identified information requirements is used as the basis of subsequent analysis and design. This leads up to the Systems Specification.

As stated previously, the amount of effort required at any step depends on the installation and the project. To define specific standards for all interim documentation *it is vital to first establish detailed methods standards.* For example, to define the contents and format of a checklist/interview guide requires standards for how interviewing is to be carried out. (This is unlike, say, defining standards for a System Specification, the contents and format of which can be specified without laying down standards for *how* analysis or design are to be done.) The development of methods standards is outside the scope of this book. The interim documentation reviewed below, therefore, relates to data organization—a formal checkpoint. The techniques described for documenting a manual system can be used in specifying manual procedures in the new system, as documented in the System Specification.

The documents used to describe an existing business environment are:

System Documentation

- Organization Chart (who is what and who reports to whom)
- Function Chart (what is done)
- Document Flowchart (information flow)
- Data Analysis Chart/Matrix (data characteristics and usage)
- System Description

Note that the Function Chart and Document Flowchart can be, and often are, combined into one chart. It is the combined approach which will be discussed here.

Organization Chart: The formal organization chart is usually drawn in a hierarchic tree form. It is drawn to show the mechanistic structure of a department. (Working copies can be annotated to show informal lines of communication.) Note that where an organization chart contains company confidential personnel data, it must be prepared, circulated, and held with appropriate security arrangements. An example chart is shown in Figure 4.2. General conventions are given below:

1. Do not show too much on one chart. Be consistent in what is shown in a box. For example, Figure 4.2 shows a relatively simple structure with each box representing one job position—one man—and containing the job title and present incumbent. The exception is where there is a group of personnel doing the same job, as in the lower-level boxes in Figure 4.2.
2. In a complex structure or where it is politically expedient to show job holder's names independently, use the two-chart approach, as in the examples shown in Figure 4.3. In this case note that Figure 4.3(*b*) can be superimposed on the outline chart (Figure 4.3(*a*)) to get personnel information. Unless there is to be a very restricted circulation, do not include salary information.
3. The firm connecting lines are used to show formal lines of authority. Distinguish, therefore, between "Assistant" and "Assistant to" positions: For example:

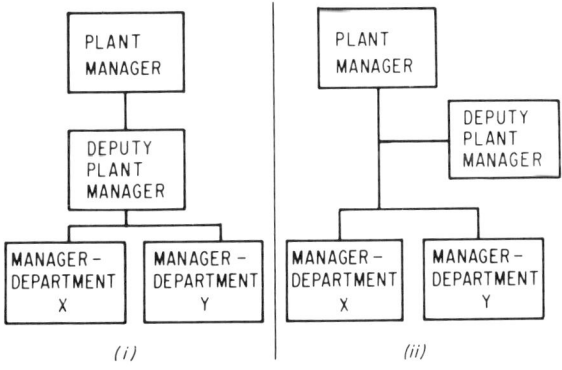

(i)   *(ii)*

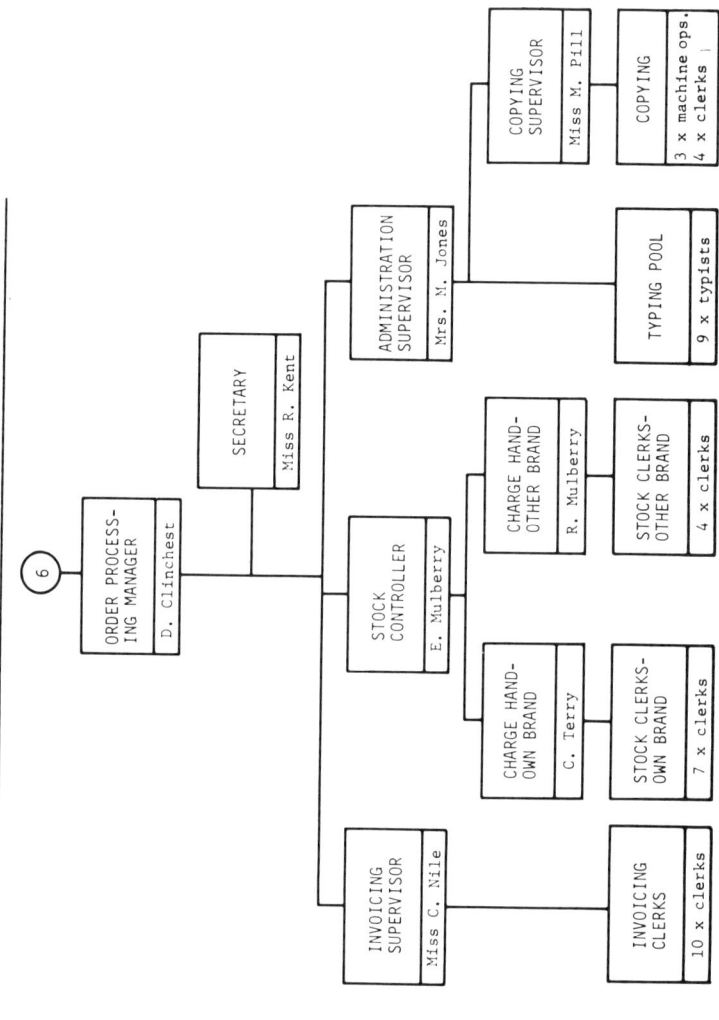

FIGURE 4.2 Sample Organization Chart—I

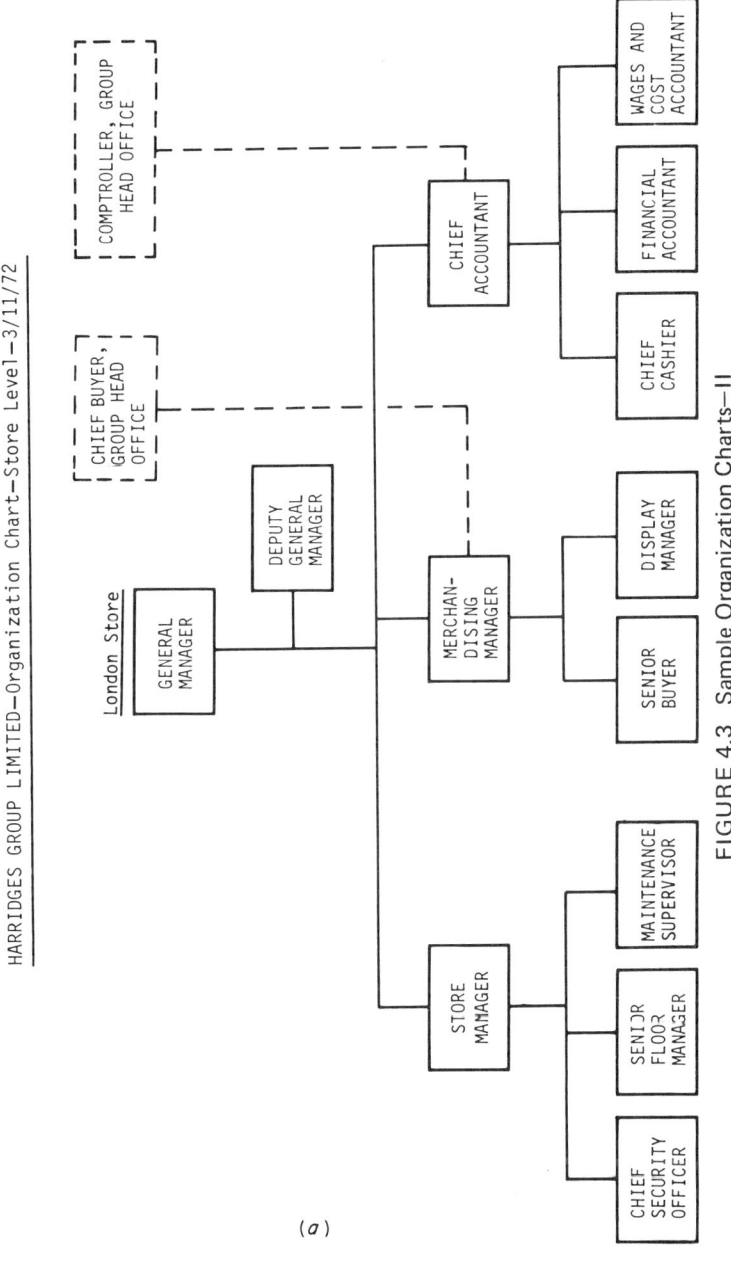

FIGURE 4.3 Sample Organization Charts—II

HARRIDGES GROUP LIMITED—Personnel Assignments—London Store—3/11/72

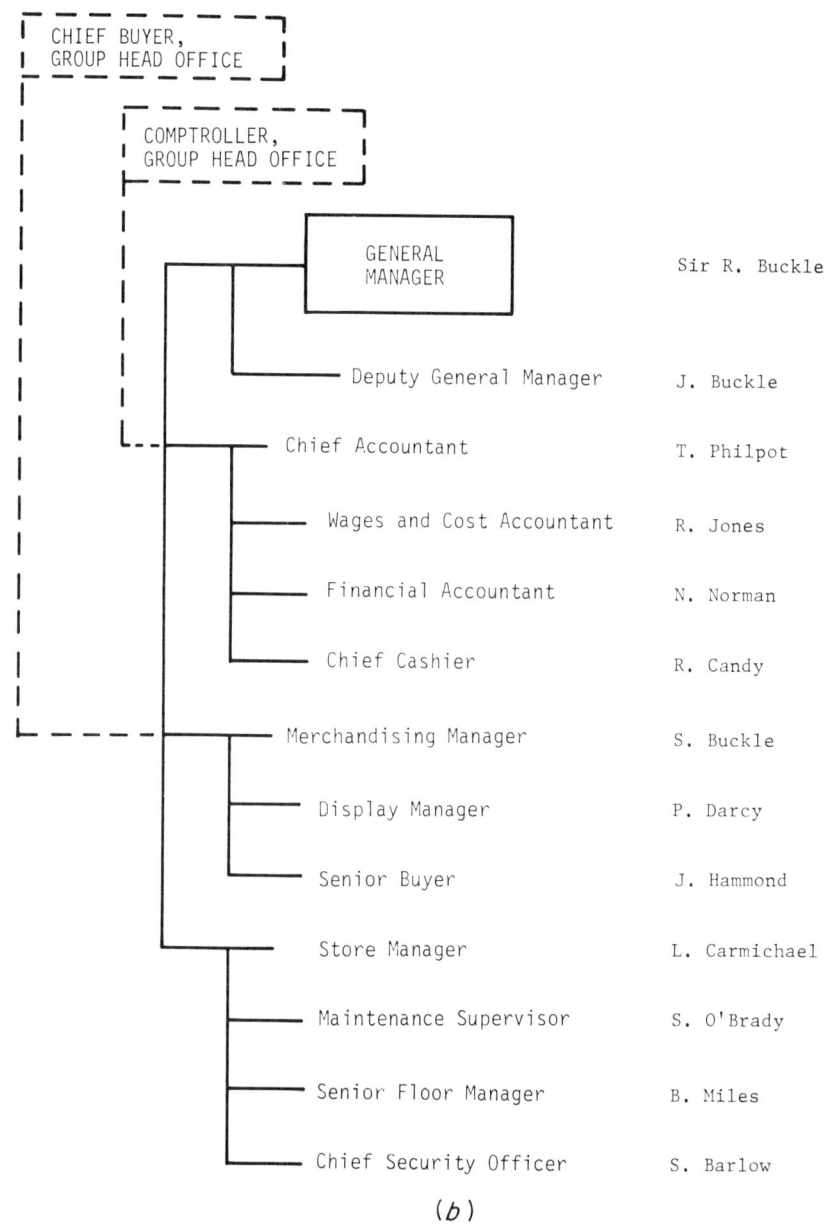

GENERAL MANAGER	Sir R. Buckle
Deputy General Manager	J. Buckle
Chief Accountant	T. Philpot
Wages and Cost Accountant	R. Jones
Financial Accountant	N. Norman
Chief Cashier	R. Candy
Merchandising Manager	S. Buckle
Display Manager	P. Darcy
Senior Buyer	J. Hammond
Store Manager	L. Carmichael
Maintenance Supervisor	S. O'Brady
Senior Floor Manager	B. Miles
Chief Security Officer	S. Barlow

(*b*)

System Documentation

In example (*i*) there is a formal line of authority with Managers of Departments X and Y reporting to the Plant Manager *via* the Deputy Plant Manager. In example (*ii*) the Deputy Plant Manager serves a supporting (possibly administrative) role in the sense of "Assistant to" the Plant Manager.

4. Formal "staff" reporting can be shown by broken lines. An example of this is shown in Figure 4.3. The formal line of authority (firm line) shows that the Chief Accountant reports to the General Manager. The dotted line indicates that there is some form of "advisory" reporting from Chief Accountant to the Group Head Office Comptroller.

THIS IS A NARRATIVE DESCRIPTION OF THE PROCEDURES SHOWN IN CHART FORM IN FIGURES 4.5, 4.6, AND 4.7.

1. An approved order for goods comes from a salesman. It is handwritten and a master copy is typed then photocopied. Three copies are produced: Transport Copy, Advice Note and Delivery Note. The original order and the typed master copy are filed together in a Master Order File.

2. The Transport Copy is passed to the Transport Supervisor who prepares a schedule of vehicle loads and routes. As he allocates a load to a vehicle, he notes the vehicle number and driver on the Transport Copy. He then files it in a pending file after giving instructions for the delivery to the workers in the Dispatch Department.

3. The Advice Note and Delivery Note pass from photocopying to the warehouse (Assembly Gang) who pick the required goods from the shelves. The two documents (plus the goods) are then passed to Dispatch where the order is loaded and delivered as instructed by the Transport Supervisor.

4. When delivery is made the customer checks the goods against the documentation. The Advice Note and Delivery Note are altered to show any damaged goods, short deliveries, etc. The customer signs them, keeps the Advice Note and returns the Delivery Note to the driver who brings it back to Dispatch, to the Transport Supervisor.

5. The Transport Supervisor matches the returned Delivery Note against the appropriate filed Transport Copy. The Transport Copy is removed from the file and destroyed. The Delivery Note is then passed on to the next process. (This step is a simple "proof of delivery" procedure. All Transport Copies remaining in the file at the end of a certain period represent "non-deliveries" or lost Delivery Notes which the Supervisor must chaseup. The Transport Copy pending file also serves as a record of work in progress.)

FIGURE 4.4 Narrative Procedure Statement

DOCUMENTATION STANDARDS

5. If the hierarchy of jobs is not clear from the job titles, a hierarchy must not be accidentally implied merely through the positioning of boxes. In the construction or presentation of a chart do not confuse *status* with a job position hierarchy of authority.
6. *The basic rule for preparing any organization chart is: It must have a title, a date—and it must be kept simple.*

Function/Document Flowchart*: The object of this chart is to show the sequence of processes and the information used. There are many methods for representing manual procedures. Three example methods are shown in Figures 4.5, 4.6, and 4.7; they are summed up in a narrative description in Figure 4.4.

---

*We are concerned here with the documentation of manual procedures. The documentation of computer-based procedures will be discussed later in this chapter.

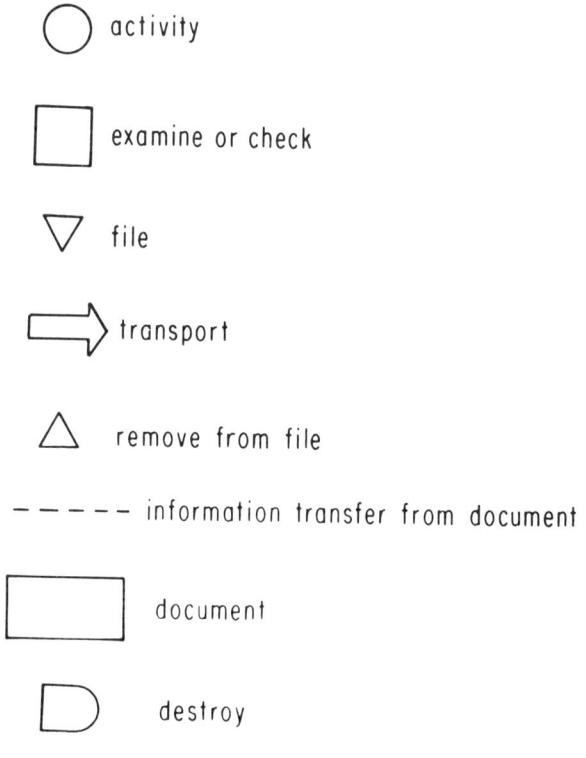

(a) Symbols

FIGURE 4.5 Manual Procedure Charting Conventions, American Society of Mechanical Engineers

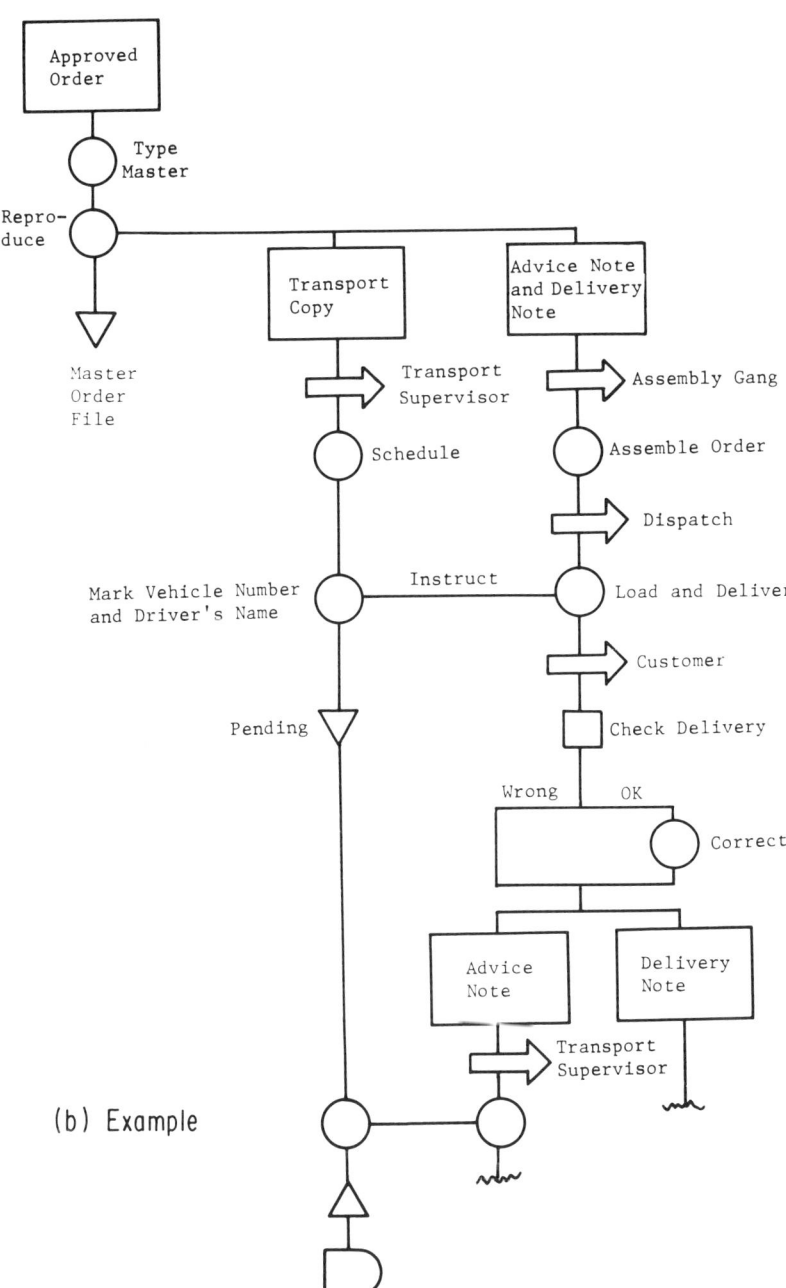

(b) Example

FIGURE 4.5 Continued

Each approach has its advocates. To a large extent, the adoption of any technique is based on the historical development of the company (e.g., from Organization and Methods)—and, of course, personal preference. The technique preferred by the author is the one shown in Figure 4.7. The main reason is that it is similar to (and based on) accepted techniques for flowcharting computer-based procedures. Additionally, the technique uses an outline approach, rather than step-by-step clerical detail. (Additional charts to a detailed level can be produced in special circumstances and included as necessary as part of the System Description.)

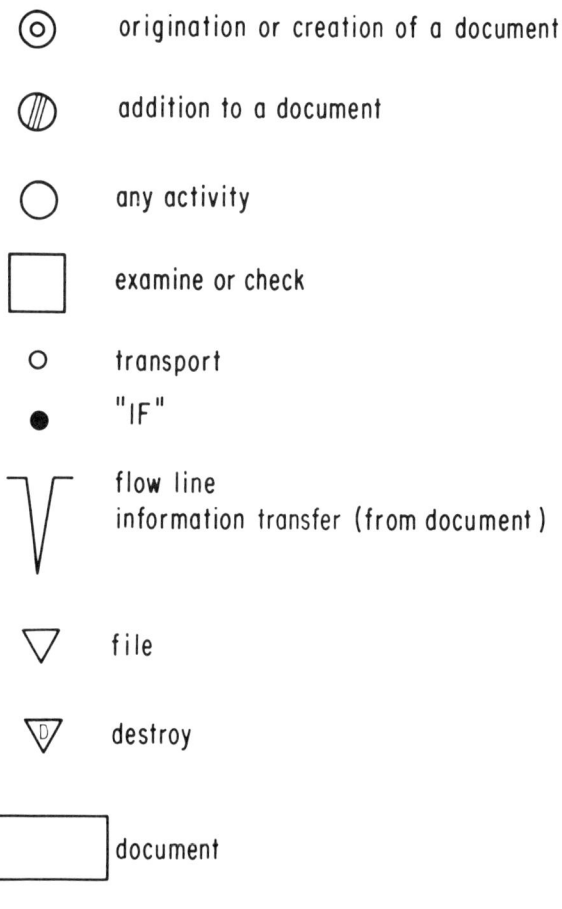

(a) Symbols

FIGURE 4.6 Manual Procedure Charting Conventions, Horizontal-Form Flowchart

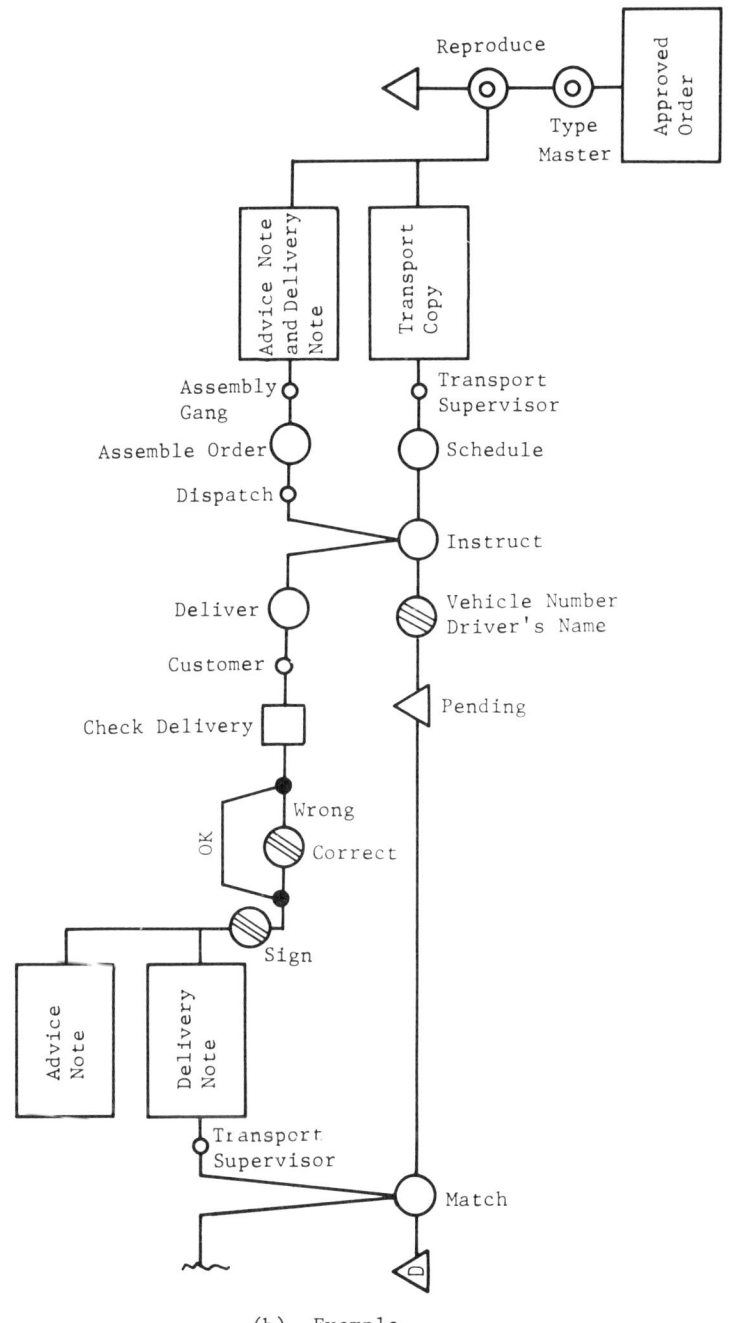

(b) Example
FIGURE 4.6 Continued

DOCUMENTATION STANDARDS

The principle is that the flow of major documents is traced through the system. Note that the manual process symbol represents a clerical process—*not* an organizational unit. For example, Figure 4.8 (*a*) shows too much detail. It confuses, in this case, a department or very general "STOCK CONTROL" function with the many procedures which it comprises; it also confuses procedures which take place at different times. The diagram in Figure 4.8(*b*) shows the same procedure, this time using flow, with the boxes containing procedure identifications.

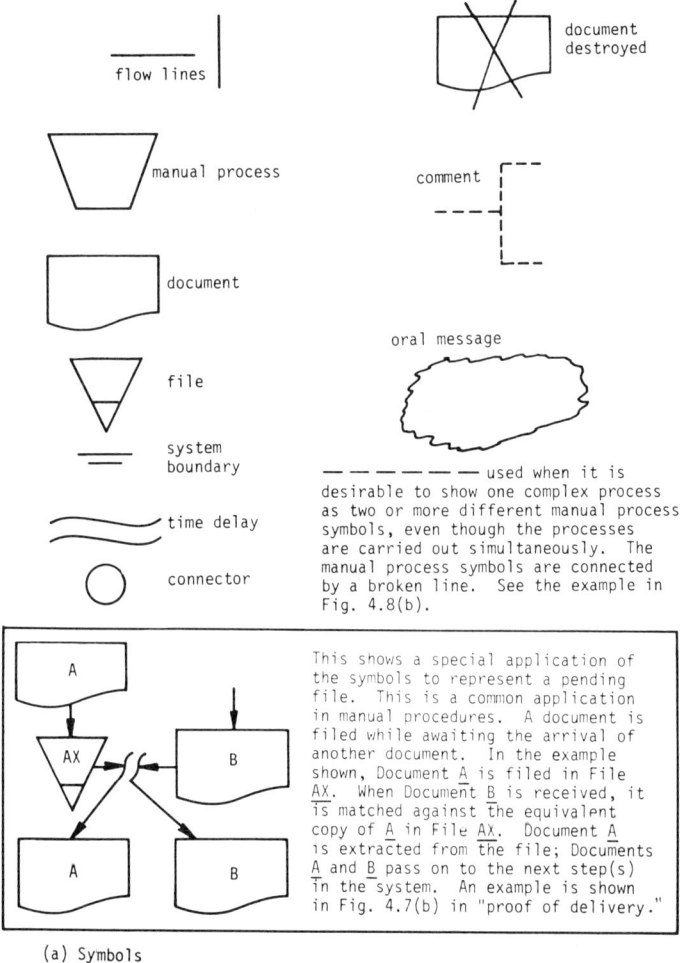

(a) Symbols

FIGURE 4.7 Manual Procedure Charting Conventions, Computer Flow-charting Adaptation

System Documentation

Basic guidelines for preparing the Function/Document Flowchart are given below.

1. The key to preparing the chart is to identify the major flow. Ancillary procedures such as file maintenance should be shown as a separate diagram or separate string on the main diagram.

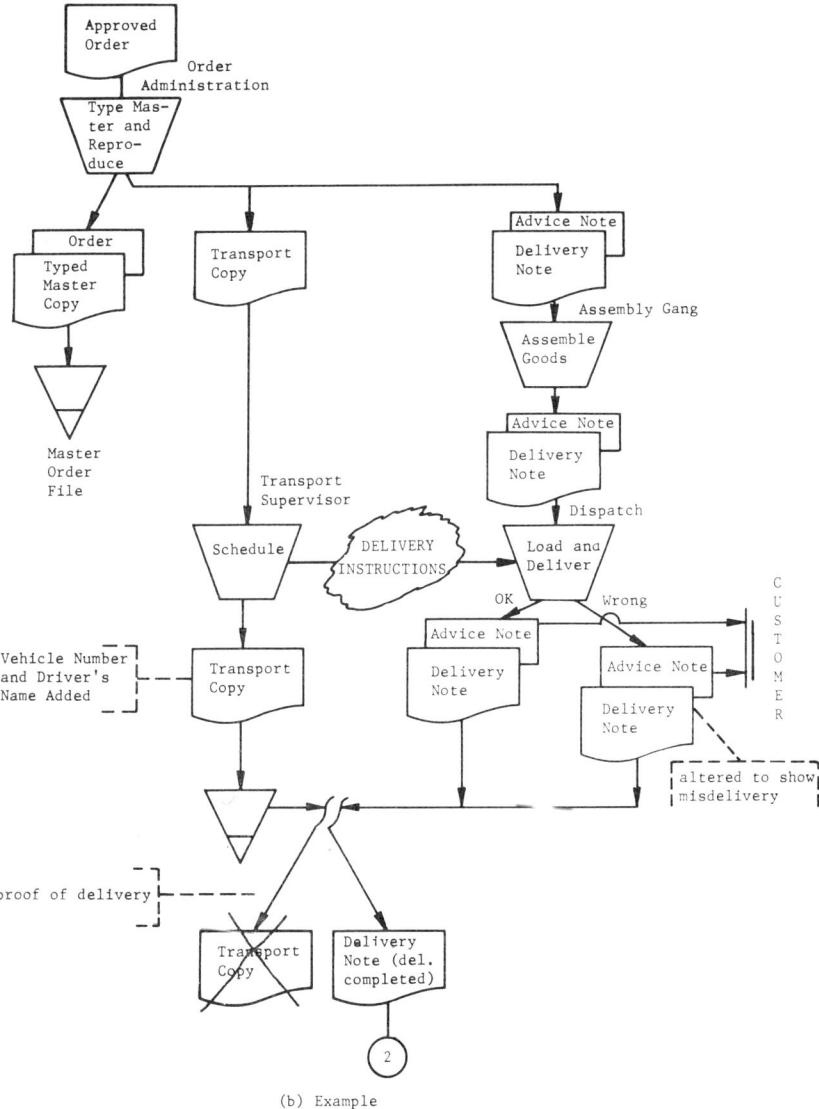

(b) Example

FIGURE 4.7 Continued

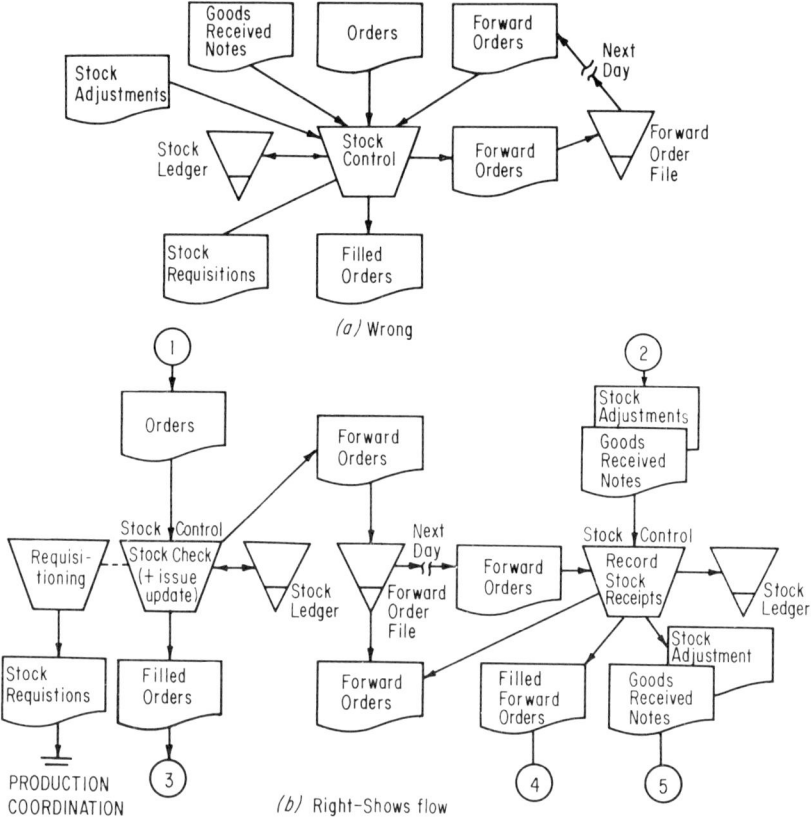

FIGURE 4.8 Example Function/Document Flowcharts

Notes: 1. Note that the two processes of *stock check* and *requisitioning* take place at the same time, but for clarity are shown as two processes (connected by a broken line).
2. Forward orders are prepared for those items which have been ordered but are not in stock. They are processed the next day when new stock is received.

2. The manual process symbol can be annotated with the department, section, or job title, etc., where the process is done. One convention is to note the location/job title over the top of the process box as in Figure 4.8(b). Names of individuals should be avoided.
3. Where volumes and timing are important, they can be noted on the document/process symbols.
4. Note that a document can change its function as it passes through the system. This change in type or function should be noted on all documents where appropriate. For example:

System Documentation

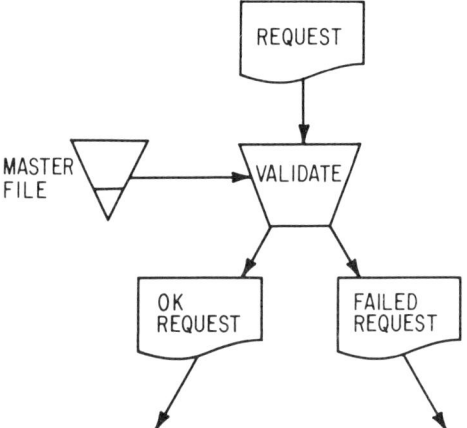

This shows a simple validate which has two outcomes: pass or fail. This will lead to two different sets of actions. This is important in checking the operation of the system as represented on the chart; see point 5 below.

5. Two basic checks can be made on the completeness of the chart and, indirectly, the analyst's understanding of the system.
   (a) Are the volumes of data known or noted? This can only be checked if point 4 has been followed. In the example given above, the analyst can check: how many REQUESTS are validated; how many REQUESTS are OK; how many REQUESTS FAIL.
   (b) Are all documents accounted for? A document entering a process must either come out and pass on, be filed, or be destroyed. For example, Figure 4.8(*b*), right-hand side of diagram, starting with connector 2, shows a GOODS RECEIVED NOTE (GRN) going into the manual process RECORD STOCK RECEIPTS (etc.). What happens to the GRN?

Data Analysis Chart/Matrix: The objective of this document is to record the data in the current system, its characteristics and usage. It expands the document/oral message/file symbols shown on the Function/Document Flowchart. It is used to define data duplications and redundancies, and to give the analyst a good grounding in the data usage in the existing system as the basis for the input, file, and output design in the new, computer-based system.

The exact format and content of the data analysis documentation will depend on the installation, the project—and the working method of the analyst on the next stage of analysis and design. A two-step approach is shown in Figures 4.9. and 4.10. Figure 4.9 shows a chart describing the contents of a document; this information will come from the interview summaries and annotated samples. Figure 4.10 is a matrix showing the usage of a document/ file in the various processes in the existing system. This is prepared from the Function/Document Flowchart and is a useful summary of usage. The extension is a data usage matrix which combines the two, showing data element against usage in the various processes; see example in Figure 4.11.

System Description: The objective of this document is to describe the exist-

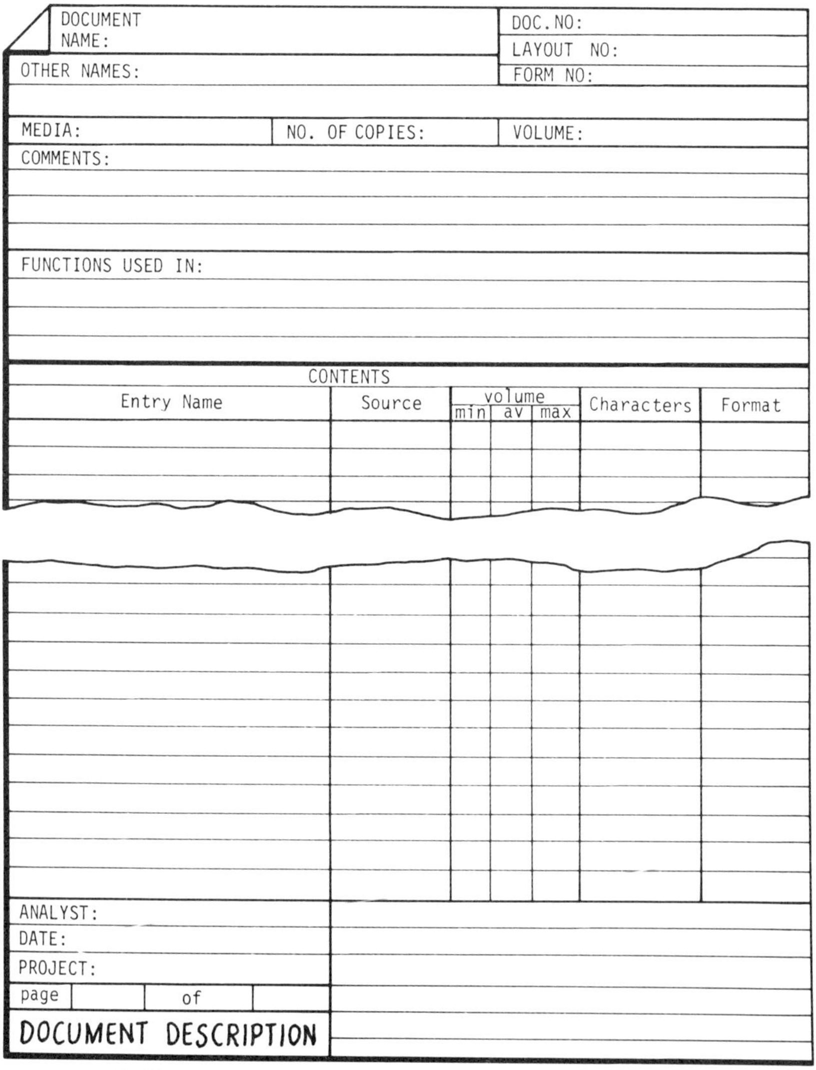

FIGURE 4.9 Data Analysis Chart—Document Content

System Documentation

PROJECT:	P 23 ORDER PROCESSING								page	1	of	2
ANALYST:	J. KENT	DATE:	11 JAN 1973									

DOCUMENT/FILE FUNCTION/PROCESS	Original Order	Forward Order	Sales Ledger	Stock Ledger	Order Requisition	Transport Copy	Delivery Note	Advice Note	Goods Received Note	Bin Card	Invoice	Invoice Copy
Sale	X											
Credit Check	X		X									
Stock Check	X	X	X				X		X	X		
Stock Req.				X	X				X			
Transport Schedule						X						
Assembly							X	X		X		
Load							X	X				
Delivery							X	X				
Proof of Delivery						X	X					
Invoicing			X				X				X	X

FIGURE 4.10 Data Analysis Matrix—File/Document Usage

ing system. It is an outline description of the system, which pulls together all the other items of documentation described above. The System Description can be narrative, with flowcharts or decision tables used to describe the important, complex procedures or decision-making logic.

Thus far in this chapter, some items of documentation which are prepared during systems investigation and analysis have been discussed. It has been stressed that this documentation must be based on the specific methods standards employed in an installation. The interim documentation described here has been concerned with the representation of the current environment, principally for a formal review checkpoint before proceeding to detailed analysis and design. The next major formal document produced will be the Systems Specification.

NAME: DELIVERY NOTE		DOC. NO: P23107					page 1 of 1			
ANALYST: J. KENT		DATE: 12 JAN 1973				PROJECT: P23 ORDER PROCESSING				

DATE ELEMENT \ FUNCTION/PROCESS	SOURCE	Reproduce	Assemble	Load	Deliver	Proof of Delivery	Stock Adjustments	Forward Order			CROSS REFERENCE
Invoice Number	Banda (Serial List.)	X				X	X	X			
Customer N/A	From Original Order In Banda	X	X	X	X			X			Note 1
Delivery Name Address	"	X	X	X	X			X			Notes 1 and 2
Order Date	"	X						X			
Cust Order Number	"	X					X	X			
Product Code		X	X				X	X			
Quantity Ordered	"	X	X	X	X		X	X			
Quantity Delivered	Assembly Gang/Customer		X	X	X		X	X			Note 5
Quantity to Follow	Assembly Gang / Customer		X		X		X	X			Note 5
Remarks	Assembly Gang/Driver Customer		X		X	X	X	X			
Customer Signature	Customer				X	X					

FIGURE 4.11 Data Analysis Matrix—Data Usage (in Document or File)

THE SYSTEMS SPECIFICATION

The systems development process can be said to begin with the production and approval of the final analytical documentation and the authority to proceed with the project. As discussed in the previous chapter, the level and scope of this analytical documentation will depend primarily on the type of project. Detailed investigation, analysis, and design then take place. The major output from the systems development process is a *Systems Specification*. The Systems Specification is the basic medium of communication between the system design function, the programming function, and the user. It forms a permanent record of the structure, functions, flow, and control of the system.

System Documentation

The successful completion of the Systems Specification may be taken as indicating the completion of the systems design process. However, the systems analysis and design personnel will also participate in the system implementation process (e.g., user training, assistance with programming, file conversion, parallel running).

The production of a document of such scope is of necessity a lengthy process. The level and content of the information is detailed and the number and type of intended readers many. Thus, the organization of the document and the method of presenting material must be carefully planned. One suggested approach described below is to consider the Systems Specification as comprising a number of documents. This approach requires the production of six subset specifications, namely:

- Systems Summary
- File Specifications
- Transaction (Input) Specifications
- Output Specifications
- Processing (Program) Specifications
- Systems Test Plan

Each of the above specifications is described below, in terms of content, usage, suggested methods of presentation, and the relationship with the previously produced analytical documentation.

As a general note, however, the size and scope of the Systems Specification are dependent on the type of project development work required. Thus, a major systems revision or completely new system would require a full Systems Specification. However, the production of a new report from existing data sources, or the modification of the physical layout of a file, may only require a concise one- or two-page specification.

As a matter of procedure, however, a standard should be laid down that a formal Systems Specification of some kind must be prepared for all project work. For minor revisions, the Systems Specification may simply be some form of analytical documentation with a few details added. However, to have the positive presentation of a specification with a formal agreement/acceptance procedure establishes a clear "freeze" procedure before the subsequent programming and implementation tasks are undertaken.

PROBLEMS AND SOLUTIONS OF THE SYSTEMS SPECIFICATION

The importance of producing a complete, accurate, and unambiguous Systems Specification cannot be stressed too strongly. The approval of the Systems Specification represents the last "go/no go" decision before the expensive tasks of programming, testing, and conversion/implementation begin.

Changes to the specification, for any reason, after the subsequent tasks are begun can be very expensive indeed. Because of the importance of the Systems Specification, it is necessary to look deeper at the factors which lie behind the preparation and approval of the specification.

Systems/Programming Demarcation: Much has been written about the division of responsibilities between systems design and programming, and the arrangements for the formal handover of work. Organizing a workable systems/programming interface is one of the most important aspects of managing a data processing department. It is fundamental to the development of the Systems Specification. Problems can arise if the division between systems and programming is ill defined. For example, if the systems analysts are mainly exprogrammers they may be able to develop the Program (processing) Specifications in some depth. This may lead to problems on the programming side with cries of "they (the systems people) are doing *our* job." It must be realized that the preparation of the Systems Specification is commonly a joint exercise with the participation of systems, programming, users, operations, and so on. *But one job function must be given the responsibility for coordinating work and insuring that the finished document(s) is complete, accurate, and unambiguous.* This is normally the responsibility of the lead analyst, project manager, or the equivalent.

Phased Programming: The objective is to get full approval of the Systems Specification before subsequent programming work begins. On a large project with intensive pressure to meet a tight delivery schedule, however, this might not be practicable. This can mean that Program Specifications are prepared one after the other with programming beginning immediately each specification is completed and released. This situation is best avoided if at all possible. If it becomes necessary through outside pressures, the phased preparation of the Systems Specification must be very carefully controlled.

One approach is to arrange approval in two steps:

- *Step 1*: approval of Systems Summary and major files, inputs, and output specifications
- *Step 2*: using step 1 as a base, approval of each Program Specification as required

This is useful if the data relationships and structures are relatively straightforward; if they are complex then step 1 may be too time-consuming within the schedule. An alternative approach is to arrange the design and approval of the whole system in stages, each stage being at a greater level of detail. For example, stage 1 would be the approval of the Systems Summary, the input and output specifications, and the file *content*. Stage 2 would be the development of overall computer processing with file content and structure in detail. Stage 3 would be the development of each Program Specification.

Checkback: Some installations have experienced problems with excessive referrals from programming back to systems for more detail or clarification. These can be expensive and time-consuming, especially when programming is done physically remote from the systems staff, or when the systems staff schedule is such that analysts are unavailable to answer queries. There will invariably be some points to be queried and clarified in any large specification. An objective of the system documentation standards is to minimize incomplete or ambiguous descriptions and thus reduce clarification referrals.

Getting the Approval: A comment which is made by many systems analysts is: "It is all very well to lay down the standards for documentation but the hardest task in *my* installation is to get approval—and get the user to stick to it!"

This is really a matter which goes right to the heart of the policy and techniques for developing systems in any company. Effective documentation standards must be designed with this problem in mind; they cannot of themselves solve the problem but they can assist in getting a meaningful signing-off on the specification. Some general points are discussed below.

A mandatory standard must be laid down stating that all development schedules *must* allow sufficient time for the preparation *and review* of the Systems Specification. The review of the specification may take two to four weeks, possibly longer for a large, complex system. (Some schedules seen by the author have shown "Systems Spec. to user 27th, programming begins 28th"!)

The presentation of material should be so organized as to be readily and easily assimilated by the reviewer. A pressure working against this aim is that the Systems Specification is commonly a multipurpose document. It is circulated for review to user management (of different levels or departments), programming, and operations. Following the approval, it becomes the terms of reference for subsequent action and must thus be sufficiently detailed for this work to be carried out. The arrangement of the material so that the Systems Specification serves all the functions but does not take excessive time to prepare is a key factor in developing standards in this area. A suggested approach is described later.

Although the importance of a *formal* acceptance checkpoint has been stressed, it is important that there be cooperation and contact between all parties *before* the Systems Specification is formally presented. The use of a formal checkpoint does not mean that the Systems Specification is presented as a rabbit out of a hat or a fait accompli. It should be regarded as the culmination of a particular phase of work. Indeed, many installations arrange the systems development work so that all parties know the content of the specification in some detail before it is formally presented.

SYSTEMS SUMMARY

The *Systems Summary* is a general description of the complete system or system change.* The summary serves three main purposes.

1. To present a nontechnical description of the proposed system to non-data processing management to enable them to understand, approve and participate in the system.
2. To present an overall description of the system to show the relationship between the files, inputs, outputs, and logical processing steps which are later considered as separate entities.
3. To present specific cross-referenced lists and to define essential terms used in the other specifications.

A sample of a formal table of contents is shown in Figure 4.12. A description of the possible contents is given below and is related for explanatory purposes to the sample table of contents.

Management Summary

The *Management Summary* should be written in concise nontechnical terms for user management. As shown in Figure 4.12, the systems designer is restricted to a logical format of four subsections:

- Purpose and Function
- Files Maintained and Affected
- Input and Input Sources
- Output and Output Users

It is also good practice to establish a maximum length standard restricting the systems designer to producing a Management Summary of from one to three pages.

The *Purpose and Function* subsection is used to explain what the system or system change is intended to accomplish and how these objectives are achieved. In most cases a few sentences only are adequate to explain why a system or system change is necessary and to place it in the context of the working environment.

The *Files Maintained and Affected* subsection identifies those principal files used in the system and also those files which are affected in other systems. This may be presented by giving a simple summary list showing name, brief definition of content, type of storage medium, and how the file is used.

---

*An extension to the Systems Summary can be used to give final cost/benefit analysis for acceptance or revision of the system developed in detail. These revised figures will be a refinement of the initial estimates given in the Systems Proposal.

System Documentation

The *Input and Input Sources* subsection may be a summary list, showing input name, brief definition of content, and the source (originator) of the input.

The *Output and Output Users* subsection deals with outputs from the system which are intelligible to the user, i.e., reports and messages rather than

```
              SYSTEMS SUMMARY - I

              Table of Contents

    1.0  Management Summary
         1.1  Purpose and Function
         1.2  Files Maintained and Affected
         1.3  Input and Input Sources
         1.4  Output and Output Uses

    2.0  System Flowchart
         2.1  Flowchart
         2.2  Reference Lists

    3.0  Narrative Description
         3.1  Definitions
         3.2  System Flow
```

FIGURE 4.12 Sample Table of Contents—Systems Summary—I

magnetic tape or disk files. This again may be a summary list showing name of output, form of output (printed report, typewriter message, visual display, etc.), and who will use the output and how.

Note that if a detailed Design Requirements Statement has been produced during the project initiation and review phase (see page 27), much of the information presented in this section will be a summarization of information given in that report.

System Flowchart

The *System Flowchart* section is used to present a graphical representation of the overall logic of the system. The data processing system flowchart is a symbolic representation of the processes through which data will flow in a system. The flowchart illustrates input and output requirements for each major step of the system, whether or not equipment processing is required. The System Flowchart should indicate the relationship between each of the logical elements in the system, where a logical element may be considered as a program, off-line machine operation, or manual/clerical operation (in user or data processing department). Since the flowchart will be supported by various narrative descriptions (subsections 2.2 and 3.2 in terms of the sample table of contents in Figure 4.12) the flowchart should simply identify each operation, the data affected in the operation, and when the operation takes place.

If any group of systems designers from different working environments were asked to prepare a System Flowchart of the same system the result, in terms of layout, symbology, and operation descriptions, would differ according to each personal train of thought. For ease of communication and clarity of meaning, localized standards for system flowchart preparation should be established. The main areas for standardization are listed below. An example set of standards is given in Figure 4.13.

1. *Overall layout of flowchart.* Example:
   - The chart must be as clear and simple as possible
   - Only one line of flow should be shown on a page
   - The direction of the flow should be vertical
2. *Paging and identification.* Example:
   - Within the rule that each major process (e.g., program) must be shown as one symbol, as few pages as possible should be used
   - Flowcharts should be drawn consistently on a standard-size paper
   - Each page must be identified by system reference (title and number), date of preparation, author identification, and page number
3. *Symbology.* Standard symbols should be established: an example range of standard symbols and their meanings is shown in Figure 4.14.
4. *Operation (Process) identification/description.* Example:

System Documentation

- Each operation symbol must contain a very brief description of what is accomplished in the operation
- Each program run in the system must be clearly labeled with its identification number

---

SYSTEM FLOWCHARTING STANDARDS

To achieve a common understanding of system logic, it is desirable to adopt a standard set of symbols for use in system flowcharting.

Rules for the preparation of systems flowcharts follow.

1. All systems flowcharts must be drawn on standard XYZ company flowchart paper. A margin of one inch should be maintained on the left-hand side with reasonable margins on the other sides.

2. The identification block must be completed on all flowcharts.

3. There should be one overall system flowchart for each complete system. This flowchart should, where possible, be drawn on a single sheet of A3 or A4 size paper.

4. For each subsystem, shown as a block on the overall chart, a separate chart should be drawn showing all the inputs and outputs of the subsystem including intermediate files.

5. Each block of the subsystem flowchart must be identified by a program number written on the upper right-hand side and outside the symbol.

6. The logical flow of the flowchart should be from top to bottom and from left to right.

7. The direction of data flow should be shown on all connectors

8. All system flowcharts must be drawn using the standard symbols shown in Fig. 4.14. The actual size of the symbols may vary (according to the manufacturer's template employed), but the overall shape of a symbol must conform to Fig. 4.14.

9. An example flowchart is shown in Fig. 4.15.

FIGURE 4.13 Example System Flowcharting Standards

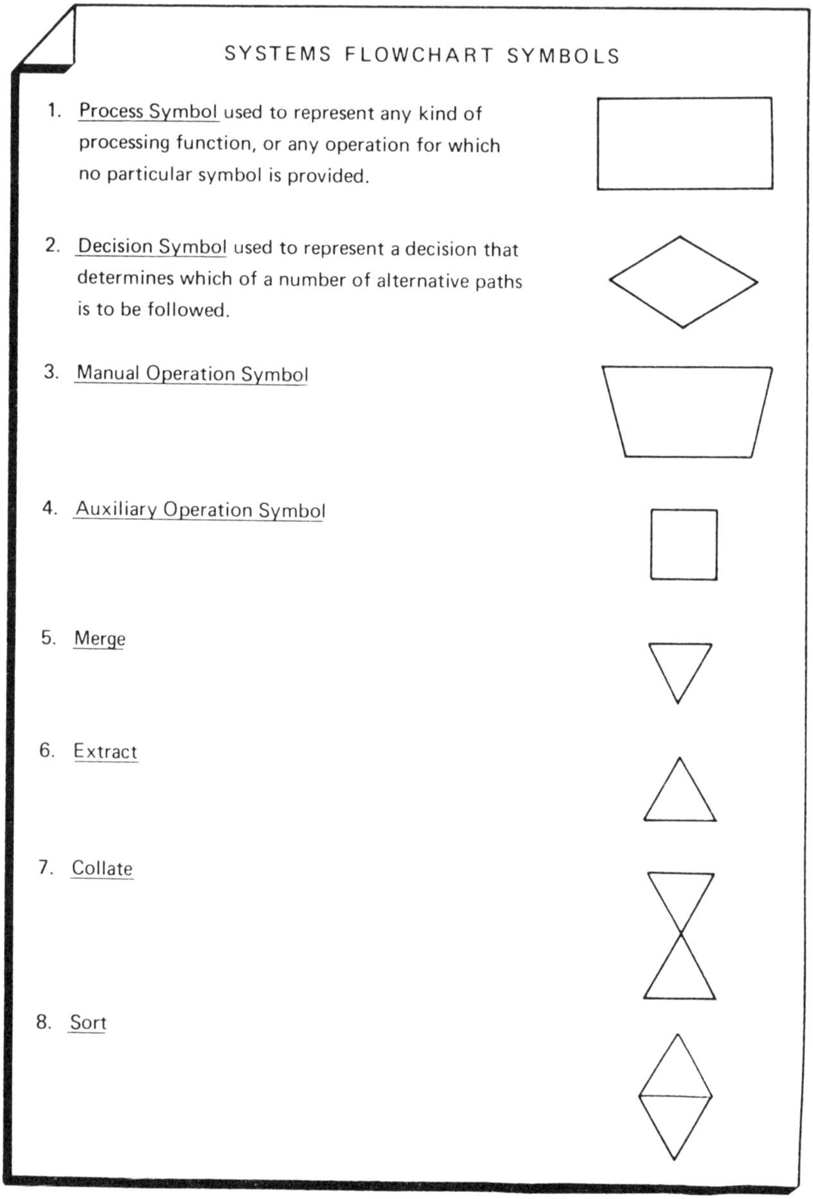

SYSTEMS FLOWCHART SYMBOLS

1. <u>Process Symbol</u> used to represent any kind of processing function, or any operation for which no particular symbol is provided.

2. <u>Decision Symbol</u> used to represent a decision that determines which of a number of alternative paths is to be followed.

3. <u>Manual Operation Symbol</u>

4. <u>Auxiliary Operation Symbol</u>

5. <u>Merge</u>

6. <u>Extract</u>

7. <u>Collate</u>

8. <u>Sort</u>

FIGURE 4.14 Standard Symbols for System Flowcharts

SYSTEMS FLOWCHART SYMBOLS

9. Manual Input

10. Generalized Input/Output Symbol

11. On-Line Storage Symbol represents the use of any kind of on-line backing, store, i.e., disc, drum or magnetic tape

12. Off-Line Storage Symbol represents the function of storing information off-line, regardless of the medium on which the data is recorded.

13. Document

14. Punched Card

15. Deck of Cards

16. File of Cards: this symbol represents a collection of related punched card records.

17. Punched Tape

18. Magnetic Tape

FIGURE 4.14 Continued

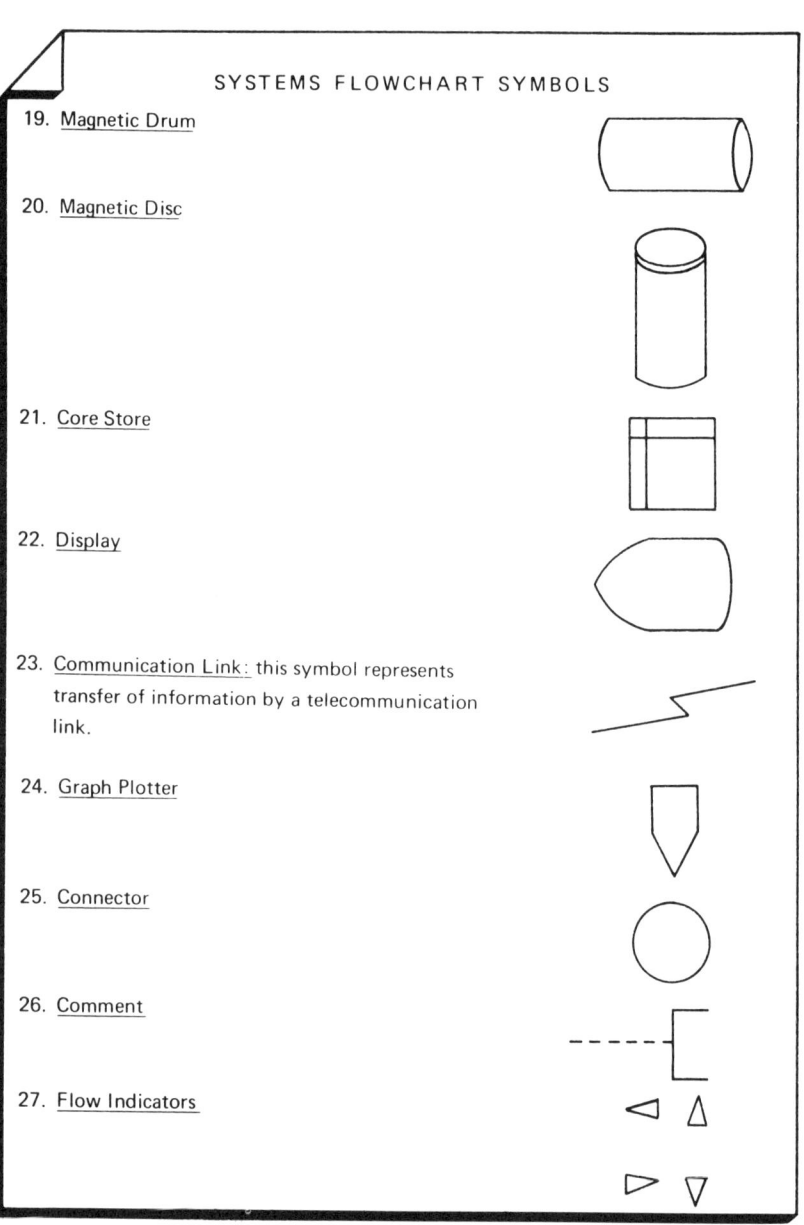

FIGURE 4.14 Continued

- Each data element symbol (e.g., file, input, or output symbol) should be labeled with the appropriate reference number*
- Processing cycle (e.g., whether an operation is performed daily, weekly, monthly, as required, etc.), should be clearly indicated on the systems flowchart

5. *Use of connector symbols.* Example:
    - Connector symbols must be used to indicate:
       (a) off-page connections for continuations
       (b) alternative flow within system
       (c) interface with other systems
    - Off-page connectors for continuations and alternative flow must indicate the page number and connector identification number of the continuation
    - Connectors referencing other system flowcharts should contain the page number and connector identification number of the referenced chart. The system reference number and the date of preparation of the referenced chart should be shown by means of a comment symbol

A sample systems flowchart drawn in accordance with the above rules is shown in Figure 4.15.

In some cases, it may be desirable to provide *Reference Lists*, i.e., summary lists and tables, to support a complex system flowchart. Whereas the system flowchart is logic-flow oriented, reference lists can be, for example, program, file, or report oriented. Thus, programs could be listed by frequency and sequence in the processing cycle and files listed by frequency of use and status, again within the processing cycle.

Decision tables (described in Chapter 8) may be included to support the flowchart. Decision tables will be useful to indicate and explain multiple-flow systems where the processing flow taken at any one time depends on conditions present at time of processing.

Narrative Description

The *Narrative Description* section comprises two subsections: 3.1 Definitions and 3.2 System Flow (see Figure 4.12).

All terms used in the system which have a special application significance and are essential to its understanding must be defined in the *Definitions* subsection. Alternatively, where there is a company glossary of data processing and application area terms, this may be referenced.

---

*The reference number referred to here assumes a system in which each file, input, and output is assigned a unique identification number. This number indicates the type of data and the reference number within that type—this is explained in more detail later in the chapter.

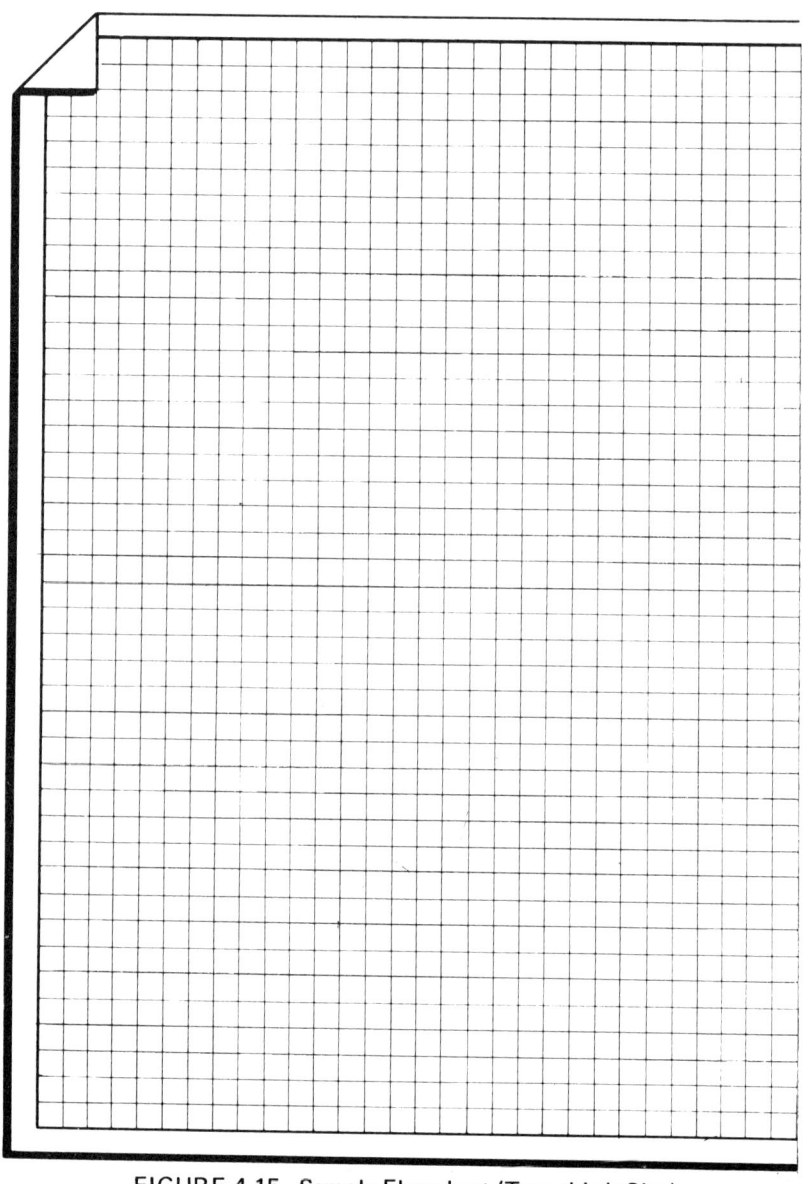

FIGURE 4.15 Sample Flowchart (Two-thirds Size)

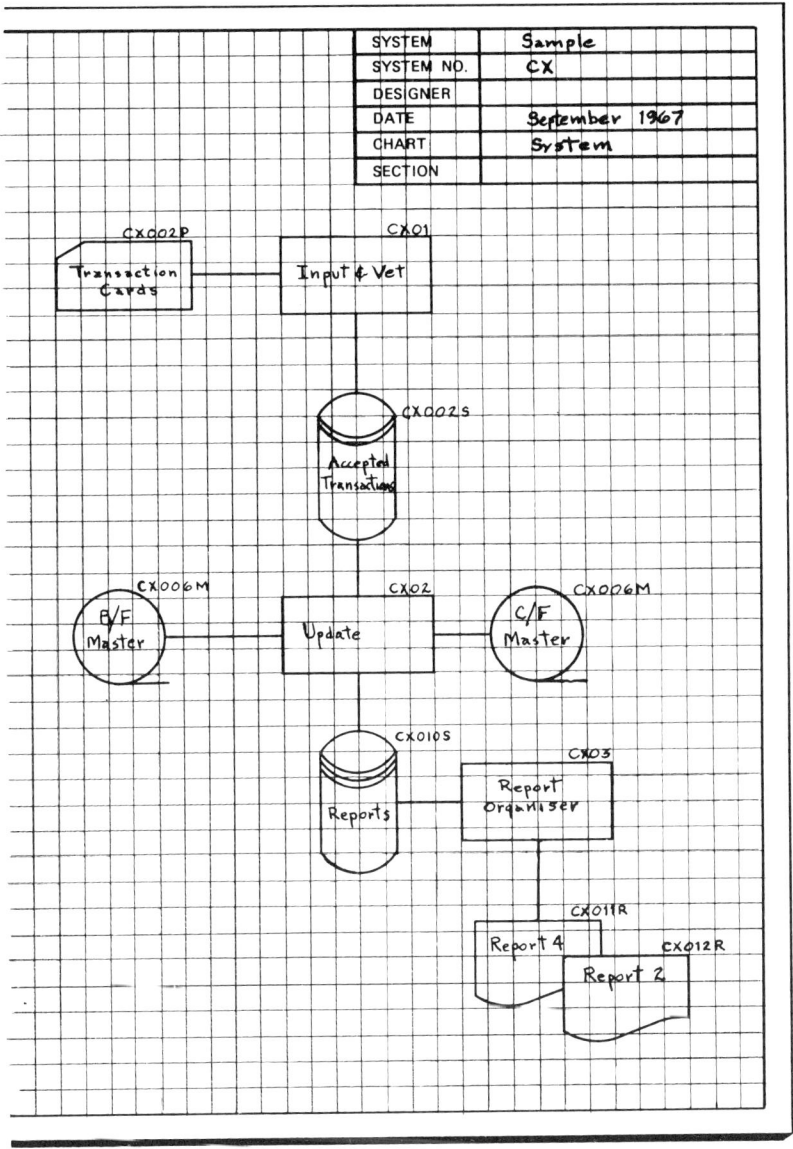

FIGURE 4.15 Continued

System Flow is a narrative description of the processes shown in the System Flowchart. The description should always enhance the understanding of the flow rather than form a simple narrative restatement of what the flowchart shows. The narrative should be cross-referenced to the flowchart. This may be done by placing identification letters or step numbers against the process symbols on the flowchart (or in the margin) for reference to paragraphs in the narrative description. Alternatively, each narrative paragraph should be identified by a heading which corresponds to identification on each processing block.

AN ALTERNATIVE APPROACH TO THE SYSTEMS SUMMARY

In some instances, the sample table of contents for the Systems Summary given previously may not be adequate to define a complete system. A very large organization, with a rigid reporting structure and complex systems or hardware/software requirements may require a Systems Summary in greater detail. An alternative table of contents is thus shown in Figure 4.16.

Note that sections 1.0, 2.0, 3.0, 7.0, and 8.0 correspond in content (if not by breakdown) to the Systems Summary presented earlier in this chapter. In addition, however, provision is made for descriptions of hardware and software environment (sections 4.0 and 5.0). Section 6.0, "System Segments," presents the system as a number of individual processing segments. Each segment is described briefly and the relationship between each segment defined. In a subsequent set of Processing Specifications, the data and processing requirements for each segment are described in detail.

FILE SPECIFICATIONS

A *File Specification* document is a detailed description of the purpose, contents, and organization of a file. Use of this document generally requires that each file be defined in a File Specification. A possible exception to this rule could be where an existing file is to be used in the system; the previously prepared File Specification may be referenced or duplicated in the System Specification.

For the purposes of this book, a file is defined as a series of related records, each identified by a key, which is processed more than once. Information will be required on the file as a whole—such as general organization, storage medium, sources of data, etc. At the next level, the format of a record must be described. At the lowest level, each of the constituent data elements comprising a record must be described.

A File Specification comprising this information is essential for communi-

SYSTEMS SUMMARY - II

Table of Contents

1.0 General Information
- 1.1 Cover Page
- 1.2 Table of Contents
- 1.3 Revision Page
- 1.4 References[1]

2.0 Problem Description
- 2.1 Definition
- 2.2 Solution
- 2.3 Results

3.0 System Description
- 3.1 Capabilities
- 3.2 Assumptions
- 3.3 Limitations[2]
- 3.4 Restrictions
- 3.5 System Interface[3]

4.0 Software Environment
- 4.1 Required Operating System Components
- 4.2 Interrelationships and Dependencies
- 4.3 Language Utilization
- 4.4 Special Software Packages
- 4.5 Subroutine Library Utilization

5.0 Hardware Environment
- 5.1 Computer and Peripheral Equipment
- 5.2 Instruction Set[4]
- 5.3 Auxiliary Equipment
- 5.4 Interrelationships and Dependencies

FIGURE 4.16 Sample Table of Contents—Systems Summary—II

6.0 System Segments

    6.n.1 Function
    6.n.2 Interrelationships
    6.n.3 Language
    6.n.4 Timing and Size Estimates
    6.n.5 Interface

7.0 System Logic

    7.1 Description
    7.2 Flowchart

8.0 Glossaries

    8.1 Mnemonics/Terms
    8.2 Symbols

9.0 Bibliography

Notes
1. Contains administrative information, correspondence, etc.
2. "Limitations" may be taken as being self-imposed constraints and "Restrictions" as environmental constraints.
3. This is the link or interface points with other systems.
4. This contains a list of special equipment capabilities, e.g., special floating-point facilities.

FIGURE 4.16 Continued

cation to the programmer, as a permanent record as to the nature of a file (for subsequent use by other systems, system amendment, and system modification). It will also serve as a valuable communication aid to the user by means of a formal review step. For example, an established checkpoint by review of the specification can validate that the file *will* grow by not more than 5 percent per commercial period—the product code *does* require not less than five characters—the quantity field *can* contain an arithmetically negative quantity, and so on.

A suggested table of contents for a File Specification is shown in Figure 4.17. A breakdown of the content and methods of presenting information in the File Specification is given below.

File Identification and Characteristics

The first section comprises two subsections: General Description and File Abstract.

The *General Description* is a brief (one- or two-paragraph) narrative description of the sources and general functional characteristics of the file. The information that should be included is

- Brief (two- or three-sentence) definition of file contents and purpose
- Identification of systems in which file is used
- General statement of the source of data and how the file is generated
- General statement of the updating cycle and retention requirements

The *File Abstract* is a succinct definition of the physical or technical characteristics of a file in quick reference format. Use of a simple preprinted form is an ideal method of representing the required information. A sample form is shown in Figure 4.18, and examples of the types of entries are listed below.

File Medium and Code

- Punched cards/paper tape; magnetic disks/disk packs/cards: ASCII, BCD, EBCDIC

File Organization

- Sequential; indexed sequential; controlled sequential; random; serial

Record Type

- Fixed length; variable length

Update Cycle

- Days in processing cycle when file is brought up to date; date from which information in file is valid; reference numbers/titles of programs performing the updating.

FILE SPECIFICATION

Standard Table of Contents

1.0 File Identification and Characteristics

        1.1 General Description
        1.2 File Abstract

2.0 Record Format

3.0 Data Element Descriptions

4.0 **Appendixes**

        4.1 Record Layouts
        4.2 Edit Lists
        4.3 Cross-Reference Lists

FIGURE 4.17 Sample Table of Contents—File Specifications

File Abstract Form

File Name _____

File Medium and Code _____

File Organization _____

Record Sequence _____

Header Label _____ Trailer Label _____

Record Type _____ Maximum Length _____

Blocking Factor _____ Maximum Size _____

Update Cycle _____

File Security Classification _____

Current Volume _____ Growth _____

Retention Characteristics _____

_____

_____

Remarks _____

_____

_____

_____

_____

_____

_____

_____

_____

FIGURE 4.18 Sample File Abstract Form

Current Volume

- Number of records in file at present

Growth

- Rate of increase/decrease/fluctuation in number of records in file, expressed in terms of percentage increase/decrease per unit time, or as specific number of records per unit time

Retention Characteristics

- Number of generations maintained; period of retention of generation before purging

A form similar to that shown in Figure 4.18 should provide an adequate technical description of the basic file characteristics.

Record Format

The next section of the File Specification, *Record Format*, deals with the record-level information. Again, use of some sort of printed form will aid the presentation of information about record structure, use, and content. A sample Record Format form is shown in Figure 4.19. One form is prepared for each record type in the file. The information recorded is defined below.

Relative Positions

- This may be specified by the systems designer at the time the document is prepared or, alternatively, it may be completed by the programmer

Field Label

- This is the title given to the data element (and is a means of cross-reference to a Data Element Description described later)

Program Mnemonic

- Unless a centralized authority assigns mnemonic label for use in the program(s) referencing the data element, this is completed by the programmer

Length

- This defines the length of the data element

Type

- This defines the data element as being numeric, alphabetic, alphanumeric

An alternative system of representation is the use of a free-form graphic description similar to the sample shown in Figure 4.20. Note that the field usage

RECORD FORMAT

File Mnemonic _____ Date _____

Record Type _____

Relative Positions		Field Label	Program Mnemonic	Length	Type
First	Last				

FIGURE 4.19 Sample Record Format Form

RECORD LAYOUT FORM

Record Name _____ DS Name _____ Page ____ of ____
Organization _____ Record Length _____ Date _____

Field Label
Field Description
Field Usage

Field Label
Field Description
Field Usage

Field Label
Field Description
Field Usage

Field Label
Field Description
Field Usage

Files: Processes:
                        Input to: Output from:

Usage Code
A – Alphanumeric
B – Binary
F – Floating Point
N – Zoned Decimal
P – Packed Decimal

FIGURE 4.20 Sample Free Form

System Documentation

rank indicates the type of field (by means of a simple usage code as shown) and its length. For example, an entry A.6 could mean the field comprises six alphanumeric characters.

Data Element Descriptions

Thus far, a method of file description documentation has been presented which has been concerned with the characteristics of the file as a whole and with the composition of records. In the latter case, however, the content of a record was defined solely in terms of the relative position, name, length, and type (alphanumeric, etc.) of each data element. As discussed previously, one purpose of the Record Format definition is to act as an index to a number of individual Data Element Description forms, each of which contains all the information required to define a field. The main reason for using this three-level system of file definition is that the same data elements may appear in a number of files (and also in inputs or outputs). Thus, one description of a data element may be prepared and the description cross-referenced whenever necessary. Further, there may even be a case in some installations for establishing a central control point for the approval/assignment of data element names. Again, use of a preprinted form may prove worthwhile to discipline the systems designer in presenting specific information about a data element in a standard manner. A sample form is shown in Figure 4.21 and a description of the contents is given below.

The form is headed with the Field Label (cross-referenced from the Record Format), the file name or mnemonic, the date and the author's name. A short description of the data element and source is then given, followed by the definition of length, format, and values. In some cases, a field may be defined for future use; i.e., space is provided for a field in a file but at the time the field is defined it has no processing significance. Thus, provision is made for stating a "reserved" category and defining the present contents of the field. For example, under the Reserved heading may be "for future use" and the entry under Contents may read "filler 9s."

Similarly, some organizations employ a security classification system which defines the levels and methods for personnel to access information held in certain data elements. Thus, the contents of a field may be "scrambled" and only certain approved personnel given the means to interpret information. On the sample form shown, provision is made for recording the security classification. Under "Addenda" any other relevant information for the understanding of the data element is entered. The information recorded should include such items as:

- Scaling factor
- Description or reference to coding system employed
- Units of measure

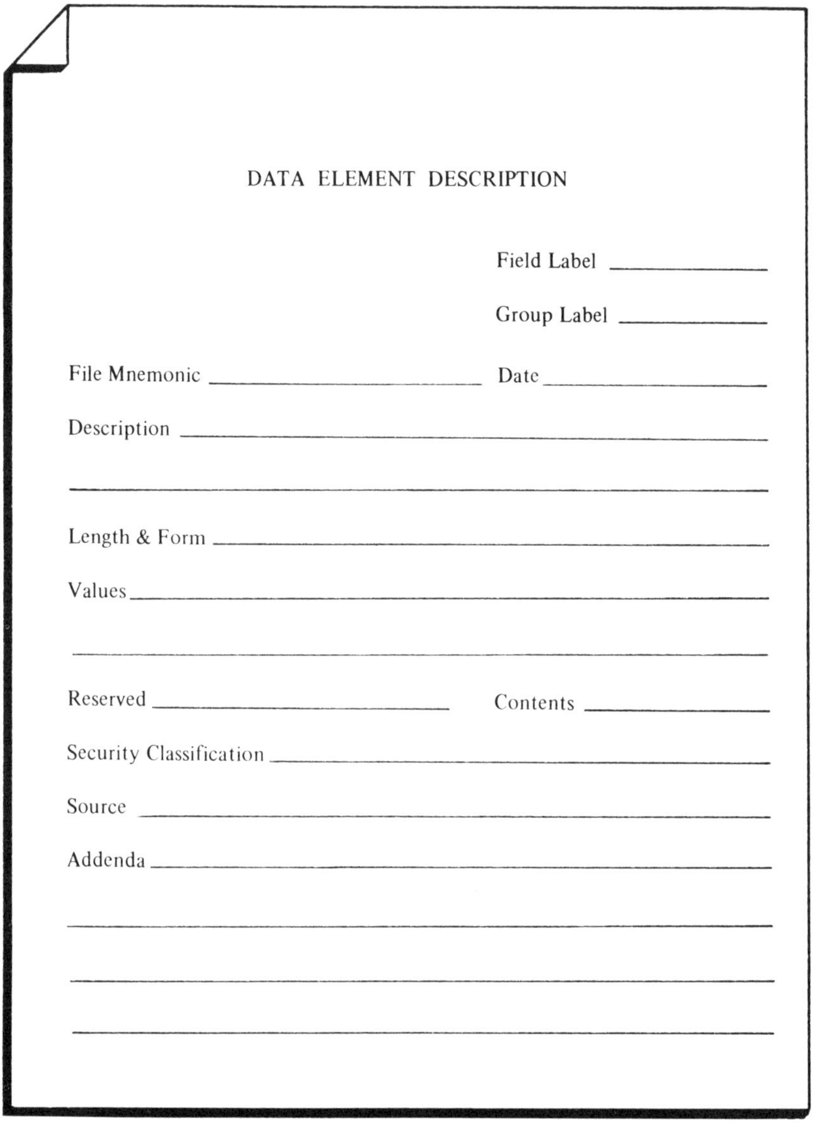

DATA ELEMENT DESCRIPTION

Field Label _____

Group Label _____

File Mnemonic _____ Date _____

Description _____

_____

Length & Form _____

Values _____

_____

Reserved _____ Contents _____

Security Classification _____

Source _____

Addenda _____

_____

_____

_____

FIGURE 4.21 Sample Data Element Description Form

Appendixes

The remainder of the File Specification, the *Appendixes*, can be used to record additional optional information which will assist in use of the specification. Examples of possible appendixes are

- Record layouts: graphical representations of tape, disk, or card record layouts
- Edit lists: tabular representation of editing criteria for acceptable and unacceptable conditions and values of various data elements in a file
- Cross-reference lists: various lists produced as required, which may include index to data elements, reference list showing which transactions produce which file data, and summary tables showing the frequency and use of files within a system

TRANSACTION (INPUT) SPECIFICATIONS

The *Transaction Specification* document describes all the inputs to the system. For the purposes of this book, a transaction is defined as an input which generates some activity in the system, e.g., changes to a file. In addition, the Input Specification describes these transactions in the form in which they enter the computer system, not as they appear at some earlier or later stage of their processing.

For example, if a source document is entered into the computer processing system, the information punched in cards, and the contents of the cards written onto magnetic tape (to form, say, a daily order file), the punched-card form of the transaction is then described in the Input Specification.

A sample table of contents for an Input Specification is shown in Figure 4.22; the contents and methods of presenting information are discussed below.

Identification

The *Identification* simply identifies the report by referencing the system, the author, and the date of preparation.

Transaction Listing

A *Transaction Listing* is a convenient method of summarizing the characteristics of all inputs to the system. As in the File Specification report, preprinted forms or predefined formats may be used to discipline the systems designer to present the required information in a standard manner. A sample form is shown in Figure 4.23 and its contents discussed below.

Transaction Title

- An assigned short name identifying the transaction; if a transaction coding system is used, the transaction identification number may be specified here

```
                INPUT SPECIFICATION

             Standard Table of Contents


       1.0  Identification

       2.0  Transaction Listing And
            Transcription Descriptions

       3.0  Input Layouts and Samples
```

FIGURE 4.22 Sample Table of Contents—Input Specification

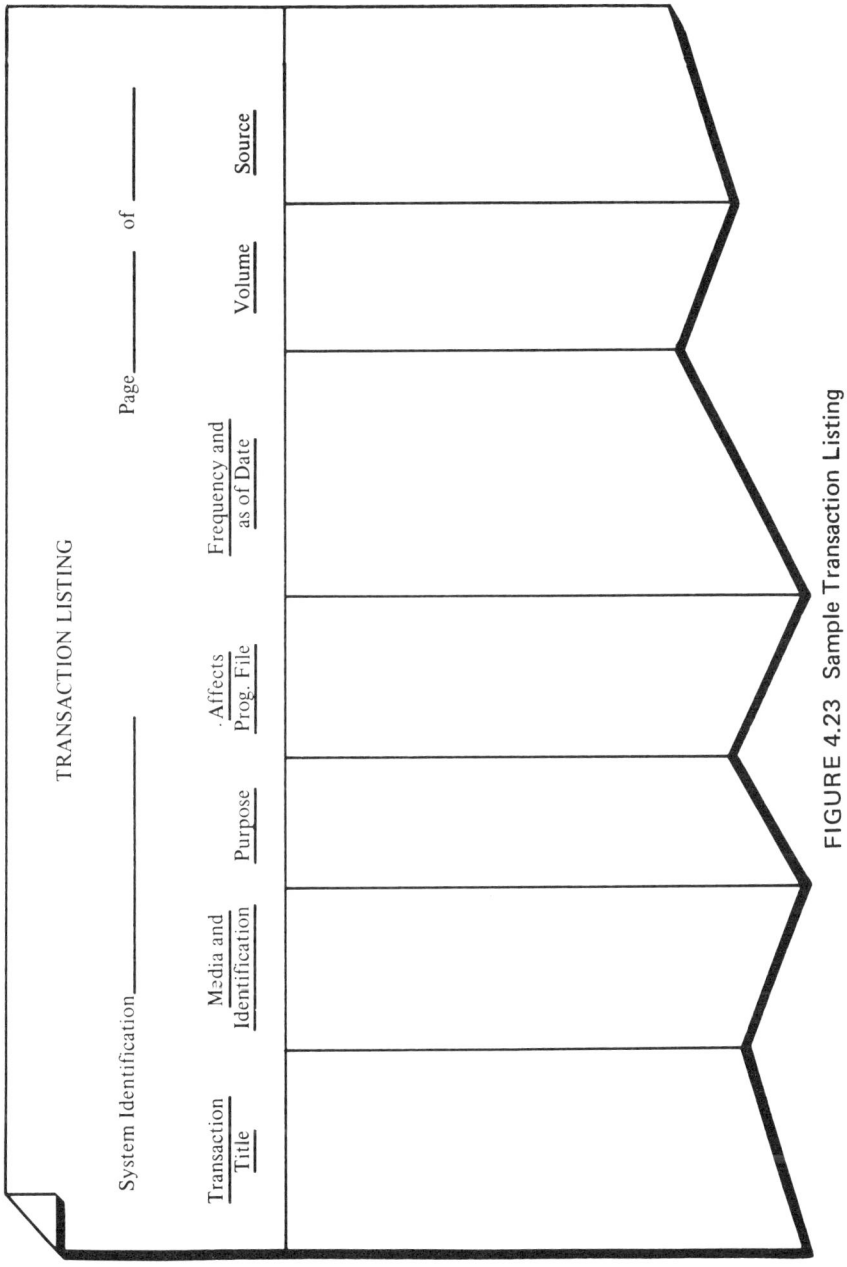

FIGURE 4.23 Sample Transaction Listing

Media and Identification

- The medium on which the transaction is recorded is stated (e.g., magnetic tape, punched card, or paper tape), together with the identifying name of the medium and transaction. For example, the media identification for a punched-card transaction would be the card format; however, one card format may hold a number of different transaction types, and thus the particular card-type code must be specified for each transaction type

Purpose

- A brief statement of the purpose served by the input in a system

Effects

- This should show the program name/number(s) of the program(s) which process the transaction, and a reference to the files that are changed by the transaction

Frequency

- This states the processing cycle of the transaction, i.e., the frequency with which the input will enter the system, together with the date at which the information is accurate

Volume

- An estimate of approximate volume of this transaction type

Source

- A reference to the originating source of the transaction

Transaction Descriptions

The Transaction Listing identifies and presents a general description of all inputs to the system. The Transaction Description, however, presents a detailed description of the contents of each input. A sample preprinted form is shown in Figure 4.24; use of this form requires that each input be described on one form. An explanation of the contents is given below.

Field Label

- An assigned name to identify the field

Field Length and Type

- This defines the length of the field and the type (e.g., numeric, alphabetic, binary, etc.)

Transaction Description

Transaction Name _____

Relative Position	Field Label	Field Length and Type	Values	Edit Criteria

FIGURE 4.24 Sample Transaction Description

Values

- The range of values (minimum and maximum, special conditions) that the field may hold

Edit Criteria

- This is a summary of the acceptable and unacceptable data conditions and values for entering the system. The acceptable conditions and values should be listed first, followed by the unacceptable ones. The latter should be accompanied by a statement of required action for each unacceptable condition

Note that a system of Data Element Descriptions as described on page 73 may be used to supplement or replace part of the Transaction Description.

Input Layouts and Samples

The *Input Layouts and Samples* section should list the input formats to be used in the system. Each format should be documented by showing

- A layout; in rough form or final copy
- A reference list of transactions to layout
- Samples of filled-out formats

The samples need only be included if they will aid the understanding of the input.

OUTPUT SPECIFICATIONS

The *Output Specification* details the systems outputs—why and when produced, contents, formats, and recipients. By output is meant here any product of the system which is to be used elsewhere. Thus, under this definition, messages to equipment operators and intermediate files (interfacing two or more segments in the same system) are excluded from the Output Specification. The Specification does include descriptions of such material as reports, messages to remote terminals, output, magnetic and paper tape for input to a data transmission process. A sample table of contents is shown in Figure 4.25. Note that the method of treatment is similar to Input Specification, i.e., outputs are listed, formats shown, and the individual data elements defined.

Identification

The *Identification* simply identifies the output by referencing the system, the author, and the date of preparation.

OUTPUT SPECIFICATION

<u>Standard Table of Contents</u>

1.0   Identification

2.0   Output Listing

3.0   Output Description

4.0   Output Formats

FIGURE 4.25   Sample Table of Contents—Output Specification

Output Listing

The *Output Listing* is a list of all outputs from the system in the general sequence in which they are produced. For each output, the following information is given (possibly on a preprinted form as shown in Figure 4.26).

Output Name

- The assigned name of the output and possibly a reference number; where a number of output types are produced, such as a number of message types, classed as one output, each output type is defined

Program Number

- The reference number of the program generating the output

Media and Media Identification

- The type of output medium (printed reports, punched cards, magnetic tape, etc.) and the output media identification number or symbol (label or card number, etc.)

Purpose

- The purpose and content are briefly summarized

Frequency and Volume

- This defines the day or date in the processing cycle when the report is produced; the approximate volume should be shown in the appropriate unit of measurement

Number of Copies (Distribution) and Destination

- For a printed report, the number of copies should be specified and a distribution list given; for other outputs, the destination should be specified; e.g., the system reference and point of entry for an output magnetic tape file

Output Description

Having defined the general characteristics of the output in the Output Listing, the detailed contents of each output are defined in the *Output Description*. An Output Description is prepared for each output of the system: a sample preprinted form is shown in Figure 4.27. The entries are described below.

Positions

- The positions occupied on the output file report or message. Where the exact format of a message card or tape output has not been formalized, the relative position may be stated

System Documentation

Field Label

- The assigned name of the field

Source

- The source of a data element in a field is specified (i.e., cross-referenced to a specific input data element or file data element)

		Output Listing			
System Identification _____					
Output Name	Program No.	Media and Media Identification	Purpose	Frequency and Volume	No. of Copies and Destination

FIGURE 4.26 Sample Output Listing

Length and Format

- The length and format of field are defined, e.g., number of characters and edit requirements—position of sign, currency symbol, decimal point, zero-suppression requirements, etc.

Positions	Field Label	Source	Length and Format	Program	Layout Reference

Output Description

Output Name _____

FIGURE 4.27 Sample Output Description

Program

 • The program reference number of the program generating the output

Layout Reference

 • A cross reference to the pictorial layout in Section 4, Output Formats

Note that the Output Description describes only data fields: indicative data such as printed headings, etc., should be shown in Output Formats. Again, a series of Data Element Descriptions may be used as described previously to define the contents of fields.

Output Formats

Samples of output should be included in the form of layouts or copies, keyed to names and/or numbers in the Output Listing. Report formats would customarily be finalized at the system design stage. However, in some organizations precise formats of messages, card, or tape layouts may be omitted if these have not been defined at the design stage. When report layouts are shown, standards should be laid down for their presentation. For example, the difference between printed and preprinted headings should be apparent, layouts should be drawn on a standard form, sample values should be included showing minimum/maximum/special values, and so on.

PROCESSING (PROGRAM) SPECIFICATIONS

In the method of system documentation used as an example in this chapter, a Program Specification comprises the File, Input and Output Specifications, and a Processing Specification.

The *Processing Specification* is essentially a statement of the design requirements and general logic for a program. It is prepared by the systems designer (possibly with assistance from the programming function) to enable the programmer to develop processing logic. One Processing Specification is thus prepared for each program. Note, however, that in a complex system as defined by means of the detailed Systems Summary on page 64, the *segment* concept of processing may be used. In this case, each major logical segment of the system may be described by a Segment Processing Specification. This specification may encompass a number of programs. For ease of documentation, this specification should be broken down into a number of Processing Specifications. This then gives the required one Processing Specification per program.

The Processing Specification may either be "free form" within a laid-down table of contents or be based on a preprinted form with standard headings. Irrespective of the format, the information listed below must be given.

Secondly, to obviate unnecessary duplication, the information must be presented in a form such that it can readily be incorporated (as introductory material) in the program documentation. Information requirements are:

- The inputs to a program
- The outputs of a program
- The major functions performed
- The means of communication between this program and previous/following programs
- The logical rules and decisions to be followed (defined in decision tables if necessary), including a statement of how the input is to be examined, altered, and utilized
- The validation and edit criteria
- The action to be taken on error or exception conditions
- Special tables, formulas, and algorithms
- The parameters to be entered if a utility program is to be used, e.g., sort sequence and keys for a sort program

One method of presenting the above information is by using a preprinted form similar to that sample shown in Figure 4.28. The form is completed according to the following three rules:

1. Define each file and input to the program by

    - Showing the appropriate input/file symbol and connecting it to the input line
    - Entering into the symbol the appropriate file name and identification number
    - Drawing a connector symbol above the input/file symbol, and stating the origin of that input/file in the symbol

2. Define each output and file produced by the program by

    - Drawing the appropriate output/file symbol and connecting it to the output line
    - Entering into the symbol the appropriate output/file name and identification number
    - Drawing a connector symbol below the output/file symbol and stating the destination of that output/file in the symbol stated

3. In the processing box, enter the purpose and function of the program, and refer to supplementary sheets giving the additional material. Decision tables, as described in Chapter 8, can be used to define complex processing logic.

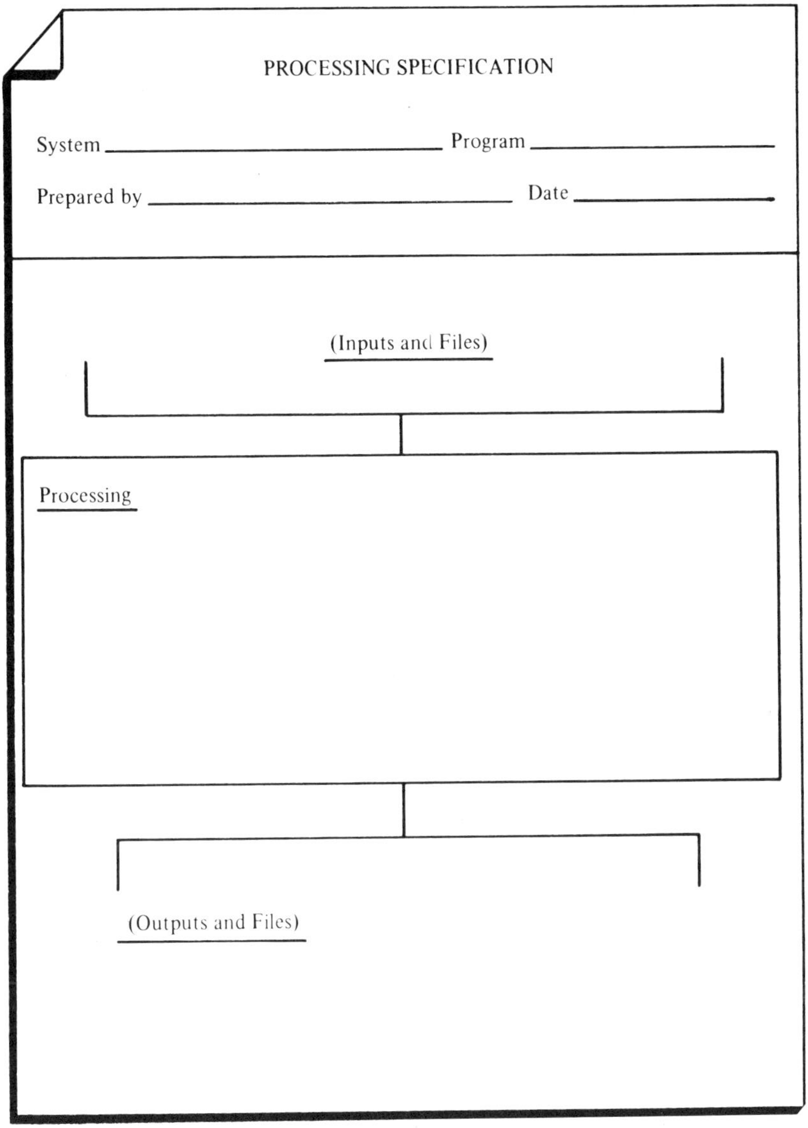

PROCESSING SPECIFICATION

System _____ Program _____

Prepared by _____ Date _____

(Inputs and Files)

Processing

(Outputs and Files)

FIGURE 4.28 Sample Processing Specification

SYSTEMS TEST PLAN

The *Systems Test Plan* is a permanent record of the testing procedure to prove the system prepared by the systems design function. Note that it is distinct from the program test plan which includes a series of test cases prepared by a programmer to prove a program.

The Systems Test Plan should

- Explain the purpose of the test designs
- Define test inputs and files
- Specify test procedures
- Define outputs to be achieved

Thus, the test plan establishes the requirements to be met before the system can be considered as being operational.

A sample table of contents is shown in Figure 4.29.

Identification

The *Identification* references the Systems Specification of which the test plan is a part.

Test Organization

The *Test Organization* summarizes

- Test objectives for the system
- Responsibility allocation for conducting the tests, for coordination with runs and data sources, and for maintenance of the test material
- References to other systems which have provided tests of some components of this system; e.g., existing files and inputs previously tested for another system

Validity Criteria

The *Validity Criteria* section may be considered as comprising a "quality control" specification for data and procedures. It is a description of the test criteria for all conditions in the system. These conditions include: control, processing, and output test criteria.

Control conditions include criteria for such functions as

- Permissible error tolerances
- Provision of checkpoints for error recovery
- Preprocessing requirements
- Acceptance of files and file records
- Acceptance of input

SYSTEMS TEST PLAN

Table of Contents

1.0 Identification
2.0 Test Organization
3.0 Validity Criteria
    3.1 Control
    3.2 Processing
    3.3 Output
4.0 Test Schedule
5.0 Test Cases
    5.1 Test Case 1
    5.n Test Case n

FIGURE 4.29 Sample Table of Contents—Systems Test Plan

Processing criteria should be included for such functions as

- Valid and invalid combinations of input and file data
- Invalid codes and code combinations
- Invalid parameter options

Output criteria should be shown for such conditions as

- Message length and format
- Output designations and codes
- Report spacing limits

Test Schedule

The *Test Schedule* section lists the sequence of operations for performing a complete systems test. The steps required and the appropriate sequence can be defined by means of a standard preprinted form similar to the sample shown in Figure 4.30. The required information is summarized below.

Step Number

- All operations in the test are assigned a number to indicate the sequence in which the tests are applied

Test Number

- All test cases are assigned an identification number

Program Number

- The program involved in this step is listed by its identification number

Inputs Required

- The inputs required for a test are listed here by input name (and/or reference number); the source and date of the test data should also be shown (e.g., whether the data is artificial test data or selected live cases)

Files Required

- The files required for a test are listed here by file name (and/or reference number); the source and date of the file data should be identified (e.g., whether the data is artificial or live)

Results

- The desired results for each step in the systems test should be stated; this may be by reference to the documented test cases as defined below

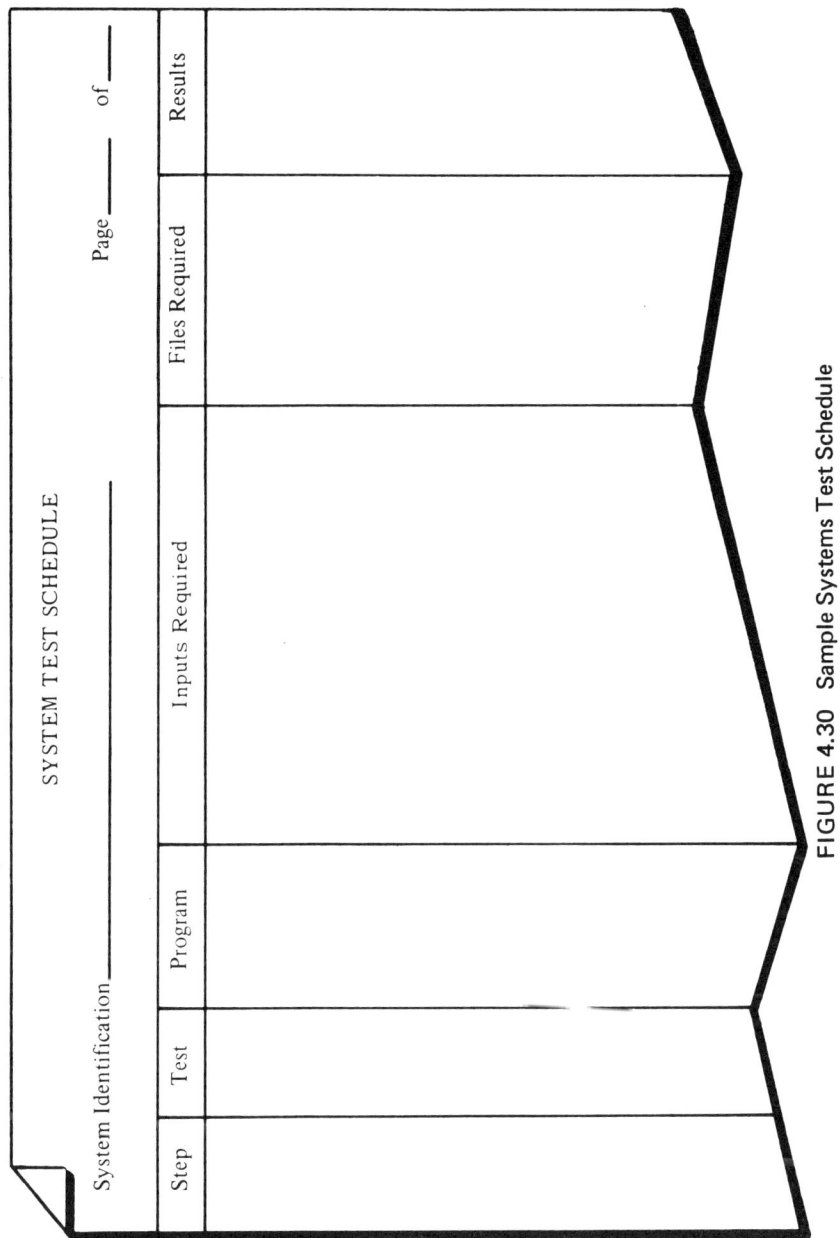

FIGURE 4.30 Sample Systems Test Schedule

Test Cases

Each *Test Case* should be described in a subsection and the subsection identified by the test number. For each test case, the test inputs, files, and outputs should be defined.

A Test File should be explained in terms of

- Organization and contents of the file
- Test-file data identification and printout of files permanently maintained for test-file purposes

Test Inputs should be defined in terms of content by transaction type. Permanently maintained test inputs should be shown by layout or print-out.

Test Outputs should show a sample of each derived output from each step in which the test case is involved.

Test files and input descriptions should include a statement of the purpose of the data, i.e., the section criteria for a transaction type of test-file records. Test outputs should state what is being tested in the production of each output.

COMPOSITE DESCRIPTIVE FORMS

The file, input, and output documentation described previously in this chapter used a technique of Data Element Description forms. This technique gives a modular approach to documentation and, by having separate descriptions of data elements, it obviates the need for including a description of the same data element in every file, input type, or output type containing that element.

Appendix B presents an alternative approach. Essentially, this approach attempts to use one basic form to record all the information concerning file, input, and output.

SUMMARY

1. The documentation requirements for the investigation and analysis tasks must be designed with the methods standards for these tasks; examples have been given.
2. The basic output from the systems analysis and design phase should be a Systems Specification.
3. The Systems Specification is the definition of the system in terms of its function, scope, flow, and controls.

4. A suggested approach to the preparation of a Systems Specification is the preparation of a multisection document comprised of

- Systems Summary
- File Specifications
- Transaction (Input) Specifications
- Output Specifications
- Processing Specifications
- Systems Test Plan

5. The contents of the File, Transaction, and Output Specifications were discussed in terms of a free-form or preprinted-form approach. The use of a three-level document system was suggested in which

- Level one was an overall description of the file, or list of transactions or outputs
- Level two was a description of the format and overall content of a file, transaction, or output record
- Level three was a Data Element Description which described the format, contents, and use of each field.

CHAPTER 5

Program Documentation

The limits and responsibilities of the programming function are perhaps easiest to define in terms of a start and end point. The programming function can be said to commence with the provision of a problem definition and specification for a solution. From this initial input, detailed program logic is designed, and the program coded and tested. The output is thus a proved and documented program ready for operation, although probably it will be operated initially under a test environment.

Within this simple functional definition, there is a wide range of applicational differences. At one end of the spectrum are the scientific/engineering problem-solving applications in which one man determines that a problem exists, defines the problem, and prepares a solution-giving program. The program may well serve a one-time purpose, the input and file data may be generated solely by the problem originator, and the output may be examined and interpreted by the user alone. In such instances there may be one nebulous documenting step from "back-of-envelope jottings" to proved object program listing.

At the other end of this application-type spectrum, the input to the programming function may be a detailed Systems Specification, comprising a number of Program Specifications describing a complex business data processing system. The programming tasks in such a case will be performed by many programmers, possibly with the use of outside contractors. Since communication becomes much more of a problem under such conditions, this chapter is primarily concerned with business data processing programming. Further, it assumes as a starting point the provision of a Systems Specification comprising a number of Program Specifications with the level of content described in the previous chapter.

The first part of this chapter is concerned principally with application programming; some notes at the end of this chapter are given on software development documentation.

Program Documentation

PROGRAMMING—TASKS AND COMMUNICATION

Historically, the tasks of the programming activity have usually been the most clearly defined of all the data processing functions. The actual personnel assignment of the tasks however is still the subject of much debate. The recognized programming tasks are

- Logic analysis
- Coding
- Desk checking
- Test data preparation
- Assembly/compilation and testing
- Specification of operating requirements
- Final documentation
- Installation

Associated with these clearly defined tasks is a traditional concept of types and levels of documentation, and agreed lines of communication. These may be stated by briefly reviewing the aims of program documentation. The results of the first five tasks in the above list must be recorded so that

- A change in programmer task assignment may be effected with the minimum of disruption
- Program modifications and corrections may be made efficiently and effectively
- Conversion may be made to new equipment
- Management can assess the progress and quality of the work performed
- The programs may be turned over to operations for day-to-day running and maintenance

From the above, it can be seen that the two main users of program documentation will be programmers and data processing management. Operations will also be a prime user of that part of the program documentation relating to computer operating instructions. These will form part of the total program documentation but will be discussed in greater detail in Chapter 6, *Operations Documentation*. Note, however, that computer or program operating instructions form only a part of the required operating documentation (with data preparation, auxiliary equipment, output dispersal instructions, etc.).

Users may also reference program documentation. However, in a commercial environment, users in the operating departments will generally be more interested in the general program description and in the Program Specification.

Given the above programming tasks and documentation requirements, what is the minimum level of program documentation?

THE PROGRAM MANUAL—THE TRADITIONAL APPROACH

The term *Program Manual* is used in this book to describe the complete final documentation of a program. The *Traditional Approach* quoted in the title of this section refers to a technique of program documentation which has come to be accepted as an "industry standard" over the past few years. In some instances, it is still a valid approach. It thus forms an excellent starting point for a detailed discussion of program documentation. As we shall see in the next section, however, the changing techniques and environment of programming requires in many instances that a different structure and level of program documentation be used.

The Program Manual should contain (or reference)

- A general description of the function, use, and methodology of the program
- Descriptions of input, files, and output used or produced by the program
- Flow diagrams showing the logic of the program
- Descriptions of instructive output messages (e.g., output on console or printer)
- Coding information (e.g., an assembly listing, memory print, descriptions of matrices or tables used)
- Test plan
- Program test and operating instructions

The content and method of presentation of the above are discussed below in terms of the traditional methods of pure narrative description and flowcharts. The description also assumes original development, i.e., a Program Specification, without the elaborate use of application packages or software routines. Alternative methods of representation, the impact of application packages, and use of standard software will be discussed later in this chapter.

A sample table of contents for a Program Manual is shown in Figure 5.1

Identification

Each Program Manual should be identified by at least a system reference (name and number), a program reference (name and number), the author's name, position, and location, and the issue date.

Program Description

As shown in Figure 5.1, the *Program Description* can be considered as comprising two subsections: a Processing Specification and a description of Program Methodology.

The *Processing Specification* corresponds to the section in the Programming

Specification (described on page 85) prepared by the systems designer. If a Programming Specification is prepared as described in the previous chapter, the Processing Specification may be extracted for inclusion in the Program Manual.

The *Programming Methodology* subsection is usually prepared by the pro-

```
              PROGRAM MANUAL

             Table of Contents

    1.0   Identification
    2.0   Program Description
          2.1   Processing Specification
          2.2   Program Methodology
    3.0   Data Specifications
          3.1   File
          3.2   Input
          3.3   Output
    4.0   Program Logic
          4.1   Logic Flowchart
          4.2   Tables and Techniques
    5.0   Listings
          5.1   Post-assembly Listing
          5.2   Label and Symbol Tables
          5.3   Instruction Listing
          5.4   Switch List
    6.0   Program Test Plan
```

FIGURE 5.1 Sample Table of Contents—Program Manual

grammer, although sufficient information may have been given in the Processing Specification as to make this subsection unnecessary. Essentially, Program Methodology records, in brief terms, the programmer's approach to the Processing Specification.

This is done by recording such information as

- General logic
- Equipment configuration requirements and constraints (special features required, core storage required, etc.)
- Subroutines called and their calling sequence
- Special formulas used
- Any other information of a specialized nature which is not recorded elsewhere

Data Specifications

The file, input, and output specifications as described (pages 64-85) should be included. If the finalizing of layouts is the task of the programming function, layouts and samples (if available) should be included.

Program Logic

Traditionally, program logic is represented by means of flowcharts supported by descriptive narrative.

Supporting the diagrammatic representation of logic is a subsection *Tables and Techniques*. This is generally an optional subsection: it can be used to describe any special techniques or tables. Tables and techniques which are self-explanatory by reference to the program listing do not require any special description. However, some explanatory notes may be required for such items as

- Complex table structures
- Special search techniques
- Randomizing formulas
- Special access formulas
- Core storage layouts for small machines with wiring boards or where buffering techniques are complex

Listings

The coding of the program should be shown by including

- Postassembly listing
- Label and symbol tables
- Machine code instruction listing
- Switch list

The listing of the source language program should be a copy of the final assembly listing. The label and symbol tables and machine code instruction listing may be included in the postassembly listing. When they are not so included, separate listings should be produced and incorporated in the Program Manual.

The switch listing should record a list of all program switches under the programmer's control. Notes should be given on the purpose of each switch and the alternate (on/off) settings or conditions.

The coding of a program, as shown in the computer listings, should itself represent a major documentation aid. For example, an assembler or low-level language program may be written in accordance with rules which govern program layout and use of labels or symbols. Examples of areas in which rules may be specified are as follows.

1. Layout of introductory comments by use of comment cards showing program and programmer identification, equipment requirements, program options, etc.

2. Layout and content of data defining part of a program, e.g.,

- Sequence in which various areas of memory are assigned such as input/output areas, work areas, tables, constants (data and address), messages, headings, halts, and so on
- Use of standard identification characters and format for labels. This can include rules of use of first character of label field to show type of field area, e.g.,

    A = accumulator/count field
    D = disk input/output area
    H = halt constant/address
    S = program switch
    K = data constant
    L = table
    M = message
    N = address constant

    Further rules may specify how the remainder of the label is to be made up.
- Use of comment cards and comment fields to explain the purpose and use of the field or area

3. Layout of program in terms of blocks, use of block identification comments and block identification character, and listing spacing.

4. Format of source statement (instruction labels). This could include a system which cross-references macro- and micro-flowchart to the listing. For example,

first character = B (Branch Point)
second character = block identification character
remainder = numeric character corresponding to the identification sequence numbers on micro-flowchart symbols

5. Use of comments to describe processing statements. Rules may be specified governing the use of comment cards or the comment field in the processing part of the program. Such rules may include these:

- Abbreviation of comments should be avoided
- Comments should be a meaningful description of an operation rather than a simple restatement of an instruction in English language form
- During program testing and alteration, comments as well as instructions should be updated

The actual format and content of comments to certain processes may be standardized as in, for example, the description of entry, processing, and exit conditions from a loop.

By the application of such rules, a source program listing of a low or intermediate level language may be constructed so as to form a meaningful document for reference.

Program Test Plan

The preparation of a program test plan is a fundamental technique of program preparation methodology. The basic purpose and use of a test plan is summarized below.

A test plan is essentially a schedule of sequenced operations to test a program. Program testing is perhaps the most inexact science within the programming function; however, it is possible to structure a hierarchy of testing objectives. A suggested breakdown of program test steps is as follows.

1. Rectify clerical or punching errors as indicated by error flags in program listing; i.e., produce "cleanlisting."

2. For each program block, test using artificial data of simplest cases to test major logic; if the processing reaches end of block compare output to expected result. If correct, test next "logic type." If incorrect or program hangs up, begin major check-out by establishing last point that program was functioning correctly and work from there, checking the contents of key fields, arithmetic accuracy, possibly by use of a trace/diagnostic routine.

3. Continue test using more complex cases and combinations of test cases, to prove each block.

4. Test the overall logic of the program, e.g., interblock communication.

Program Documentation

From the above simplified description it can be seen that a good testing technique is a modular technique. Further, testing must not be assumed to be a one-time process. Any but the simplest corrections to a proved program must be followed by a complete testing cycle. Testing is also generally the most time consuming and expensive of the program development tasks. For these reasons, it is important to have a record of the test plan.

The test plan incorporated in the Program Manual should normally comprise

- A summary of method
- List of test cases, sequence of application and expected results
- Listing of test data

A major cause of wasted machine time is that program errors are corrected but the test data is not updated. Often, test data is as much in error as the program. Thus, test data, where faulty, should be corrected at the same time as program bugs and documentation are updated. Subsequent testing for program modifications and amendments may thus be made without complete redesign of test data. The other aspect of the test plan is as a control document recording the number of test shots, types of errors, and so on.

This then, is the traditional Program Manual. But as observed at the beginning of this section, it has a number of basic limitations and does not make use of a number of modern techniques.

THE PROGRAM MANUAL—ALTERNATIVE APPROACHES

There are a number of limitations to the arrangement of a Program Manual as described above. There are alternative ways of presenting data other than flowcharts, for example, by the use of decision tables. Secondly, there are a number of factors in the current methodology of programming which need to be considered when determining the type, level, and scope of a Program Manual.

The Program Manual as described above would probably be best suited to an installation which has:

- The majority of its programs written in a low-level assembly language (such as Autocoder and Easycoder)
- A personnel breakdown in the programming function to program logic designer, coder, and tester
- Little or no elaborate use of application software
- A medium to low level of programmers using conventional approaches and techniques

A number of factors which influence the program documentation techniques for different environments are discussed below. These are:

- Logic Representation by Decision Tables (see Chapter 8)
- Impact of High-Level Languages
- Impact of Application Packages
- Use of General-Purpose Software
- Use of Documentation Aids (see Chapter 9)

As a summary, we may say that the only areas which are not affected by any differences in working environments are Identification, Data Descriptions, and Test Plan.

Use of High-Level Languages

The traditional Program Manual as described previously was mainly oriented toward the lower-level assembler-type languages. In such a case, it was suggested that reference to program structure and content could be streamlined by using an identification method which directly relates macro-flowchart to micro-flowchart to coding. The use of a high-level language would to a large extent make such a system unnecessary and unwieldy. However, to insure clarity of meaning in the listings a number of simple rules may be laid down. For example, program layout standards may be established for COBOL programs. These could cover such areas as

- Rules for the use of an identification character preceding the label to identify it as an accumulator, block, constant, data, etc.
- Rules for forming labels (e.g., avoidance of nonstandard abbreviations)
- Rules for use of comments and paging
- Rules for use of margins for lining up source statement entries and for the use of indentations

The required level of flowcharting for a high-level language should be at least a macro-level flowchart and, possibly, to micro-level flowchart.

For example, a COBOL program which merely produces a number of reports from a file may have a complex "logic structure" but since the program may be a series of similar operations, no micro-flowchart may be required.

Impact of Application Packages

With the wide range of application packages (wide both in terms of scope and quantity) coming onto the market, it is difficult to make generalizations about their impact on program documentation. A prime requirement for an application package is that it be well documented. This is essential, for an inadequately documented package prevents the user from understanding the techniques and methods used. One result of this is that the user is prevented from evaluating its efficiency or effectiveness. In addition, the format and content of the programming and operations documentation may not be written in accordance with the installations standards and therefore require alteration and expansion.

As a basic rule, the level of documentation required for programs comprising an application package should be equivalent to the Program Manual. At least the Identification, Data Description, and (probably) the Program Description must be written by the user. Ideally, the logic flowcharts/explanatory narrative/decision tables should be supplied by the developer; the program listings are invariably supplied and the test data is rarely supplied. Depending on the current status of a package, no logic flowcharts may be supplied if the package is at an early state of development. In this case, the user will probably have to undertake the task of preparing flowcharts from the listings. (Alternatively, the flowcharts may not be up to date.) If the package is in a more advanced state of development, detailed logic diagrams *may* be available, but, more probably, they will be in outline (with brief narrative) only.

One of the criteria for selecting a particular package must be the availability and level of documentation supplied.

If the package program documentation is considered adequate, the required Program Manuals may be treated the same way as for the use of general purpose software, as described below.

Use of General-Purpose Software

Program documentation should be produced for all programs in a system, including standard utility programs, e.g., sort/merge programs and transcription programs. However, since such software programs are well documented when initially written, the user program documentation can be much abbreviated.

For compatibility, a Program Manual similar in form to the one described can be produced for each utility employed. The manual content would be amended as follows:

Program Methodology—statement of routine name, version number, source, reference to descriptive material, and basic description of parameters (such as sort keys).

Program Logic—detailed list of parameters (e.g., blocking factors, record formats, sort control keys) and parameter card layout and contents; if the software used is a Report Generator, the completed specification forms should be included.

Program Coding—listings need be included only for a report generator and similar generator programs.

Similarly, where standard subroutines are incorporated into a program (other than basic input/output subroutines called by an assembler or compiler), these subroutines need not be documented in detail. Standard subroutines used in a program should be referenced in Program Methodology by listing:

- Subroutine name
- Source/reference
- Brief purpose and description
- Calling sequence

SUMMARY

1. The start of the development programming phase is considered to be the provision of authorized Program Specification(s).

2. The end of the development programming phase is the output of proved program(s), fully documented in Program Manual(s).

3. The basic steps in programming are:

- Logic Analysis
- Coding
- Desk Checking
- Test Case Preparation
- Assembly/Compilation and Testing
- Specification of Operating Requirements
- Final Documentation
- Installation

4. The work in the tasks listed above should be documented in a Program Manual. The basic content of a Program Manual is:

- A general description of program functions
- Specification of program logic
- Coding information
- Description of inputs, outputs, files, and instructive output messages
- Test plan
- Program test and operating instructions

5. The establishment of program documentation standards should take into account:

- The level of the language used
- The use of decision tables
- The use of general purpose software
- The use and selection of application packages

CHAPTER 6

Operations Documentation

In the areas of analytical, system, and program documentation discussed in the previous chapter, it was seen that the three documentation classifications corresponded reasonably well with the functional areas of systems design, project management, and programming. Operations documentation cuts across the boundaries of these functional areas. Some operations documentation will be prepared by the systems function and some by the programming function. Similarly, some operations documentation must be prepared for the user and some for the data processing operations staff; this is discussed in the next chapter. Thus, it is important to realize that in this chapter we are considering documentation produced by several functional areas. The two basic operations documents are: Program Test Instructions and System Operating Instructions; the latter has a major subset: Program Operating Instructions.

PROGRAM TEST INSTRUCTIONS

The *Program Test* document comprises those instructions which are necessary to guide the computer operator in running a program test; it is prepared by the programmer. The responsibilities for insuring that adequate test instructions are prepared should rest with the programming supervisor (chief programmer, team leader, lead programmer, etc.). An additional checkpoint should be considered whereby the senior computer operator may withhold or abandon a test shot if the test instructions are ambiguous or incomplete.

In effect, the Program Test Instructions may be prepared with a format and content similar to the Program Operating Instructions discussed later in this chapter. However, it is good programming practice in operational programs to minimize the amount of external communication with the operator. On the other hand, during program testing, additional provision should be made in the test instructions for special procedures, e.g., for programmed breakpoints and even programmer-specified intervention under certain conditions.

SYSTEM OPERATING INSTRUCTIONS

This document comprises a list of processing steps, in the sequence in which they are to be executed, defining, in detail, all the operating requirements. A major subset of this document is the Program Operating Instructions discussed below. Other information which may be included in the System Operating Instructions is:

1. Summary workflow/schedule
2. Data collection and preparation instructions
3. Input control instructions
4. Job assembly instructions
5. Output review and control instructions

At this point in the chapter, a major qualification must be made defining the relationship between the operations documentation and user aids. In some installations functions 2, 3, and 5 may be classed as user functions. That is, the user is given the responsibility for submitting clean data in a form ready for input to a computer. The data processing operations function is simply responsible for performing the required computer processing and possibly some ancillary equipment processing. The user is responsible for the subsequent output validation and distribution. However, in another installation the responsibility for these functions may be assumed by data processing operations. In the latter case the user is responsible for providing, in conjunction with the data processing development staff, explicit instructions as to how data is to be handled on receipt from source through to final dispatch. In the former case, the information given for functions 2, 3, and 5 would comprise part of the System Operating Instructions.

The relationship between the contents of the two documents is thus primarily one of functional responsibility between user and data processing operations. For explanatory purposes in this and the next chapter, it is assumed that the user is responsible for submitting source data in accordance with an agreed time and quality schedule. All processing is then performed by data processing operations. The operations documentation therefore conforms to the brief listing of contents as shown on page 108. The required user aid information would include the agreed schedule of times, input quality control information, and notes for the interpretation of output reports. Thus, for any other type of working environment the content of the System Operating Instructions and User Aids may be altered or switched according to the division of responsibility. The major requirement is that the information must be available in some formal document and the assignment of responsibilities between operations and the user clearly defined.

Basic Approaches to Organization

The structure of the System Operations Instructions depends on the internal organization structure of operations group. One method of preparing the System Operating Instructions is to produce one complete specification as shown in the example table of contents on page 000. The material is divided into a logical grouping by functional responsibility within the operations group, prefaced by a summary which shows all the processing steps in sequence. A master copy of the manual may then be kept in the library, a working master by the Operations Manager (or equivalent), and Section 1 plus other relevant section(s) retained by the appropriate operations functions.

Note that this documentation is all job dependent and must be supplemented by general housekeeping documentation such as: tape/disk, library documentation, computer and ancillary equipment usage recording, general quality control requirements, job scheduling and control procedures.

There is a multiplicity of methods for presenting the material, ranging from a multiplicity of different methods for presenting the material, ranging from the use of general narrative within standard headings to the use of preprinted forms. In both cases, the responsibility for insuring the preparation of Systems Operating Instructions must be assigned to the project leader or equivalent. A formal checkpoint should be established for the handover of the operational system and documented instructions to the operations function. The example shown on page 106 is primarily based on the narrative approach. An alternative approach is to use standard preprinted forms and to describe each processing step in sequence. For each process type (e.g., a program run, keypunching a transaction, or an ancillary equipment operation like a tabular listing) there is a standard form to be completed. The forms are bound in the sequence in which they occur, the whole document being again prefaced by an overall workflow summary and schedule. Each operations function holds a complete set of the System Operating Instructions.

Of the two approaches, the latter has been found to work well in most instances. It imposes a strict discipline on the systems analysts and programmers, is easy to use provided the summary section is adequate, and is easy to amend. It is especially useful where the system operation comprises a number of clerical and ancillary operations between computer runs, or where a number of transaction types are to be processed at a different time in the operating cycle. Where most applications comprise a series of more or less consecutive runs, with few intervening clerical or ancillary machine operations, the narrative approach to documentation will probably be adequate. For the purposes of this book, the preprinted form with one form per operation type filed in sequence by operation will be used for explanatory purposes. However, for all but the simplest clerical operations, the printed forms will reflect the physical characteristics of the equipment used. In the following discussion therefore, the minimum headings on the forms will be listed; these must be supplemented where necessary with additional hardware-oriented headings.

The first step in establishing standard System Operating Instructions is to design the required range of forms. A basic range of forms would include

- Workflow summary
- General clerical
- Data preparation—(i.e., keypunching)
- Ancillary machine (by machine category)
- Computer operating (by computer type)

A sample Workflow Summary Form is shown in Figure 6.1. Note that the form basically consists of a process flowchart and a process step number column. In the example shown, additional summary information is given for operations control such as volumes and schedule. Each process symbol corresponds to one or more operating instruction forms referenced by the step number. Where the sequence of operations is variable, e.g., the sequence is dependent on the conditions prevailing at the time, alternative sequences may be shown by means of a decision symbol and alternative flow lines.

Process Step No.	Operation (Process) Flowchart	Specification No.	Volumes	Latest Time To This Operation	Latest Time Out From This Operation
1	Check receipt of batches from all stores	1.1	17 batches of approx. 900 to 1200 documents	10.00 Tuesday	12.00 Tuesday
2	Punch/Verify Issue/Receipts	1.2	17,000 cards	12.00 Tuesday	17.00 Thursday
3	Balance Batches	1.3	N/A	17.15 Thursday	19.00 Thursday
4	Agreement / Error Check to Source	2.0		Variable	
5	Prepare Monthly Parameter Cards	1.4	N/A	08.45 Friday	09.00 Friday
6	Take-on Program 'JM 37'	1.5	17,000 cards 120 forms	09.00 Friday	11.45 Friday

System: Stores Stock (1)   Date: 5-6-67   By: J.M. Dumf

FIGURE 6.1 Sample Workflow Summary

Operations Documentation

Each operating instruction form should bear the basic identifying information comprising at least

- System identification
- Operation identification (brief title)
- This operation step number
- Previous operation step number/next operation step number
- Date of issue
- Originator/authority

Similarly, a number of standard entries may appear beneath the identification block on all forms. These may include

- Responsibility for performing the operation
- Input: description and source
- Output: description and destination
- Process: summary of process

A *General Clerical Form* should be used for any manual machine independent operation and thus contains only the above standard identification block and headings. The remainder of the form is "free form" and is completed as required with a detailed specification of the operations to be performed. Entries for various types of operations will be discussed later in this chapter.

The *Keypunch Form* should have provision for recording (or referencing) the following information:

1. Format of Punching Document and Media. This specifies

- The punching code
- An annotated copy of a punching document (if complex), referenced to the appropriate card columns/character positions to be punched
- A brief list of card columns/characters stating content of field as alphabetic, numeric, fixed-length or variable-length, and special punching codes (e.g., nonstandard field separators and special punching codes in data fields)

2. Special Procedures. This lists any nonstandard error correction procedures or special labeling requirements. For example:

- Special batch or file labels
- Nonstandard error repunching procedure for paper tape
- Error procedure for obvious mistakes or illegible entries on punching documents
- Special requirements for batch control checking

3. Punch Document/Media Destination. This specifies the procedure for disposing of the punching documents and the destination of the punched media.

4. Machine Set-Up. This specifies

- Copy of program card/wiring diagram
- Switch settings

A preprinted *Ancillary Equipment Form* should be prepared for each major ancillary machine type. The form should provide for a statement of

- Disposition of input/output on machine
- Switch settings
- Wiring diagrams
- Special error/batch checking procedures and a step by step summary of operation, if warranted by complexity of the operation

It is often useful in a large installation running complex applications to have separate *Job Assembly Instructions* prior to the operating instructions for each program. The job assembly instructions list the complete data/program availability requirements for the job to be run. The required material may thus be checked off and assembled in the computer room prior to the program being run. Where it is the responsibility of the job assembly function to prepare parameter cards, the contents, format, and, if necessary, the position of the card in a data file of each parameter card should be given.

The *Computer Operating Instructions* will vary according to the size and type of machine. Note that the operating instructions included in System Operating Instructions are backed up by the relevant program manuals (including the detailed data specifications); thus the operating instructions should provide only a concise but complete specification of the procedures to be followed by the computer operator. A general summary of the contents of the computer operating instructions is given below.

A three-sheet approach is recommended, each sheet being identified by the program name/number, with

sheet 1 = summary data and set-up
sheet 2 = running
sheet 3 = take-down

The summary data on sheet 1 should appear below the standard identification block and contain information such as

- Brief description of program functions
- Summary of peripheral and core storage usage
- Priority (for a multiprogramming system)
- Estimated running time (average or by volume)

For program set-up, the following information should be given:

1. The exact program name, media, and source.

2. The peripheral on which the program is to be loaded (if necessary).
3. For each item of input data

- The name of the input (for operator identification)
- Input peripheral type
- Actual peripheral (if necessary)

4. For each item of output data

- The name of the output (for operator identification)
- Output peripheral type
- Actual peripheral (if necessary)
- Peripheral preparation instructions, e.g.,

printer: paper type and size, number of copies, control loop to be used, lining-up instructions

card/paper tape: card or paper tape type/color, parity checking requirements if variable, visual labeling to be made.

5. Initial switch settings (if any) on console or peripherals.

Items 1 to 4 may be shown on an annotated system flowchart for the program. The additional output preparation instructions in item 4 may be shown by preprinted headings for each peripheral type. Similarly, if the hardware comprises a switch panel console, a diagrammatic representation of the switches may be shown with provision for marking off the settings.

For sheet 2, program running, the action required for the following should be shown

- Normal running
- Program error
- Peripheral failure
- Unexpected halts or looping
- Restart procedures

The take-down instructions, sheet 3, should specify the visual labeling required on the output and the disposal instructions.

General Clerical Instructions. It is in the area of the above machine-oriented instructions that the use of formal preprinted instructions sheets will be most useful. It is a rigid checklist approach for standard presentation ensuring that all the required information will be given in a form for each and quick reference by the operations personnel. However, as discussed at the beginning of this section, a general clerical procedures form should be used for nonmachine-oriented instructions. These include instructions for input data collection, proving, and coding and for output review, dispatch, and control. Below are some general checklists for the contents of these instructions. Again it is necessary to emphasize that some of these instructions will be given as user aids, depending on the arrangement of responsibility.

The input data collection, proving, and coding instructions should specify

- Methods for evaluating acceptability of data
- Methods for establishing control over batches of input
- Methods for identifying erroneous input
- Procedures for tracing input not received as scheduled
- Procedures for handling uncontrolled input

To achieve the above, the instructions may include

- Lists of originators of source documents/messages by source and document type
- Data reception schedules
- Source document specimens
- Criteria for valid and invalid data
- User personnel directory for query references
- Procedures for coding source documents (if required)
- Batching procedure in terms of batch size, batch totaling, and "batch receipt register"
- Disposition of source documents/messages

The output review and dispatch instructions should specify procedures for

- Correct formats and acceptable deviations
- Number of report copies
- Decollating and binding instructions
- Labeling and classification instructions
- Authorized distribution
- Methods of distribution and special handling procedures

These procedures are essentially concerned with the overall format, completeness, and distribution of reports. A more rigorous quality control check is generally required on the content and the appropriate instructions for this may include

- Rounding and truncating formulas
- Cross-footing controls
- Invalid data field conditions
- Valid and invalid combinations of data
- Tests of reasonability to be applied
- Tolerances for accuracy
- Meaning of special diagnostic codes and flags
- Methods for isolating errors and their causes

Operations Documentation 113

SUMMARY

1. Two types of operations documentation are required. There are those instructions which must be given to the user so that he may participate in the running of the system, and there are those instructions required by the data processing operating function.

2. The classification of "user" and "data processing" operations documentation depends on the local division of responsibilities for pre- and post-computer processing.

3. This chapter has assumed that the majority of the processing work (i.e., all operations other than data origination and report interpretation) is the responsibility of the data processing operations function.

4. Data processing operations instructions are defined in a document called Systems Operating Instructions. This is prepared jointly by the systems and programming functions, although responsibility for preparation is usually assigned to a senior member of the systems team.

5. The contents of the Systems Operating Instructions were discussed in terms of a Workflow Summary which indexes or references one set of instructions for each discrete operation.

6. The contents of the instructions for each operation type were discussed.

CHAPTER 7

User and Management Aids

User and management aids are the two areas of development documentation that are perhaps the most nebulous in scope and content. Therefore, before presenting some suggested documents, the purposes of user and management documentation should be defined.

User aids comprise that documentation which presents information to enable the user to understand and approve his system, and later to participate in the running of the system. The aspect of user involvement is often overlooked during the systems development work. Often, the user may not actively participate in the systems development because of a past experience of poor relations with data processing or because the failure of data processing personnel to present information in nontechnical form suggests a "closed-mind" attitude. More likely, the user may accept and participate passively in the systems development work and in the subsequent system operation. This passive user involvement is perhaps most critical in the area of systems maintenance and improvement. When a system is implemented, data processing staff participation is reduced and the user is forced to accept responsibilities for some parts of its day-to-day operation. When major flaws are uncovered in the operation of the system and the user has not actively participated during the development process, lack of user involvement may result in

- The user instituting his own remedies to problems, thus possibly negating certain functions of the system and countering proposed aims and benefits
- The user claiming that the whole system is defective rather than specific parts of the system
- The user placing complete reliance on data processing for controlling the operation of the system

Thus, user involvement is of primary importance and user aids are therefore essential aspects of development documentation.

Management aids comprise information to enable senior management to

User and Management Aids   115

assess the applicability of a system to their needs, assess the benefits of the system, and appreciate the necessary time scale and resources for implementation.

Thus, the distinction between user and management aids is derived from the organizational structure or responsibility assignment within a company. Their common similarity is that they are for nondata processing personnel; their differences are that user aids are primarily concerned with the operation of the system, while management aids comprise summarizations of system function and resource requirements.

Suggested areas for use of user and management aids are in

- Management Summaries
- Reference Manuals
- User Data Processing System Instructions
- User Input Preparation Instructions

MANAGEMENT SUMMARIES

The *Management Summaries* comprise that part of the System Specifications corresponding to Management Summary described in Chapter 4. The Management Summary serves two purposes. First, it informs management about current developments within their own area of responsibility. Second, by establishing a management distribution list, the collected Management Summaries may act as a "catalogue" of applications and systems. As described in Chapter 4, these instruction abstracts describe the capabilities and limitations of a system to allow management to evaluate the applicability of a system to a requirement.

REFERENCE MANUALS

The term *Reference Manual* is used here to cover those documents produced for the user as required. Provision should be made for assigning the responsibility for assessing the need for a Reference Manual to the appropriate project management. Examples of Reference Manuals are given below.

User Guides to Data Processing Services

User Guides cannot truly be classed as development documentation. They are intended to improve liaison between users and data processing personnel by defining the data processing services which are and are not available and the procedures for requesting reports and systems. These manuals may be backed up by more specific manuals relating to one system. For example, in a large system with a complete and complex data base, a *Guide to Report Requests* may be produced. This manual describes the current reports available and the data content of the files, what may and may not be requested, and the forms to be completed for the request.

Coding Manuals

Coding Manuals describe the structure of, and list in quick reference form, the codes to be used when completing input forms or transaction messages.

Conversion Instructions

System conversion from a manual system to a computer system can represent a major task. Conversion Manuals provide a step-by-step guide to conversion. They may therefore act as supplements to Coding Manuals or Training Manuals (see below).

Training Manuals

Training Manuals are prepared as required to instruct users in the system. Note that they are not the same as specific operating instructions; rather than being a concise list of "who does what and when," training manuals explain the overall system and the background to the various aspects of user participation.

The actual contents of the various Reference Manuals will vary widely by type and function. As a general rule, however, as much as possible of the existing system documentation should be used in the preparation of Reference Manuals. The following are some general rules for the preparation of Reference Manuals.

1. Each manual should include a standard introductory section stating

- The name of the manual
- Its purpose and aims
- Its intended readership
- The prerequisites for use
- The authority for preparation
- Its organization
- How it should be used and updated

2. The manual should be written in simple, nontechnical language, directed at the level of the particular audience for which it is intended.

3. Illustrations should be used as necessary, e.g., to show how a form is filled out, how equipment is operated, and the flow of work. When forms are illustrated, they should contain representative sample entries; instructions for completing the form should be keyed to these sample entries.

User and Management Aids

4. If it appears that there will be a large number of Reference Manuals produced, standard house rules should be prepared covering general methods of presentation, e.g.,

- Basic manual level (e.g., to section, chapter, and subject level)
- Page numbering system
- Illustration numbering system
- Standard paragraph numbering system
- Standard amendment handling and distribution

USER OPERATING INSTRUCTIONS

User Operating Instructions are prepared to instruct the user in the procedures for input data preparation and for control of output reports. As discussed in Chapter 6, there will always be a requirement for User Operating Instructions. At the simplest level, these instructions specify the procedures for such operations as completing source documents, the timetable for submission of data, brief descriptions of the content of a printed report (e.g., meaning of error flags).

If the user has a direct responsibility for detailed proving of input, etc., the relevant parts of the System Operating Instructions will be the user reference. The complexity of the system may demand additional operating instructions. For example, if the user has access to remote terminals, detailed instructions will be required on their operation and use. Similarly, an off-line data transmission system will require special instructions for call-up and closing messages, batching procedure, transmission times, and so on.

SUMMARY

User aids comprise those documents submitted to the user so that he may participate in the design and running of a system.

PART THREE

SPECIAL
TECHNIQUES

CHAPTER **8**

Recording Complex Logic

CONDITIONAL LOGIC IN DATA PROCESSING

Conditional logic can be defined as the decision-making process when there is an alternative set of actions to be taken. The action or actions to be taken in a particular instance will depend on the circumstances or conditions that prevail at the time. In narrative, conditional logic takes the form of "IF . . . THEN . . . " statements. Where there is a series of conditions or exclusions of conditions, they are linked together with a series of conjunctions such as "and," "with," "but not," "or," and so on.

The study and design of systems is based largely on understanding and specifying conditional logic, often complex logic. Indeed, it can be said that it is the conditional logic of procedures which makes systems development a difficult and time-consuming process. For example, consider the following two questions:

- What makes a complex form-completion procedure?
- What makes a complex computer program?

A complex form is one in which the entries vary according to the circumstances of its completion. For example, on an order form:

> If it is a home order, enter items A, B, C, and E, unless it is covered by a government subsidy in which items A, B, and D must be entered. If the order is placed by a subsidiary company of a trading group, then A must contain the head-office reference not the local reference. If it is an export order, then . . .

and so on. (A study of the notes which accompany a Revenue Service tax form will emphasize this point!)

A complex program is one which contains a large number of condition tests (branches). For example, a data vet or validate program which deals with many data types and with many relationships between them will consist, in flowchart form, of a series of condition test diamonds.

Simply, if a procedure does not have an element of conditional logic, then we are dealing with a sequence of serial actions which will be relatively easy to understand—and to document.

There are many reasons why a conditional procedure must be committed to paper. A complex procedure may have to be studied during the systems investigation. This procedure may be documented informally to help the analyst understand it and to check it for completeness and accuracy with the appropriate user shortly after the interview. The procedure may be formally documented and presented as part of the System Description as described on page 48. New manual and computer-based procedures will have to be documented during system design. These will include conditional procedures which must be approved and implemented. The programmer will be vitally concerned with detailed conditional logic during program design, coding, and testing.

Defining standards for the effective presentation of conditional logic is thus of primary importance. The key areas for documenting complex conditional logic are summarized in Figure 8.1. Other important areas are in the specification of *any* complex operating procedures.

The techniques commonly used for recording logic are narratives, flowcharts, and decision tables. Each technique has its uses; it is not technically feasible, nor indeed desirable, to use one approach to the exclusion of the others in all documents shown in Figure 8.1.

Summary of Basic Methods

The three traditional methods for recording conditional logic are narratives, flowcharts, and decision tables. Three examples are shown in Figures 8.2, 8.3, and 8.4 respectively. The narrative (Figure 8.2(*a*)) describes a rather complex pay agreement between employers and union. This is difficult to understand because of the restatement of numbers in narrative form and, more importantly, because of the complex arrangement of "ifs," "ands," "howevers," and so on. It is certainly possible to simplify the description of the procedure by taking a step-by-step approach as shown in Figure 8.2 (*b*). This approach will require one paragraph for each set of conditions and would be very lengthy. This demonstrates an important factor in the choice of logic recording method: *the ratio of size to sense and the use to which the documentation is to be put.* If the pay agreement is to be documented for general agreement, then the narrative approach in Figure 8.2(*a*) is preferable to that shown in Figure 8.2(*b*). If it is to be documented as a set of procedure instructions for clerks to perform, the Figure 8.2(*b*) is a better approach—provided that the clerks do the job in a semimechanical manner. That is, finding the paragraph which applies to a particular case by examining each paragraph, one after the

Recording Complex Logic

other. Method (*b*) could also be useful if the analyst were reviewing the procedure with a user, with each paragraph being checked in turn.

An alternative is to use a flowchart representation (Figure 8.3). To draw a flowchart, only four components are needed.

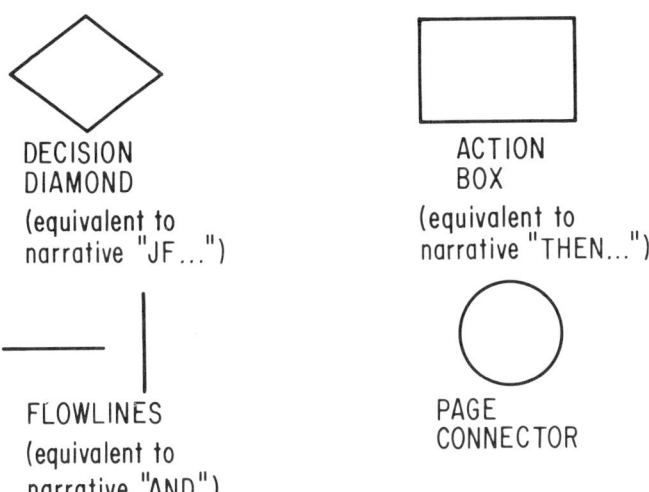

DECISION DIAMOND
(equivalent to narrative "IF...")

ACTION BOX
(equivalent to narrative "THEN...")

FLOWLINES
(equivalent to narrative "AND")

PAGE CONNECTOR

As we shall see later, there are many variations to these symbols to denote, for example, type of action, type of connector, etc. The principle advantage of a flowchart over narrative is a reduction in word length by replacing the "IF ... THEN ... AND/OR" expressions by symbols. Most data processing technicians have been "weaned" on flowcharts. Indeed many installations use them with blind faith without even considering an alternative, such as decision tables.

Let us consider the use of flowcharts in three main areas

- Documenting an existing decision-making procedure during systems investigation (as in Systems Description)
- Specifying processing requirements from analyst to programmer (as in the System Specification)
- Documenting processing logic in program development (as in the Program Manual)

Flowcharts have been used with varying degrees of success for analyst/user communication. Over a period of time, users have certainly gotten used to dealing with flowcharts. Some, however, still react against the arrangement of lines and symbols—"Oh, that's far too complex for me to understand." With the graphical spacing on a flowchart, a complex procedure can occupy many pages and sheer bulk may be a problem.

Step	Document	Example Usage
Interim System Documentation	Interview Summary	Understanding complex decision-making logic
	System Description	Checking logic with users
System	Processing (Program) Specification	Definition of processing logic from systems function to programming
	Narrative Description System Flow in Systems Summary Description in Systems Summary	General presentation of processing logic for all people who receive the System Specification
	Systems Test Plan	Specification of test cases
Programming	Program Logic	As in Logic Flowchart
	Program Test Plan	Specification of test cases
Operations and Management/ User Documentation	For all complex procedures, as in involved operating instructions	

FIGURE 8.1 Documenting Conditional Logic

The use of a flowchart in specifying processing requirements presents many interesting problems. First the specification should be primarily concerned with *what* should be done, not *how* it is to be done (unless there is a specific standard which puts program design in the province of the analyst in the Program Specification). There is a tendency to use a flowchart to specify both decision-making requirements and *procedures*. This can lead to "demarcation disputes" between systems and programming functions. It can result in excessive time being spent on program logic design, possibly without a sufficient knowledge of programming. The major problem here is using *flow*chart, when *flow* is not necessarily important.

Flowcharting is the accepted method of recording processing logic during program development. This serves two purposes. The first is as an aid to design, a means of mapping out logic in outline prior to detailed coding. The

This Agreement between Associated United Conglomerated Limited (AUCL) and the National Union of Machine Grinding Operatives (NUMGO) shall apply to all machine operatives as from the First Day of May, 1969.

ASSOCIATED UNITED CONGLOMERATED LIMITED PRODUCTIVITY PAYMENTS
Phase 1—Base Rates of Pay and Bonuses for Machine Operatives.
To be reviewed on the last Friday in June and December.

If an operator has worked on a job for at least six months and has spent at least fifty percent (50%) of his clocked time to that job, then his base rate of pay will be increased by five percent (5%) and his bonus rate will be decreased by seven percent (7%) on all parts produced in excess of the standard established quota. If an operator has worked on a job for at least six months but has spent more than seventy percent (70%) of his clocked time as above, then his base rate of pay will be increased by twelve and one-half percent (12½%). In addition, his base rate of pay will be increased by one percent (1%) for each full five percent (5%) of clocked time over seventy percent (70%). The bonus rate will be decreased by one tenth of one percent (.1%) for each one percent (1%) increase in the base rate as described previously. If an operator has worked for less than six months of a job, he will receive an increase in base rate of pay of two and one half percent (2½%) until the sixth month qualification is reached, when the above terms will apply.

Operators will be eligible for a premium bonus based on an inspection quality rating of good work produced, such as rating to be calculated as in Appendix 1, paragraph 12, of this agreement. A premium bonus of fifteen percent (15%) for each fifteenth part of the rating will be paid to all operators who have reached the six months qualifying period and who have an inspection rating of at least fifteen (15). This premium will be paid only if the operator has recorded at least fifty percent (50%) of his clocked time to that job. If an operator has worked for less than six months on a job, then he will be eligible for a premium bonus of ten percent (10%) for each fifteenth part of the rating, subject to his attaining a quality rating of at least fifteen (15), providing that at least fifty percent (50%) of his time is clocked to that job. If an operator has worked for less than six months and has less than fifty percent (50%) of his time clocked to that job, then he will only be entitled to a bonus if he has attained a quality rating of at least fifteen (15), when the bonus will be two percent (2%) of base rate for each rating point over fifteen (15).

In addition, any operator, regardless of the length of time spent on a job, who has more than seventy percent (70%) of his time clocked to a job and who has a quality rating of at least fifteen (15), will receive a *supplementary* premium bonus of four percent (4%) of base rate for each quality rating point over fifteen (15).

The record of each operator will be inspected on the last Friday of June and December and the base rates and bonuses calculated according to the above agreement.

FIGURE 8.2 AUCL and NUMGO Productivity Payments—Narrative

Instructions for the Payment of Base Rates and Bonuses for Machine Operators

Phase 1 of Agreement between AUCL and NUMGO

1. On the last Friday of June and December, or as soon after that day if it is a public holiday, each machine operator covered by this agreement should be reviewed in terms of the following:
   - length of time spent on a job
   - clocked time on that job
   - inspectors' quality rating (see appendix 1, para. 12)

2. Operators with the following:
   - at least 6 months on the job
   - more than 70% clocked to that job
   - an inspection rating of at least 15

   will be paid the following rates:
   - base rate up by 5%
   - bonus rate down by 7%
   - base rate up by further 12½%
   - base rate up by further 1%, bonus down .1% for each full 5% of clocked time over 70%
   - a premium of $(G/15) \times 15\%$ base, where G is the inspectors' quality rating
   - a supplementary premium of $(G - 15) \times 4\%$ base

3. Operators with the following:
   - at least 6 months experience
   - at least 50% clocked time but not more than 70% clocked time to that job
   - an inspection rating of at least 15

   will be paid the following rates:
   - base rate up by 5%
   - bonus rate down by 7%
   - a premium of $(G/15) \times 15\%$ base

FIGURE 8.2 Continued

Recording Complex Logic 127

second is as an aid to testing (debugging) and maintenance. In this respect, the flowchart serves the function of a road map to enable a programmer to find his way about the detailed coding of the program.

Decision tables are an alternative to flowcharts. The principle is shown in the example in Figure 8.4. The table comprises a descriptive header and four main components:

CONDITION STUB	CONDITION ENTRY
ACTION STUB	ACTION ENTRY

The *condition stub* contains statements equivalent to entries in flowchart decision diamonds. The *action stub* contains statements equivalent to entries in flowchart action boxes.

The right-hand half (the entry portion) is divided into vertical columns called *rules*. The *condition entry* part of the rule contains entries equivalent to the notation which would be used on the exits of a decision diamond; "Y" = YES, "N" = NO, "–" = indifference (does not apply or not relevant). The *action entry* indicates the action(s) to be taken; "X" = take action, "blank" – do not take action.

For example, rule 8 of the table in Figure 8.4. can be written in narrative as follows:

> *If* the operator has been on the job for less than six months *and* has more than 49% of his time clocked to that job *and* has an inspection rating of less than 15, *then* increase base by 2½% (no change in bonus).

And in flowchart form as:

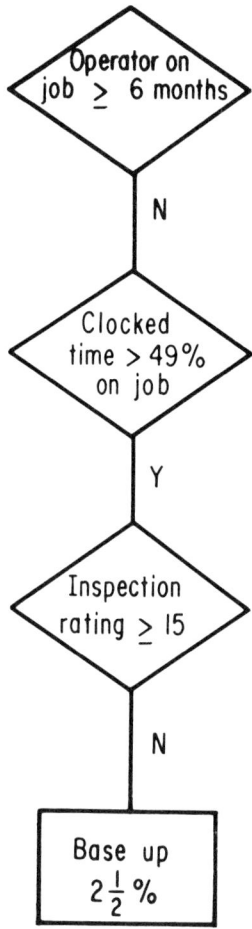

Three more important definitions are:

Limited-entry table: a table which contains only Y, N or — entries in the condition entry quadrant. This is the equivalent of a flowchart with only two exits of a diamond used, and annotated "Y" and "N."

Extended-entry table: a table which contains specific condition values in the condition entry. This is equivalent to multiple exits on a decision diamond. For example,

Recording Complex Logic 129

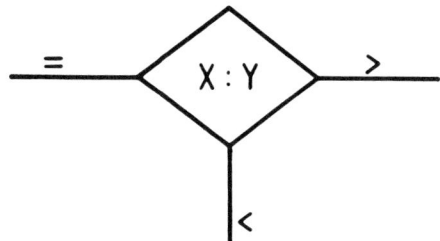

The first two conditions in the example table in Figure 8.5 are extended entry.

Mixed-entry table: a table which contains both extended and limited entries (e.g., Figure 8.5).

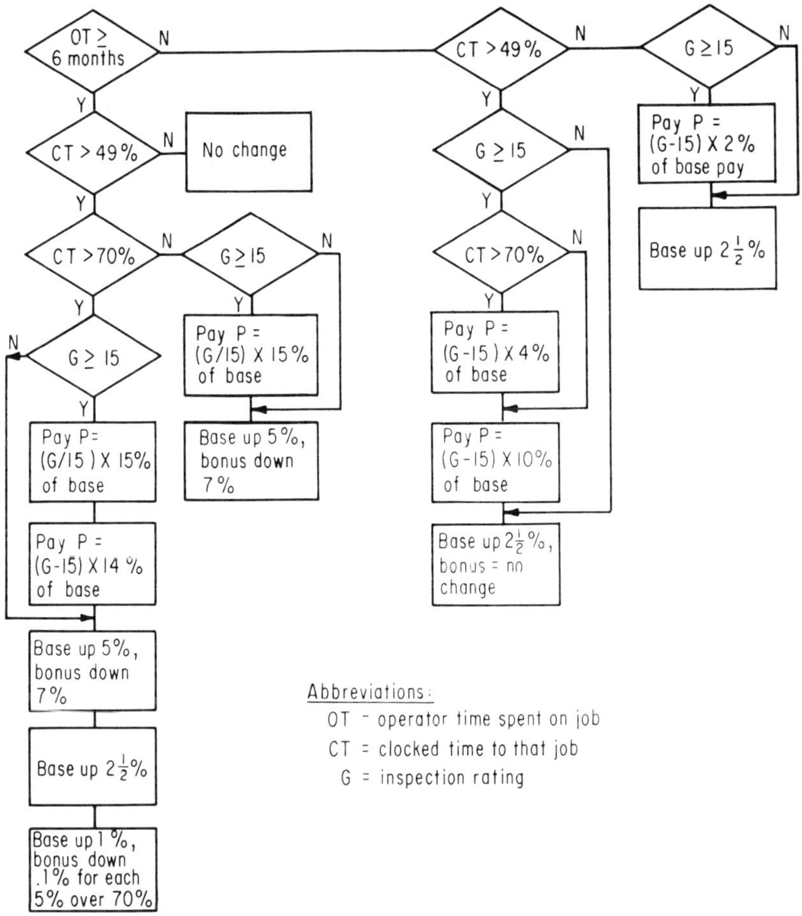

FIGURE 8.3 AUCL and NUMGO Productivity Payments—Flowchart

Title of Table "AUCL & NUMGO Productivity Payments—Phase 1"		Prepared by ⎵ Date 7/1/77 Checked by SW										
		4	8	12	16	20	24	28	32	36	40	44
c1 operator on job ≥ 6 months?		Y Y Y Y	Y N N N									
c2 clocked time > 49% on job?		Y Y Y Y	Y N Y Y Y N									
c3 clocked time > 70% on job?		Y Y N N	– Y N – –									
c4 inspection rating ≥ 15%?		Y N Y N	– Y Y N N Y									
a1 no change		X										
a2 base up 5%, bonus down 7%		X X X X										
a3 base up 12½%		X X										
a4 base up 1%, bonus down .1% for each 5% over 70%		X X										
a5 base up 2½%, bonus no change			X X X X X									
a6 pay premium = (G/15) × 15% base		X X										
a7 pay premium = (G–15) × 4% base		X	X									
a8 pay premium = (G–15) × 10% base			X X									
a9 pay premium = (G–15) × 2% base			X									

FIGURE 8.4 AUCL and NUMGO Productivity Payments—Decision Table

Title of Table: "GHTV File Creation"
Prepared by KRL Date 8/5/70 Checked by SW

	1	2	3	4	5	6	7	8
c1 compare key X : key Y	>	>	=	=	=	=	=	<
c2 record type	–	–	1	1	2	2	3	–
c3 approved?	Y	N	Y	N	Y	N	–	–
a1 update file	X							X
a2 write to error file		X			X	X		
a3 write to exception file			X	X				
a4 form control totals	X	X			X	X		
a5 list for inspection	X				X	X	X	
rule count:	3	3	1	1	1	2	6	1 = 18

FIGURE 8.5 Example Mixed-Entry Decision Table

There are many techniques and conventions used in the preparation and presentation of decision tables.* They are too numerous to describe in detail here. It is useful, however, to review the general advantages and disadvantages of decision tables over the flowcharting approach.

Compactness. The decision table format enables complex logic to be expressed in a small space. The columnar rules present an easily assimilated statement of a complex situation and the courses of action possible. Flowcharts tend to spread because of their graphical nature. Whereas a decision table shows separately the conditions, actions, and relationships between them, a flowchart shows these mixed together. On a decision table, for example, it is possible to go from actions to conditions; this is not readily possible on a flowchart.

Completeness. By using formal table construction techniques, the preparer is forced into considering all possible combinations of conditions and to define them. The rather free-form nature of a flowchart makes this difficult.

Logic Sequence. Decision tables enable logic to be treated without the need to consider sequence. Thus free from procedural considerations, it is easier for *logic* to be reviewed. For example, in a flowchart, the overall processing logic can be seen only after all paths of the chart have been followed.

Error Spotting. Because of its compactness and the ability to apply formal rules for their completion, decision tables enable errors to be picked up at a specification stage. The format enables checks to be readily made for completeness, redundancies, and contradictions.

Artistry. A tabular format requires the use of simple penmanship. Provided a preprinted form is used, the only penmanship on a decision table is the drawing of a straight line which divides the condition part of the table (upper half) from the action part (lower half). The penmanship required to draw a flowchart is considerable. Spacing the symbols and arranging the connecting lines require planning. Most flowcharts are drawn using some form of standard template. Given the finite space caused by drawing symbols, there is a restricted space for writing entries. This leads to abbreviation, both standard and nonstandard; without adequate controls, the excessive use of abbreviations can make a flowchart confusing and difficult to follow.

Fair Copy and Reproduction. Preprinted tables can be used which are designed for ordinary typewriter spacing. The typing and drawing of final flowcharts (where handwriting is not acceptable) can be difficult. (The author still has to determine the optimum sequence for preparation: draw flowchart first and then get secretary to type entries, or vice versa!)

Maintenance. Experience has shown that decision tables are easier to update

---

*Keith R. London, *Decision Tables* (Auerbach, 1972) gives a complete description of these.

than flowcharts. (That is, without automatic documentation aids as described in the next chapter.) Tables require the restatement of a rule or a number of conditions, etc. Redrawing a flowchart can be a tedious process, introducing the possibility of transcription errors.

Modularity. Tables force a modular approach, partly because they themselves are usually small modules and partly because actions are broken into small units handled separately from condition testing. Both development and maintenance are assisted by this.

Standardization. Because tables have a structured format, it is possible to lay down standards for their preparation. With a standard format, it is relatively easy to detect errors or deviations. It is easier to standardize the content and format of tables than of flowcharts.

There are, however, two claimed advantages for the use of flowcharts. The first is that they have been used for many years and have become an industry-wide, accepted technique. The second is that flow, not shown in a decision table, is important for developing program processing logic. If a decision table preprocessor is used, then the table logic can be incorporated automatically into the program coding.* Manual transcription from decision table logic to program coding can be a very tedious task, with considerable scope for introducing errors. It can also lead to inefficient programs.

To summarize the use of decision tables in programming: Decision tables can form an effective method of representing detailed program logic. They will usually be backed up by a general narrative description and, for a complex program, a macro-level flowchart. Decision tables, as is the case with the more conventional flowcharts, can be an integral part of the programming function. That is, they are part of the development process rather than an after-the-event recording of what has been done.

Decision tables may be used in a number of ways in the programming function. At the lowest level, they may be used only as documentation aids to show complex logical processes. In some cases, they may be used to support flowchart representation and in other cases they may be used as the sole method of logic representation. At the next level of use, the program may be coded directly from and cross-referenced to a decision table. Further, a decision table may actually be set up in memory and be used by the program during processing. At yet another level, decision tables may comprise the source language. The output from a compilation is a high-level language object program in a language such as COBOL or FORTRAN. An object pro-

---

*A decision table preprocessor is a compiler-type program which accepts input in a stylized decision table form and converts it to program coding. The output is usually a high-level language (COBOL or FORTRAN) source program which must then be run against the appropriate language compiler to produce the machine code object program.

gram thus produced would then be compiled to give a machine code object program. The use of such decision table preprocessors may well obviate the need for detailed manual documentation, since a satisfactory level of automatic documentation may be produced at compilation time.

The Scope of Standards

Specific standards are given at the end of this chapter. The main areas for the setting of standards are summarized below.

1. *Usage:* For each document produced, the basic *method* for recording complex logic must be described. This can include alternative methods with the criteria for selection. Note that the techniques employed and the level of detail shown in a logic diagram will depend on the usage of the document. For example, communication between analyst and user for system review and approval, or specification of processing requirements from analyst to programmer.

2. *Basic Format:* Standards must be laid down for the basic construction of the diagram. These include the symbol conventions, page size, and diagram format. They must also cover the limits of diagram size and complexity, and the number of levels required (see number 4 below).

3. *Content:* Rules for completing the diagram, such as types of entries and abbreviations, should be specified.

4. *Segmentation:* The basic rule for dealing with complex logic is to segment it into a number of easily manageable units and to a number of cross-referenced levels. For example, a flowchart representation of a complex logical procedure is commonly at two levels: macro-flowchart (outline) and micro-flowcharts (detail). Where a micro-flowchart does not fit onto one page, then it must be segmented across a number of pages. A similar arrangement is used for decision tables: an overall block diagram to show relationship between a number of tables (equivalent to macro-flowchart) and a further set of conventions to link tables together.

Standard abbreviations should be specified for both decision table and flowchart entries. An example set of standards is shown in Figure 8.6. All nonstandard abbreviations should be defined on a sheet accompanying the logic diagram.

Standards for Flowcharts

The standards reviewed here are flowcharting standards for programming. They are those used in Section 4.0, *Program Logic,* of the Program Manual as described on page 98.

Much has been written about representation of program logic by flowcharts

+	plus, positive, or addition
−	negative, or subtraction
±	plus or minus, positive or negative
X	multiplication—commercial use
*	multiplication—technical or coding use
÷	division—commercial use
/	division—technical or coding use
**	exponentiation—technical or coding use
~	negation
|	logical OR
&	logical AND
:	comparison
←	is replaced by
=	is equal to
>	is greater than
<	is less than
≠	is not equal to
≯	is not greater than
≮	is not less than
c(x)	contents of x
A( )	address constant
#	octal
" "	literal
( )	grouping
||	absolute value
no.	number
EØF	End of File
EØJ	End of Job
EØR	End of Run

FIGURE 8.6 Standard Symbols and Abbreviation List

and standards for their presentation. The following simple rules are suggested for the preparation of flowcharts.

1. A macro-flowchart (also known as an outline flowchart) may be prepared, if program size and complexity warrant, to show the basic logical processing steps. If a macro-flowchart is prepared, it should be cross-referenced in some manner to the second "micro" level of flowcharting.

2. The logic of all programs must be shown by micro-flowcharts (also

known as detailed flowcharts). Coding will in effect take place from the micro-flowchart.

3. Rules may be established for

- Size of flowchart paper
- Standard symbols to be used
- Methods for use of connectors and indicating director of flow
- Methods of presenting information within a symbol

4. A cross-reference system may be used to relate macro-flowchart to micro-flowchart to coding.

These, then, would be the areas in which presentation standards for flowcharting could be established. Flowcharts drawn according to the agreed conventions would be included in the subsection *Logic Flowcharts* of the Program Manual.

A sample set of standards is given below.*

A program flowchart is a symbolic representation of program logic. It serves as a communication link as well as a design tool, and must therefore have the same meaning for all data processing personnel. A uniform method of preparing flowcharts is necessary for this purpose.

There shall be at least two levels of flowchart:

1. The Macro-flowchart, which shows the major logical elements of the program.

2. Micro-flowcharts, which show the detailed logic from which the program will be written.

The relationship between the macro- and micro-flowcharts must be maintained such that each block of a macro-flowchart shall define a separate micro-flowchart, which must itself be identified by the block letter of the macro-block it represents.

Rules for the preparation of program flowcharts follow.

1. For each program, at least two levels of flowchart shall be prepared:

- Macro-flowchart
- Micro-flowchart

2. All flowcharts shall be prepared on company XYZ flowchart paper. (See Figure 4.15.) A margin of one inch shall be maintained on the left-hand side, and reasonable margins maintained on all other sides.

3. The identification block shall be filled out whenever the form is used.

---

*For industry standards see ANSI, *American National Standard X 3.5 - 1970 Flowchart Symbols and Their Usage in Information Processing* (New York: American National Standards Institute, Inc., 1971)

4. Only one side of the form shall be used for the preparation of flowcharts. The other side shall be left blank.

5. The flowchart symbols to be used for each operation shall, with the exception of the I/O symbols, conform to USASI standards. A list of the symbols and their definitions is shown in Figure 8.7. If extra description is needed for an operation, an annotation symbol should be used.

6. The abbreviations which may be used to describe special relationships and actions on the flowcharts are shown in Figure 8.6. Any nonstandard abbreviations which are used must be defined.

7. Each block of the macro-flowchart shall be assigned an alphabetic character, starting at A and continuing sequentially to Z. The letter shall be written on the upper left-hand side, and outside, the symbol. Each block of the macro-flowchart shall contain a brief description of the logic it represents.

8. For every macro-block, there will be a corresponding micro-flowchart. Each micro-block shall be assigned a two-digit number, starting at 01, and continuing sequentially to 99. The number shall be written outside the symbol, on the upper right-hand side. Later insertions to the flowchart may be given a decimal notation within the same sequence, e.g.,

02.1, 02.2, . . . , 02.8, 02.9

The general sequence of numbering shall as far as possible follow the logical flow of the flowchart. A brief description of the logic that each block represents shall be written inside the symbol.

9. The logical flow of the flowchart shall be from top to bottom, and left to right on the page. To avoid excessive use of connectors, this rule may be relaxed, but care should be taken that intersection of linkages is minimized. All linkages between symbols shall be shown.

10. When the logical flow of the flowchart is being maintained, arrowheads need not be shown on the linkages between symbols. When logic flows from bottom to top, or right to left of the page, arrowheads denoting the direction of the flow must be shown.

11. The first symbol on each page of a micro-flowchart shall be a connector. This connector shall show the number, and the corresponding macro-block letter, of the first block on the page.

12. Each exit from a page of the micro-flowchart shall be indicated by a connector. The connector shall show the number and the corresponding macro-block letter of the block to which the exit is made.

Rules 11 and 12 apply also to connectors used on one flowchart page where use of a linkage line is impossible (e.g., due to intersection with another linkage line).

PROGRAM FLOWCHART SYMBOLS

1. <u>General Operation Symbol</u>: used for any operation which creates, alters, transfers or erases data, or any other operation for which no specific symbol has been defined in the Standard.

2. <u>Subroutine (Predefined Process) Symbol</u>: used when a section of program is considered as a single operation for the purpose of this flowchart.

3. <u>Generalized Input/Output Symbol</u>: used where it is desired to stress I/O operations. The symbol is used as an alternative to the specific device symbols when:
   — at the time of flowcharting the actual device to be used has not been decided,
   — the flowchart is drawn as an example, and is not related to any specific I/O function,
   — local standards specify its use.

4. <u>Magnetic Tape I/O</u>

5. <u>Disc I/O</u>

6. <u>Drum I/O</u>

7. <u>Document I/O</u>

8. <u>Punched Card I/O</u>

9. <u>Punched Paper Tape I/O</u>

FIGURE 8.7 Program Flowcharting Symbols

PROGRAM FLOWCHART SYMBOLS

10. Preparation Symbol: used where it is desired to accentuate an operation that partially or completely determines the selection of a particular exit at given Branch Symbols.

11. Branch Symbol: has one entry line and more than one exit. The symbol contains a description of the test on which the selection of an exit is based. The various possible results of this test are shown against the corresponding exits.

12. Offpage Connector Symbol: used as a linkage between two blocks of logic that are to be found on separate pages of the flowchart. The symbol is only used on the 'exit' page, on the 'entry' page an onpage symbol is used.

13. Onpage Connector Symbol: used as a linkage between two blocks on the same page, when it is not desirable to connect them using a linkage line. The label of the block to which the connection is being made is written inside the symbols.

14. Terminal Symbol: used as the beginning or end of a flowline (e.g., start or end of a program).

15. Annotation Symbol: used to add additional information to a symbol or block of program.

16. Flowlines (Linkage Lines): used to show the flow between blocks of a flowchart. The normal flow is from top to bottom and left to right of the page. The programmer may dispense with the use of the direction arrows when the chart follows the normal flow. They must be used, however, for any portion of the diagram which does not follow the normal flow.

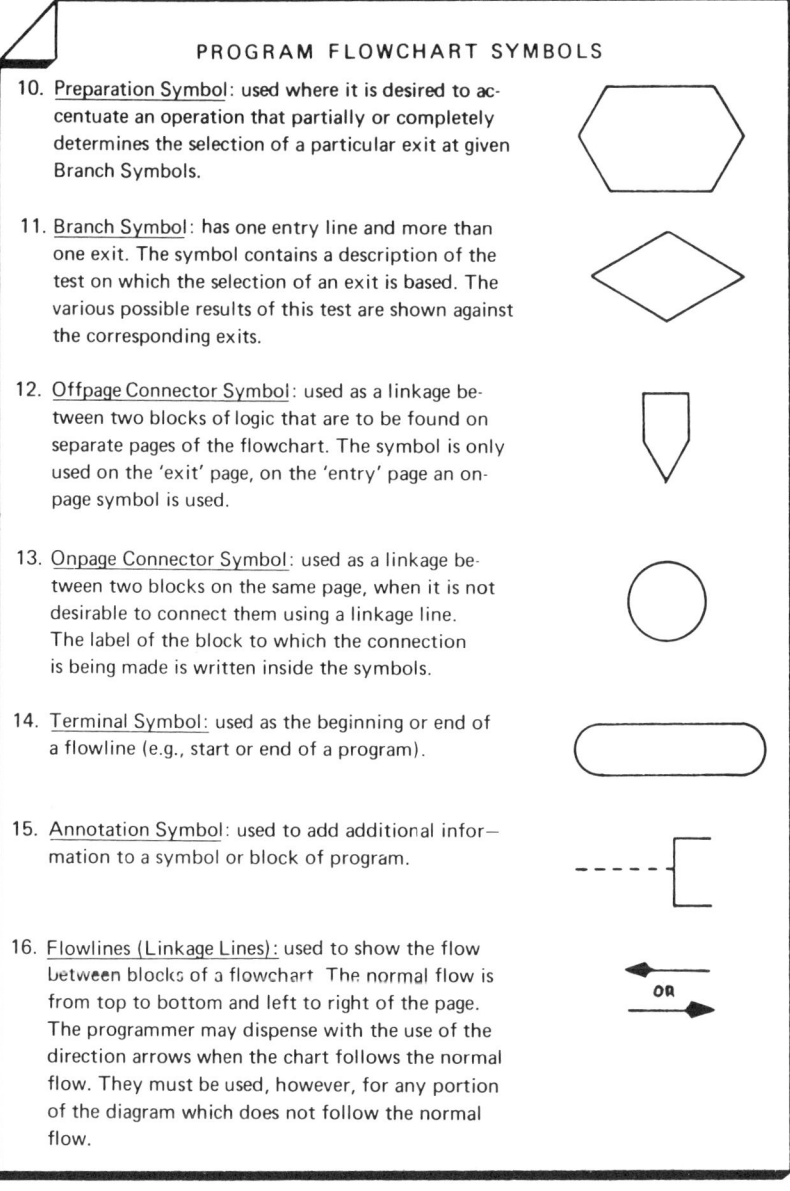

FIGURE 8.7 Continued

13. Subroutines shall be shown on the micro-flowchart by use of the Predefined Process symbol. Detailed logic shall not be drawn for these subroutines which are standard within the compiler (e.g., input/output macros) or for those subroutines which have been catalogued by Software Library.

Figure 8.8 shows examples of macro- and micro-flowcharts, respectively.

Standards for Decision Tables

The standards given below apply to the general use of decision tables in specifying processing requirements. If decision tables are used for the development of program coding, the rules of the processing software must be followed. The standards presented below in italics are examples; comments are given on each standard.

1. *Decision tables must be drawn on the standard company form, Form No. XYZ. The layout of the elements of the decision table must be:*

CONDITION STUB	CONDITION ENTRY
ACTION STUB	ACTION ENTRY

Only one table must be drawn on each sheet.

A company using decision tables should adopt the use of a standard form. Example forms are shown in Figures 8.9 and 8.10. The example shown in Figure 8.10 is more suited to limited-entry tables, the entry portion of the table being preruled into columns which enable "Y," "N," "—," or "X" entries to be made. The table in Figure 8.9 can be used for extended-entry and limited-entry conditions, because the preparer draws in the rule columns to accomodate the largest size of entry.

2. *The double (or heavy) line separating the stubs from the entries is predrawn. The preparer must draw a heavy dividing line between the condition half and the action half of the table.*

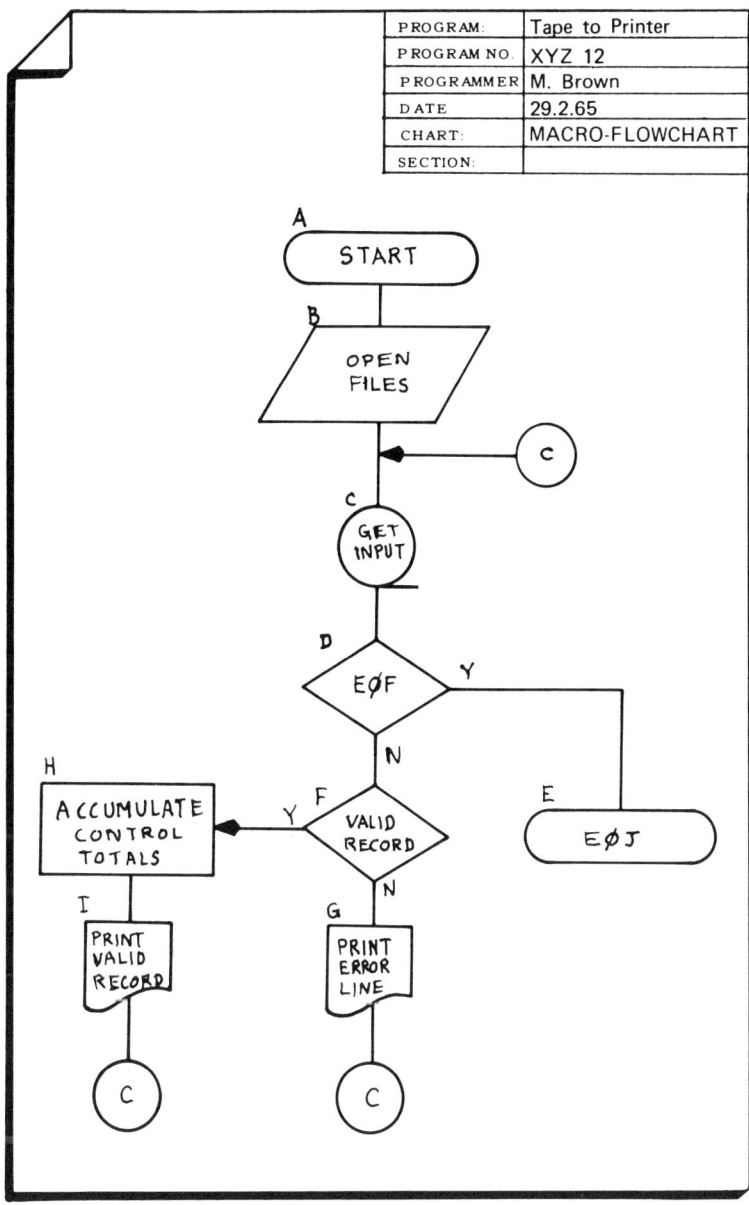

FIGURE 8.8 Sample Flowcharts

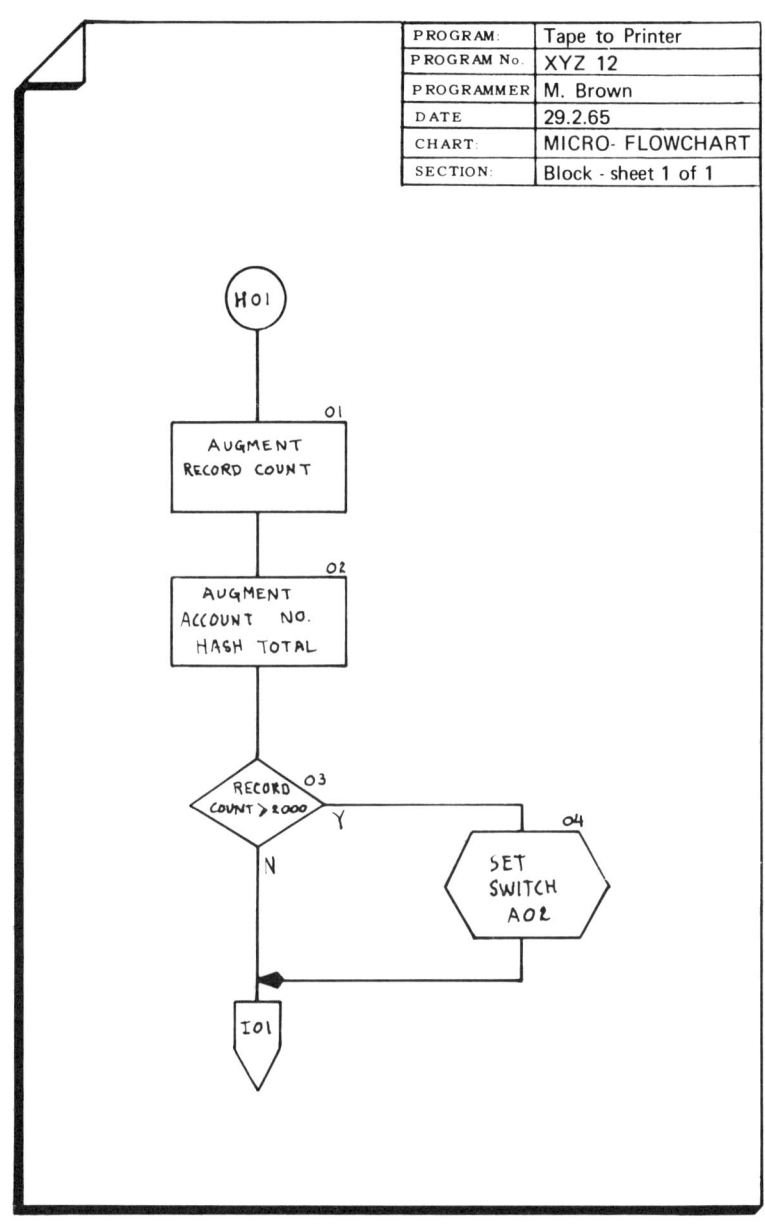

FIGURE 8.8 Continued

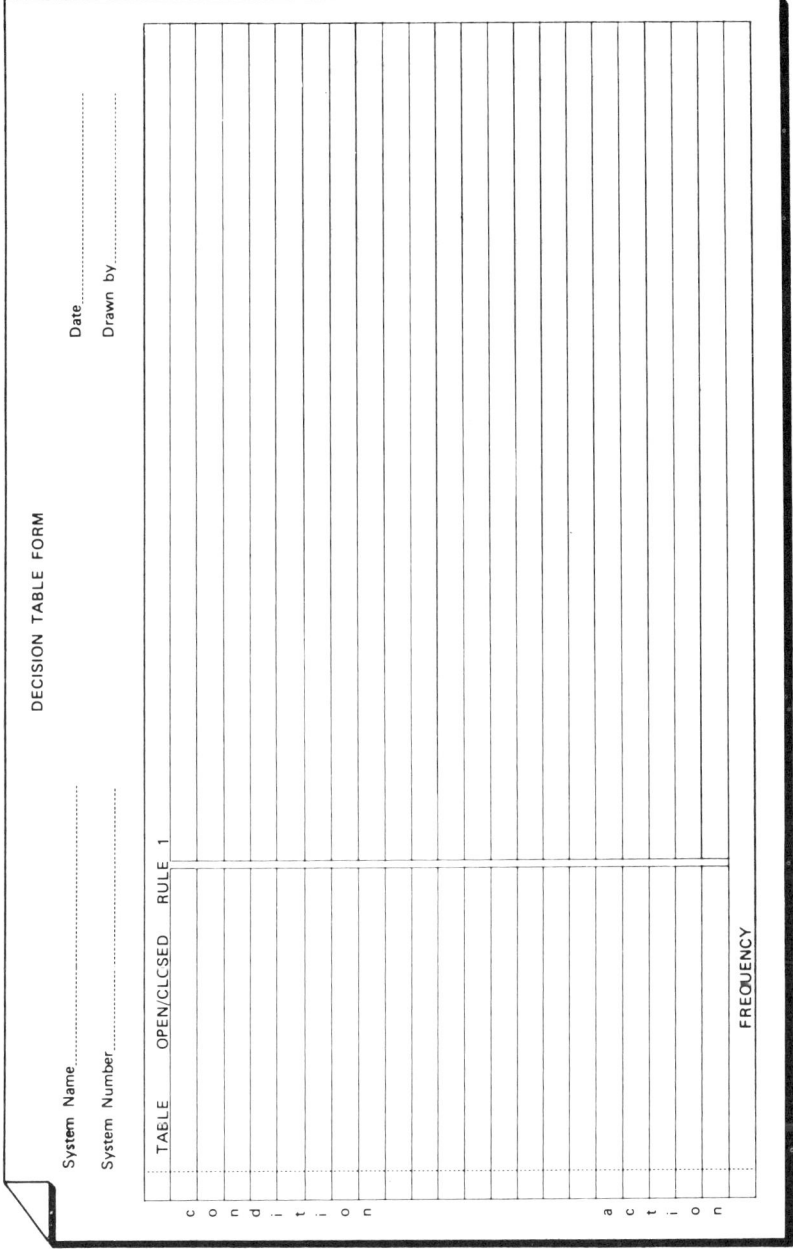

FIGURE 8.9 Sample Decision Table Form—I

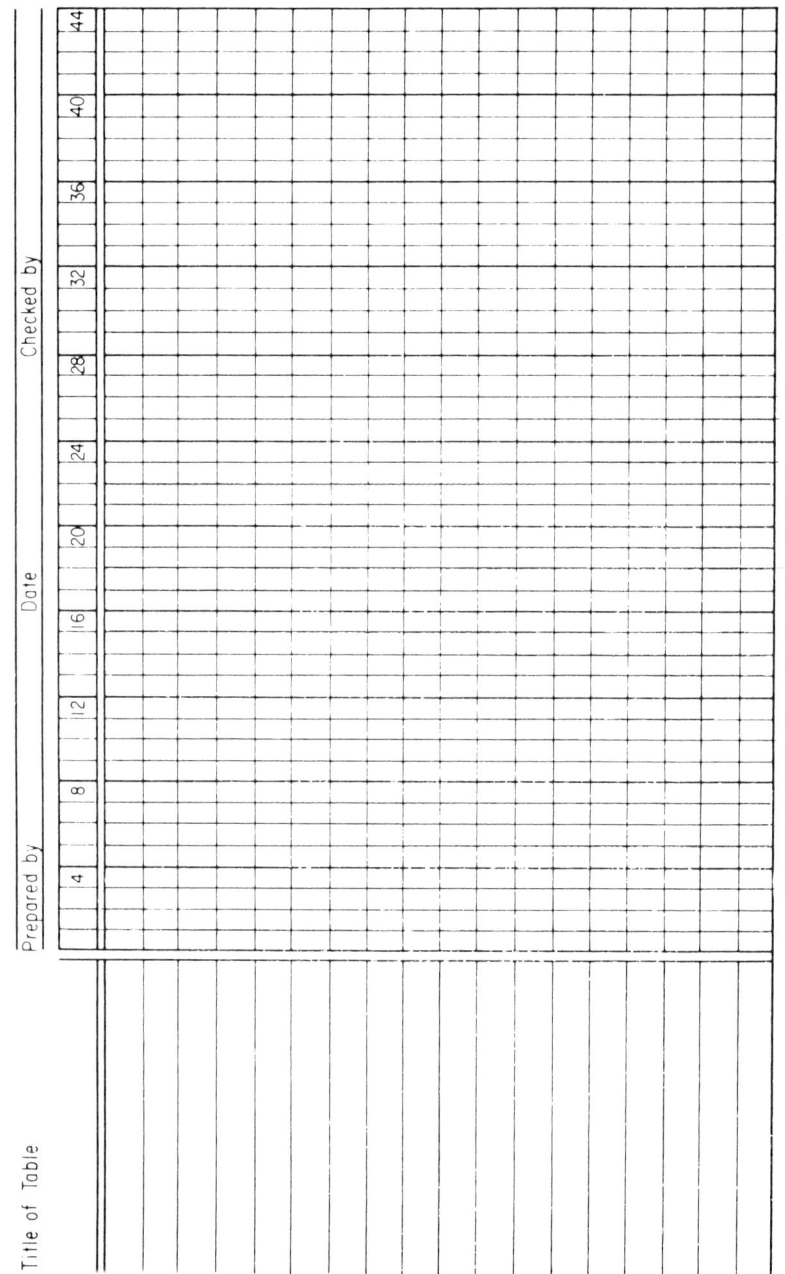

FIGURE 8.10 Sample Decision Table Form—II

Obviously, the number of conditions is variable and the dividing line cannot be predrawn.

3. *The header part must be completed on all tables.*

The header in the table in Figure 8.9 is the more explicit of the two examples shown. Note that there is provision for a TABLE NUMBER. Each table, in this case, should be identified by a unique two-figure reference number. Note that the example in Figure 8.9 requires the words OPEN or CLOSED to be deleted as necessary. (The difference is the same as for open and closed subroutines in programming.)

4. *Each condition and action in the table must be identified by a unique reference number.*

This is for ease of reference. In Figure 8.9, the conditions are numbered "1" onward and the actions from "1" onward in the left-hand column. In Figure 8.10, a simple $c_1, c_2, c_3, \ldots, a_1, a_2, a_3$, numbering system can be used (see Figure 8.4).

5. *No decision table should be drawn which has*
   (a) more than 4 condition variables, if neither indifference dashes nor an ELSE rule are used, or
   (b) more than 6 condition variables if indifference dashes and/or an ELSE rule are used;
   (c) more than 12 decision rules, and
   (d) more than 15 action variables.

This is a standard which attempts to limit the size of a table, based on the span of comprehension of the reader and ease of subsequent maintenance. Note that the number of conditions is the limiting factor, rather than the number of actions. (An ELSE rule is a special convention permitting table simplification. It is written at the end of the table and has no condition entries other than "ELSE" (or its abbreviation). Actions are stated in the normal manner in the action entry part of the rule. It is read as "take the action(s) for the condition values shown, otherwise take the action(s) shown below.")

6. *Blanks must not be left in the condition entries (except in ELSE rule). Dashes should be used to indicate that the value of a condition does not affect a particular action.*
7. *In condition entries, on a limited-entry table, "Y" should be used to indicate the truth and "N" the falsity of a condition.*

Standards 6 and 7 are agreed conventions.

8. *On the action entries, "X" should be used to indicate that an action is to be followed.*

Some standards require a tick ("√") to be used instead of an "X"; this can create typing problems because a tick is not normally available on a standard typewriter. There are a number of conventions for "do not take action."

- Leave action entry blank
- Insert a dash
- Insert an "I" (ignore)

The first is preferred by the author. The second can be confusing when scanning a table. The third is a compromise between the two.

9. *Actions must be written in the order in which they are to be executed.*

This gives a logical sequence of actions. If the sequence varies, then a standard must be laid down for how this is to be shown. For example

rule 1	*rule 2*
note status	reject
reject	note status

One method (preferred by the author) is to repeat the action:

	1	2
note status	X	
reject	X	X
note status		X

An alternative is to indicate the sequence by using numbers, thereby not repeating an action.

note status	1	2
reject	2	1

10. *Tables must be drawn up in such a way that all rules are true alternatives; rules may be stated in any order but only one rule must satisfy a given set of actions.*

This standard is, in effect, saying that no contradictions or redundancies must be present in the table.

11. *Every effort should be made to combine rules within a table (inserting indifference dashes) which give rise to the same action. It will often be found that the value of one condition is immaterial in certain combinations of conditions.*

This standard is a way of limiting the number of rules in a table by requiring rules to be consolidated wherever possible. For example, consider the four rules

Recording Complex Logic

	1	2	3	4
c1	Y	Y	Y	Y
c2	Y	Y	Y	Y
c3	Y	Y	N	N
c4	Y	N	Y	N
a1	X	X		
a2	X	X		
a3			X	X

In rules 1 and 2, the actions a1 and a2 are taken, whatever the value of c4. In rules 3 and 4, the action a3 is taken, whatever the value of c4. The rules can thus be consolidated to show two complex rules as follows:

	1	2
c1	Y	Y
c2	Y	Y
c3	Y	N
c4	—	—
a1	X	
a2	X	
a3		X

Note that the rule to consolidate mainly applies to the presentation of processing requirements from analyst to programming. An overconsolidated table, while logically elegant, may be confusing in communicating processing methods to nontechnical user staff.

Standards should be laid down for the use of all special conventions:*

- ELSE rule
- Table linkage (GO TO and PERFORM)
- Recursion (looping)
- Initialization (rule zero).

---

*See Chapter 5, "Specialized Techniques," in Keith R. London, *Decision Tables* (Auerbach, 1972).

CHAPTER 9

Software Documentation Aids

In this chapter, we are concerned with software packages which are specifically designed to produce documentation. All language processors, such as assemblers, compilers, and preprocessors produce "documentation." At a minimum, this documentation is in the form of a source program listing, possibly augmented by various reference lists. The clarity of the listing for use in post-implementation maintenance depends on many factors: the basic structure of the language, the rules for assigning labels and data names, and the use made of narrative or comment facilities. Documentation aids go further than such basic listings; they can also be used in other areas besides program coding.

The discussion in this chapter is intended to review the type of software documentation aids available, the pros and cons of their usage, and their impact on the installation documentation standards. It does not set out to be a catalogue of available documentation software. A review of current software catalogues and directories shows that there are about 100 packages available. Software documentation aids are an example of the increasing number of sources of software; the developers include computer manufacturers, software houses, commercial users, and scientific and technical institutions.* The prices of the packages range from no charge to $10,000 or more. The selection of a specific package must consider more than just the technical adequacy of the programs. The selection process must be based on many other factors as well, such as a detailed cost/benefit analysis, review of the status of the supplier, and the maintenance procedures.

Program documenters are considered first because, of all documentation packages, these are the most numerous. The impact of packages in other areas will then be discussed.

---

*Software suppliers have been very helpful in supplying technical data on their products. But technical specifications are liable to change without prior notice. The description of a package does not imply that it is commercially available at this time.

Software Documentation Aids 149

PROGRAM DOCUMENTERS

The most common type of software documentation aid is the automatic flowchart generator or flowcharter. These fall into two main groups (although there are some important exceptions). The first group operates on ordinary source programs, together with a few special parameters, to produce detailed logic flowcharts. The second group accepts special parameters plus a program description and from these, an outline flowchart is produced. A flowcharting package can also produce many types of reference lists.

The first group produces a micro-flowchart more or less to the detail of the source program coding. That is, examination of the flowchart will give the same amount of detail as the original source program. Principally, only the *form* of the program is changed. Packages are available which accept most source languages, such as COBOL, FORTRAN, PL/1, as well as assembly languages (IBM 360 Assembler, Honeywell Easycoder, etc.) These packages produce "postcoding" flowcharts, primarily for program maintenance and, to a certain extent, program debugging.

The cross-reference lists, in addition to the basic flowchart, are valuable aids to program maintenance. Some users feel that without these reference lists, the computer-produced flowcharts are not of much benefit.

The second group of flowcharts can be used for "precoding" flowcharts to a selected level of detail. A set of instructions can be used to create the chart and its entries independent of the actual program coding.

Examples of types of packages are given below. They are followed by an analysis of the most important factors in the operation of a flowcharter. Finally, there is a discussion of the advantages and disadvantages of an automatic flowcharter, and the impact of such packages on program documentation standards.

Example Packages

The first group of packages to be considered is the postcoding flowcharters. That is, they operate on a coded source language program. (Note, however, that some of these flowcharters have facilities which can be used for logic design before coding begins.) The examples are discussed below under three headings:

- Availability
- Form of Flowchart
- Reference Listings/Documentation Set

Availability: Figure 9.1 summarizes the availability of 12 sample packages (available in the USA and/or UK) by machine and languages. It can be seen that flowcharters are available for use on most popular machines and lan-

PACKAGE	AUTODOC	AUTOFLOW	COBOL DIA-GRAMMER	DOCUMATIC	FLOW-charter	FLOWGEN/F	FLOW-SORCE	QUICK-DRAW	AXIOM-ONE
Company	Data Instrument Co. (USA)	Applied Data Research Inc. (USA)	Gemini Computer Systems Limited (UK)	Data Usage Corp (USA)	J Hanwell, Data Pro- (UK)	CalComp	NCR	National Computer Analysts (USA)	Export Software Corp (USA)
Hardware									
IBM 360	X	X	X	X				X	
HONEYWELL 200	X	X						X	
SPECTRA 70		X							
BURROUGHS 3500		X						X	
ICL 1900 SERIES					X				
ICL SYSTEM 4		X							
UNIVAC 9000				X			X		
Software									
COBOL	X	X	X		X				X
FORTRAN	X	X			X	X			
PL/1	X	X			PLAN				
Assembly Language	Honeywell Easycoder and 360 Assembler	360 Assembler					NEAT/3		

	RPG		X		
Comments	Ex-Computer Time-Sharing Corp. UK Agents: Canus AG and Company	Also IBM 1400, 7070, 7080, Autocoder; plus selected support for CDC6000 COBOL FORTRAN UK Agents: Computer Analysts & Programmers Limited	ANSI COBOL	Not strictly a "flowcharter" in the diagrammatic sense, but a complete program documenter using basic English narrative for processing description	Claimed to be for any machine with a CalComp plotter and a FORTRAN IV compiler	ITT Bureau Service in the UK which provides, in addition, ICL 1900 PLAN facilities	Claimed to be computer manufacturer independent and for all levels of COBOL UK Agents: Delaware Data Services Limited

FIGURE 9.1 Sample Flowcharting Packages—I: Hardware/Software Availability

PACKAGE	AUTODOC	AUTOFLOW	COBOL DIAGRAMMER	FLOWGEN/F
COMPANY	Data Instrument Co. (USA)	Applied Data Research Inc. (USA)	Gemini Computer Systems Limited (UK)	CalComp
Form of Chart	Typically, three columns per page; choice of single or double-page chart	Typically, three columns per page	Three columns per page	One column per page
Symbols				
Decision	Diamond	Diamond	Diamond	Diamond
Input/Output	Trapezoid & Parallelogram	Parallelogram	Trapezoid	Rectangle
Process	Rectangle	Rectangle	Rectangle	Rectangle
Comment	Horizontal lines, top and bottom	Rectangle	No symbol	Rectangle
Connector*	Circle/IBM	Circle/IBM	Rectangle with points/IBM	Square
Connector References	Page, box, and special flowcharter reference (an alpha character)	Page, box, and source source program entry	Page, box, column	Page and special alpha reference character (generated by flowcharter)

| General Form | Detailed flowchart is essentially a transcription of the source program. A logic flowchart can be produced (optional) which shows only those statements which affect the logical flow of the program, notes and I/O statements. | Basic chart is a straight transcription of source program logic flow. Or, can be by grouping logically related units together, regardless of program code sequence. | Basic chart is a straight transcription of source program logic flow. High-level logic chart is available, one rectangle for each section or paragraph. | Size of chart can be determined by user (via control cards.) DO statements shown in special symbol (rectangle with points) and range of DO loop is shown by a broken line |

*can take several forms

FIGURE 9.2 Sample Flowcharting Packages—II: Chart Format and Symbology

guages. Naturally, more packages are available for use with COBOL (and IBM 360) than any other language (manufacturer).

Form of Flowchart: The details of four sample packages are summarized in Figure 9.2. The great majority produce flowcharts on a line printer; a few produce flowcharts on graph plotters. The quality of the artwork on the latter is, of course, superior to the line printer output. An example flowchart produced from a FORTRAN source program using FLOWGEN/F on a CalComp plotter is shown in Figure 9.3. There is also far more flexibility in scaling the size of the chart on a graph plotter. FLOWGEN/F, for example, permits the size of the chart to be varied according to a scale specified by the user on control cards.

Imaginative use of character patterns on a line printer can produce effective diagrams. An example is shown in Figure 9.4. There are many ways in which symbols can be produced. For example, by using "asterisks":

Or by using a combination of "plus," "minus (hyphen) sign," and "I."

and with "periods" and "slashes":

Arrowheads can be simulated in many ways. For example
  A: upward arrow
  V: downward arrow
  < > : sideways arrows by "greater than" and "less than" signs

The shapes referred to in Figure 9.2 are as follows:

Software Documentation Aids 155

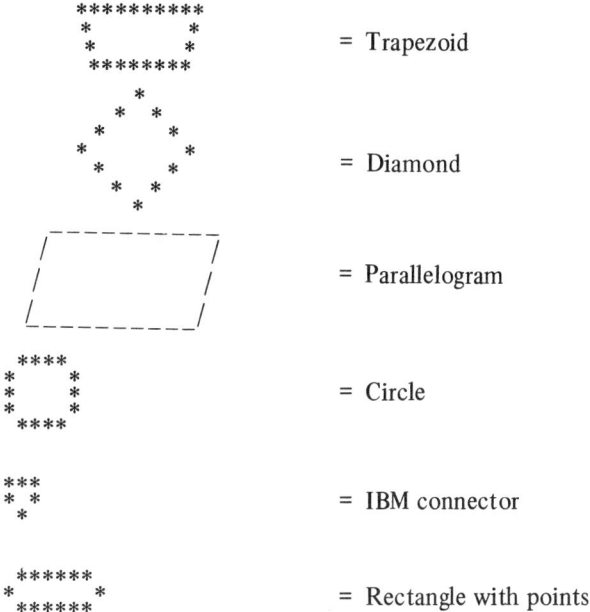

(Actual characters used depends on package.)

The symbol identification method and the cross-reference connector system are important. Let us consider some examples. COBOL DIAGRAMMER prints the chart, three columns to a page. The columns can be referenced as 1, 2, and 3, working from left to right. Each symbol in a column is identified by an alphabetic character printed on the outside, upper right-hand side of the symbol. The first symbol in a column is always "A" (other than a connector). No connector is used to show main flow when it passes from the bottom of one column to another. The flow is assumed to be continued on the top of the next column on the right (or the top of the first left hand column of the next page).

Connectors are used when there is a transfer of control. A rectangle with points is used for "transfer out" and an IBM connector on its side for "transfer in." Note that COBOL DIAGRAMMER shows a GO TO in a special symbol which gives the procedure name, followed by a connector symbol which gives the flowchart location reference number. For example:

```
*********************
*       GO TO       *     (appears in third column
* 200-NORMAL-PROCESS *      of first page)
*********************
          I
          I
```

156   DOCUMENTATION STANDARDS

A "transfer in" example is

200-NORMAL-PROCESS B

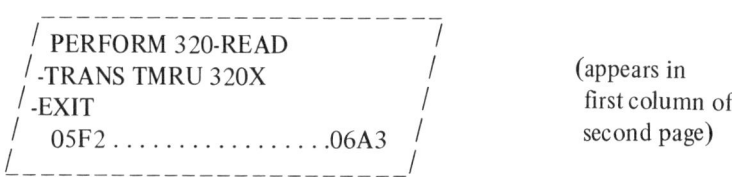

(appears in first column of second page)

The "transfer in" symbol contains the flowchart reference of the symbol which transferred control to this point. The reference system is very simple: *ppsc,* where

    pp = page number
     s = symbol character
     c = column number

In the example shown above, therefore

    02B1 = symbol B in first column of second page
    01C3 = symbol C in third column of first page

(Note that the subroutine block shown as a parallelogram contains the range of flowchart locations which show the subroutine.)

Let us now consider another example: AUTODOC. Each symbol is identified on the upper right-hand corner by the source program sequence number of the statement containing the verb which generated the symbol. The flowchart is printed in up to four columns per page. The normal flow is from top to bottom, left to right. Conditional expressions are charted with the "true" exit linking to the column adjacent and to the right of the conditional diamond. The "false" exit flows from the bottom of the conditional symbol. (Conditional statements, therefore, are never positioned in the fourth column because the flow across the page according to these rules would be impaired.)

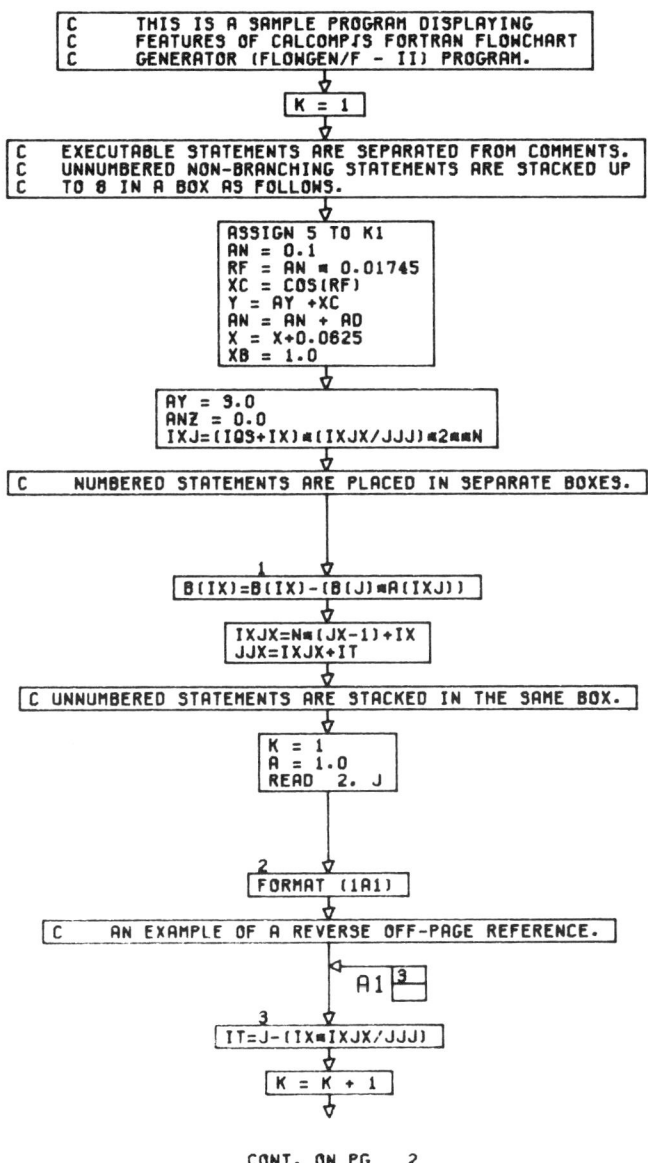

FIGURE 9.3 Example Flowchart from a FORTRAN Source Program. Courtesy of CalComp Corporation

Flow from one column into another is indicated by a connector (rectangle with points) containing an alphabetic character generated by AUTODOC.

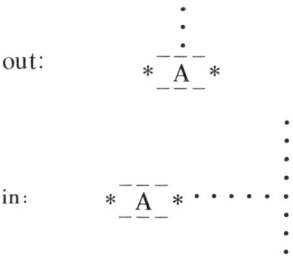

Page-to-page flow, as well as right-to-left flow (caused by the return from a "true" exit of a conditional) are charted in a similar manner. Flowlines are thus never crossed. Both off-page and on-page connectors are generated (circular). Each "out" connector contains the number of the "in" connector where the flow will be resumed. The procedure name(s) which generated the "in" connector appear to the left of the connector system. The off-page connectors contain both the page and connector number of the connector where flow is resumed.

The manner in which the flow is organized is important. All flowcharters will transcribe the sequential program flow. Some, however, have the option to present the logic in a different form. For example, AUTOFLOW automatically analyzes the program, determines which logical units of code are related, and, whenever possible, places these blocks of logic together on the chart, regardless of their input sequence.

Reference Listings/Documentation Sets

Few program documenters produce a flowchart only. Many produce a complete set of program documentation. DOCUMATIC (for RPG programs), for example, does not produce a detailed flowchart as such but an outline System Pictorial (inputs, outputs, and process box) together with a *narrative* Description of Processing. Similarly, Ancom Systems' COBOL DOCUMENTATION SYSTEM does not produce a flowchart but otherwise produces a complete set of program documentation. In fact, it can be used to improve the documentation by, for example, changing data-name mnemonics to descriptive data names; this will be discussed below.

Figure 9.5 summarizes the listings produced by six sample packages. Note that the list of outputs includes both basic outputs *and* optional, special listings. It can be seen that there is a range from flowchart only (e.g., FLOWGEN/F) to complete documentation, such as AUTOFLOW and COBOL DIAGRAMMER. Most of the outputs shown in Figure 9.5 are self-explanatory from the titles.

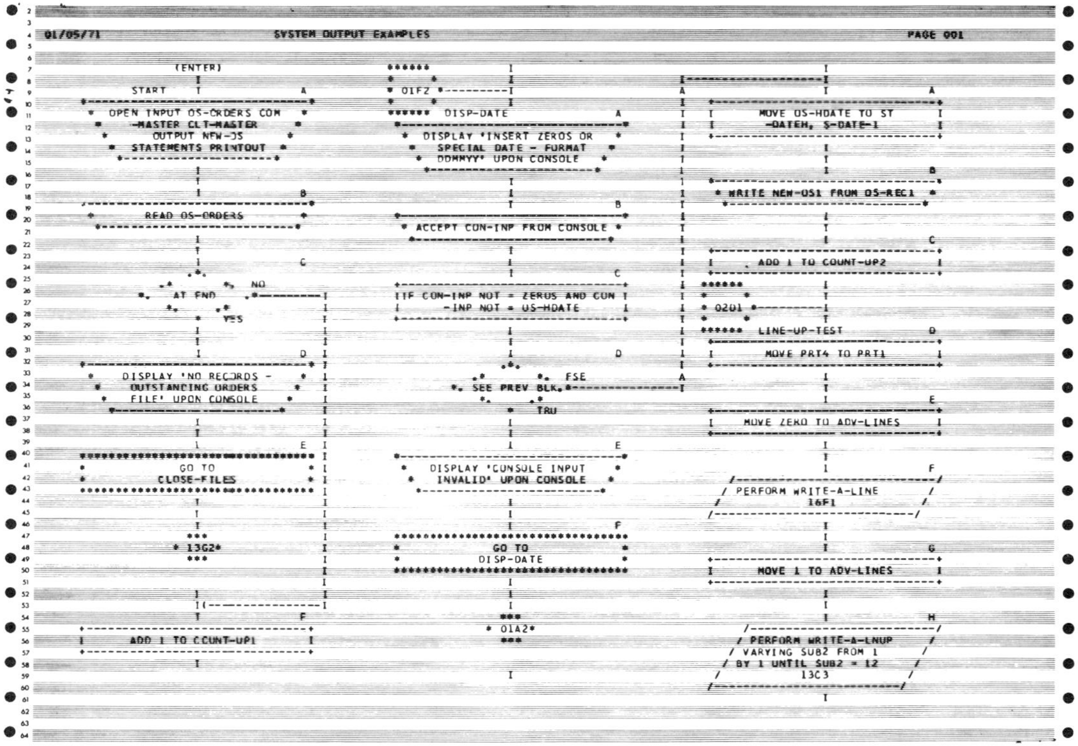

FIGURE 9.4 Example Flowchart Showing Symbols Drawn up on a Line Printer. Courtesy of Gemini Computer Systems Limited

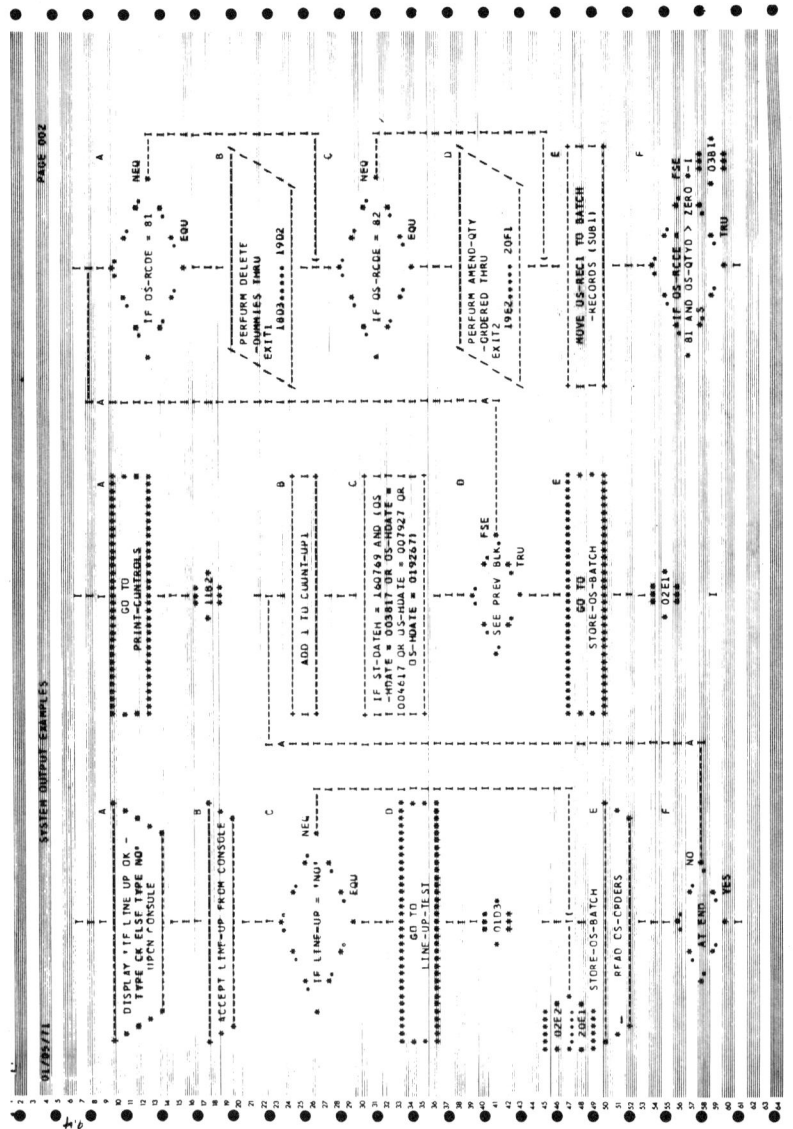

FIGURE 9.4 Continued

Software Documentation Aids

There are a number of program documentation requirements for efficient and effective maintenance. The impact of automatic documentation packages on two of these requirements will be discussed below: cross-reference lists and meaningful data or procedure names.

When maintaining a program, the programmer must identify exactly those parts of the program to be changed. Further, he must make absolutely certain that he has not introduced errors while making the change. This means that the programmer must carefully examine those parts of the program which are related in some way to that part of the program which may be affected. It is in this area that cross-reference lists can be invaluable. They are also useful in program debugging.

Sample cross-reference lists are shown in Figure 9.6. The principle of the lists is the same:

AUTOFLOW

Procedural Statement Label Index (Figure 9.6(a)):
This lists section/paragraph names, labels, or statement numbers in alphanumeric order. Against each entry is the page number and box number in the flowchart, thus providing a quick reference between source program and flowchart

Table of Contents and References (Figure 9.6 (b)):
This is a quick reference index for locating transfers of control within both the flowchart and source program. Each reference shows the source program sequence number and the flowchart page/box number.

COBOL DIAGRAMMER (Figure 9.6 (c))

Label Cross-Reference Table:
This is a listing (in alphabetic order) of all labels, i.e., paragraph and section names. Against each label is shown the source sequence number, the location in the flowchart, and the location of the statements (by flowchart coordinates) which refer to the label. (Note that flowchart coordinates are in the page, block, column format as described previously.)

AUTODOC (Figure 9.6 (d))

Data Reference List:
This is a complete cross-reference list (alphabetically) of all data items used in the program. Against each item name is given the source statement number in which the item is defined, together with the type of data item. All references to an item are indicated.

	AUTODOC	AUTOFLOW*	AXIOM ONE	COBOL DIAGRAMMER	DOCUMATIC	FLOWGEN/F
Identification Sheet	cover page	title sheet	—	—	—	—
Contents	(in cover page remarks)	(in title sheet)	—	index to report/ record layouts	—	—
Source Listing	source program list	input listing	program listing	source listing	—	—
Flowchart—Detail	detail flowchart	flowcharts	logic flow diagram	detailed flowchart	—	flowchart
Flowchart—(Logic/ Outline)	logic chart	flowcharts	—	high level logic chart	system pictorial	—
Data Descriptions	record layout	data cross reference	data matrix index	record layout	input narrative	—
		data record map		report layout	input record layout	
		data division index		input/output logic chart	output narrative	
					output record layout	

162

Procedure Description	special ref. list (external names, literals, figurative constants and system names)	procedure division analysis	—	key statement summary altered statement summary	description of processing
Cross Reference/Lists	procedure ref. list data ref. list	procedure statement label index table of contents & reference	procedure name	label cross ref. table	—
Diagnostics	error list	table of diagnostics diagnostic analysis *COBOL options	—	diagnostic table unmatched label table processing errors	—

FIGURE 9.5 Sample Documentation Packages—Outputs

```
06/16/72      PROCEDURAL STATEMENT LABEL INDEX      AUTOFLOW CHART SET -  SAMPLE  STANDARD COBOL            PAGE 1

PG.BX     NAME                          PG.BX     NAME                              PG.BX     NAME

 5.13  ADD-TRANS                         3.03  END-OF-CODE-ROUTINE                   2.14  MOVE-KEY
 3.19  CHANGE-ADDRESS                    2.20  END-OF-JOB                            5.23  NOTE
 3.25  CHANGE-CITY                       5.02  END-TO-EOJ2                           4.01  PUT-MASTER
 6.04  CHANGE-ERROR                      5.12  END-TO-EOJ2-EXIT                      4.07  PUT-MASTER-EXIT
 5.20  CHANGE-NAME                       2.27  EOJ1                                  2.05  READ-NEXT-TRANS
 3.27  CHANGE-ZA                         2.28  EOJ2                                  2.01  START
 3.26  CHANGE-ZIP                        3.17  ERROR-PROC                            2.15  TEST-OUTAREA
 2.23  COMPARE-INPUTS                    4.17  GET-MASTER-EXIT                       3.11  TEST-TRANS-CODE
 5.22  DELETE-TRANS                      5.01  GET-MASTER-EX1                        2.31  TRAANS-LOW
 5.10  END-OF-ACCT-EXIT                  4.08  GET-MASTER-ROUTINE                    2.11  TRANS-EOF
 5.03  END-OF-ACCT-ROUTINE               4.09  GET-MASTER-ROUTINE-1                  2.30  TRANS-LOW
 3.09  END-OF-CODE-EXIT                  4.15  MASTER-EOF                            3.16  TRANSACTION-CODE-ERROR
```

```
06/16/72      TABLE OF CONTENTS AND REFERENCES      AUTOFLOW CHART SET -  SAMPLE                            PAGE 1
CARD ID   PAGE/BOX   NAME                      REFERENCES  (SOURCE SEQUENCE NO. AND PAGE/BOX)


COBOL MODULE      STANDARD COBOL


CHART TITLE - REMARKS


CHART TITLE - PROCEDURE DIVISION

 012400     2.01  ADR-SAMP
 012500     2.01  START
 013000     2.05  READ-NEXT-TRANS              019800   3.18    021700   3.26     021400   3.27     026600   5. 9
                                               027100   5.21    027230   5.22
 013800     2.11  TRANS-EOF                    013200   2.06
 014400     2.14  MOVE-KEY                     013400   2.08
 014600     2.15  TEST-OUTAREA                 016100   2.26
 015400     2.18                               015500   2.19
 027700     2.20  END-OF-JOB                   014000   2.12    027233   6.01
```

```
LABEL CROSS REFERENCE BY ALPHABETIC
I---------------------I----------I--------I------------------------------------------------------
I        LABEL        I   SEQ #  I  LOC   I                                        REFERENCE BY LOC
I---------------------I----------I--------I------------------------------------------------------
I AD-LINE-COMPLETE    I 20401    I 015A2  I 015A1
I AMEND-QTY-ORDERED   I          I 019E2  I 002D.
I CFWD-RTN            I 21001    I C17E1  I 004B2
I CHK-OLD             I          I 020A2  I 004C3
I CLOSE-FILES         I 10501    I C13G2  I 001E1,004A1
I CONV-TO-PENCE       I 20701    I 016D3  I 005G2,005B3,005H3
I DELETE-DUMMIES      I          I 018D3  I 002B3
I DISP-DATE           I 06013    I 0C1A2  I 001F2
I EDIT-PRICE          I 21301    I 018F2  I 005B1,005C2
I EDIT-VALUE          I 21311    I 018A3  I 006D1,006H1,006C2,008B3,008H3,009E1,011A3,0
I                     I          I        I 017C3,017F3,018B1,018H1
```

```
PROGRAM 'AUTODOC SAMPLE'                 ** D A T A   R E F E R E N C E   L I S T **

-----------------------------------------------------------------------------------------------------
               NAME                 : REF NBR  :  TYPE  :                                  REFERENCES
-----------------------------------------------------------------------------------------------------
                                    : UNDEFINED:        :   212
 A                                  :       47 :     02 :  NO REF
 A                                  :       50 :     02 :  NO REF
 A                                  :       66 :     02 :   127    155    156    162    199    200
 AN-PRICE                           :       76 :     02 :    77
 B                                  :       48 :     02 :  NO REF
 B                                  :       51 :     02 :  NO REF
 B                                  :       67 :     02 :   127    155    156    162    199
 C                                  :       42 :     02 :  NO REF
 C                                  :       52 :     02 :   133    155    162    201    202
 COPY                               :       41 :     01 :  NO REF
```

FIGURE 9.6 Sample Cross-Reference Lists: (*a*) AUTOFLOW, Courtesy of Applied Data Research Inc.; (*b*) COBOL DIAGRAMMER, Courtesy of Gemini Computer Systems Limited; (*c*) AUTODOC, Courtesy of Data Instrument Company

Special purpose lists can be produced by many packages. For example, there is a COBOL DIAGRAMMER optional listing called the Altered Statement Summary. This is an alphabetic cross-reference index of GO TO statements, subject to an ALTER statement. The listing shows each paragraph name which is ALTERed. Against this is shown

- Location on flowchart of the paragraph name
- The flowchart location of where the ALTER statement is given
- The destination of the ALTER statement by name and flowchart location

There is also a listing (alphabetically) of important COBOL statements. This listing shows the type of statement, source line and sequence number, and up to the first 96 characters of the operand(s). The package developers define *important* as "those which are likely to be taken out when the program has been debugged, or those which an EDP manager needs for the preparation of operator instructions." "Key" statements are:

ACCEPT
CALL
COPY
DISPLAY
ENTRY
EXHIBIT
INCLUDE
ON
READY TRACE
RESET TRACE
STOP

AUTODOC can produce a Special Reference List which indexes all external names, literals, figurative constants, and system names against the AUTODOC generated source sequence numbers. AUTOFLOW can produce a Procedure Division Analysis which lists such information as ALTERed paragraphs, PERFORMed entries, I/O File Activity, STOP Summary, and DISPLAY Summary, all by name, card identification, and flowchart location reference.

An interesting approach to COBOL program documentation (not including flowcharts) is Ancom System's COBOL DOCUMENTATION SYSTEM. This accepts COBOL source programs and operates on the *content* of the statement as well as the form. For example, it will

- Change data-name mnemonics to descriptive data names
- Change data mnemonics to record-related, or qualified, names
- Change existing paragraph names to sequentially related paragraph names

An example is shown in Figure 9.7. Documentation produced includes new source listing (and source card deck), Reserved Word Usage Listing and Cross-Reference Listings (by paragraph name and data element).

High-Level Flowcharts

The preceding discussion has dwelt on the subject of postcoding detailed flowcharts produced from source programs. Many flowcharting packages have facilities for producing high-level flowcharts. These can be produced during program development or from the source program. Sample packages are discussed below.

NCR FLOWRITE is a suite of programs which processes special flowcharting instructions. Example instructions are ENTR = Entry Point, PROC = Process, PERF = Perform Routine, INOT = Input/Output, GOTO = Flow connection; 12 such instruction types are available. A detailed flowchart can be produced during coding by adding more charting instructions. Alternatively, the coded source program can be charted by means of NCR FLOSORCE. FLOWRITE and FLOSORCE are designed to operate together.

The developers of AUTODOC have taken the approach of providing a Logic Chart. This is prepared from the source program but only those statements which affect the logical flow of the program are charted. These statements include decisions, ALTER, input/output operations, and notes.

COBOL DIAGRAMMER offers two options: an Input/Output Logic Chart and a High-Level Logic Chart. The former identifies

- Input Files (one block per input or I/O file)
- Identification Division (program ID, author and remarks)
- Output Files (output and I/O files in the same format as the input files)

This is produced from the source coding and is thus not precoding. The High-Level Logic Chart is similarly produced from the source program coding. The chart shows the relationship between sections and paragraphs. Each section and paragraph in the source program is shown with its name and flowchart location in a block. Left of a paragraph block, any paragraph referring to that block is listed by name and flowchart location, under the heading TRANSFERS IN. On the right, the TRANSFER OUT paragraph names and flowchart locations are printed.

AUTOFLOW has a number of arrangements for outline flowcharts. CHART/COBOL, for example, provides for precoding flowcharting by means of simple coded COBOL Note statements. Similar facilities are available for other languages such as PL/1 and FORTRAN.

It is important for the high-level flowchart to be compatible with the source-level detailed flowchart, i.e., same layout and symbology.

```
001010 IDENTIFICATION DIVISION.
001020 PROGRAM-ID. 'DEMO'.
001030 AUTHOR. ANCOM SYSTEMS.
001040 DATE-WRITTEN. JANUARY, 1969.
001050 DATE-COMPILED.
001060 ENVIRONMENT DIVISION.
001070 CONFIGURATION SECTION.
001080 SOURCE-COMPUTER. IBM-360.
001090 OBJECT-COMPUTER. IBM-360.
001100 INPUT-OUTPUT SECTION.
001110 FILE-CONTROL.
001120     SELECT TRANS-FILE ASSIGN TO 'SYS002' UNIT-RECORD 2540R.
001130     SELECT OLD-PERS-FILE ASSIGN TO 'SYS001' UTILITY 2400 UNITS.
001140     SELECT NEW-PERS-FILE ASSIGN TO 'SYS003' UTILITY 2400 UNITS.
001150 DATA DIVISION.
002015 FILE SECTION.
002020 FD  OLD-PERS-FILE
002050     RECORDING MODE IS F      LABEL RECORDS ARE OMITTED
002070     DATA RECORD IS OLD-PERS-REC.
002080 01  OLD-PERS-REC.
002090     02  EMP-NO      PICTURE 9(5).
002100     02  EMP-NAME            PICTURE X(30).
002110     2               JBCODE
                                   PICTURE    9(6).
       02  JBNAME                  PICTURE X(24).
002130 02  BRATE                   PICTURE 9999V99.
002140 02  SHPRM       PICTURE 9V99.
002150 02  WRATE                   PICTURE 9999V99.
002160 FD  TRANS-FILE
002170     LABEL RECORDS ARE OMITTED
002190     RECORDING MODE IS F
002200     DATA RECORD IS TRANS-REC.
003010 1   TRANS-REC.
003020     02  EMPL-NO
                                   PICTURE 9(5).
003030     02  EMPL-NAME           PICTURE X(30).
003040     02  JOODE               PICTURE 9(6).
003050     02  JNAME       PICTURE X(24).
003060     02  BSRATE      PICTURE 9999V99.
003070     02  SHPREM              PICTURE 9V99.
003080     02  WKRATE              PICTURE 9999V99.
003090 FD  NEW-PERS-FILE
003120     RECORDING MODE IS F
003130         LABEL RECORDS ARE OMITTED
003140     DATA RECORD IS NEW-PERS-REC.
003150 01      NEW-PERS-REC
003153             PICTURE X(80).
003160 WORKING-STORAGE SECTION.
003170 77  NEW-PERS-COUNT          PICTURE 9(5) VALUE ZEROS.
003180 77  OLD-PERS-COUNT          PICTURE 9(5) VALUE ZEROS.
003190 77  TRANS-COUNT             PICTURE 9(5) VALUE ZEROS.
003200 77  SAVE-OLD-PERS-REC       PICTURE X(80).
```

FIGURE 9.7 Sample of COBOL DOCUMENTATION SYSTEM. Courtesy of ANCOM Systems

```
A N C O M     C O B O L     D O C U M E N T A T I O N     S Y S T E M
010010 IDENTIFICATION DIVISION.                                         DEMO
010020 PROGRAM-ID. 'DEMO'.                                              DEMO
010030 AUTHOR. ANCOM SYSTEMS.                                           DEMO
010040 DATE-WRITTEN. JANUARY, 1969.                                     DEMO
010050 DATE-COMPILED.                                                   DEMO
010060 ENVIRONMENT DIVISION.                                            DEMO
010070 CONFIGURATION SECTION.                                           DEMO
010080 SOURCE-COMPUTER. IBM-360.                                        DEMO
010090 OBJECT-COMPUTER. IBM-360.                                        DEMO
010100 INPUT-OUTPUT SECTION.                                            DEMO
010110 FILE-CONTROL.                                                    DEMO
010120     SELECT TRANSACTION-FILE                                      DEMO
010130         ASSIGN TO 'SYS002' UNIT-RECORD 2540R.                    DEMO
010140     SELECT OLD-PERSONNEL-MASTER-FILE                             DEMO
010150         ASSIGN TO 'SYS001' UTILITY 2400 UNITS.                   DEMO
010160     SELECT NEW-PERSONNEL-MASTER-FILE                             DEMO
010170         ASSIGN TO 'SYS003' UTILITY 2400 UNITS.                   DEMO
010180 DATA DIVISION.                                                   DEMO
010190 FILE SECTION.                                                    DEMO
010200 FD  OLD-PERSONNEL-MASTER-FILE                                    DEMO
010210         RECORDING MODE IS F                                      DEMO
010220         LABEL RECORDS ARE OMITTED                                DEMO
010230         DATA RECORD IS AA01-OLD-PERSONNEL-RECORD.                DEMO
010240 01  AA01-OLD-PERSONNEL-RECORD.                                   DEMO
010250     02  AA02-MASTER-EMPLOYEE-NUMBER PICTURE 9(5).                DEMO
010260     02  AA03-MASTER-EMPLOYEE-NAME   PICTURE X(30).               DEMO
010270     02  AA04-MASTER-JOB-CODE        PICTURE 9(6).                DEMO
010280     02  AA05-MASTER-JOB-NAME        PICTURE X(24).               DEMO
010290     02  AA06-MASTER-BASE-RATE       PICTURE 9999V99.             DEMO
010300     02  AA07-MASTER-SHIFT-PREMIUM   PICTURE 9V99.                DEMO
010310     02  AA08-MASTER-WORK-RATE       PICTURE 9999V99.             DEMO
010320 FD  TRANSACTION-FILE                                             DEMO
010330         LABEL RECORDS ARE OMITTED                                DEMO
010340         RECORDING MODE IS F                                      DEMO
010350         DATA RECORD IS AB01-TRANSACTION-RECORD.                  DEMO
010360 01  AB01-TRANSACTION-RECORD.                                     DEMO
010370     02  AB02-TRANSACTION-EMPL-NUMBER PICTURE 9(5).               DEMO
010380     02  AB03-TRANSACTION-EMPL-NAME   PICTURE X(30).              DEMO
010390     02  AB04-TRANSACTION-JOB-CODE    PICTURE 9(6).               DEMO
010400     02  AB05-TRANSACTION-JOB-NAME    PICTURE X(24).              DEMO
010410     02  AB06-TRANSACTION-BASE-RATE   PICTURE 9999V99.            DEMO
010420     02  AB07-TRANSACTION-SHIFT-PREMIUM PICTURE 9V99.             DEMO
010430     02  AB08-TRANSACTION-WORK-RATE   PICTURE 9999V99.            DEMO
010440 FD  NEW-PERSONNEL-MASTER-FILE                                    DEMO
010450         RECORDING MODE IS F                                      DEMO
010460         LABEL RECORDS ARE OMITTED                                DEMO
010470         DATA RECORD IS AC01-NEW-PERSONNEL-RECORD.                DEMO
010480 01  AC01-NEW-PERSONNEL-RECORD       PICTURE X(80).               DEMO
010490 WORKING-STORAGE SECTION.                                         DEMO
010500 77  7701-NEW-PERSONNEL-COUNT        PICTURE 9(5) VALUE ZEROS.    DEMO
010510 77  7702-OLD-PERSONNEL-COUNT        PICTURE 9(5) VALUE ZEROS.    DEMO
010520 77  7703-TRANSACTION-COUNT          PICTURE 9(5) VALUE ZEROS.    DEMO
010530 77  7704-SAVE-OLD-PERSONNEL-RECORD  PICTURE X(80).               DEMO
```

FIGURE 9.7 Continued

Software Documentation Aids

Flowcharters—Pros and Cons

There has been considerable controversy over the relevance of automatic flowcharters in program documentation. Some of the key arguments, for and against, are reviewed below. Their impact on documentation standards is then discussed.

First, the advantages. There are many claimed advantages of using automatic flowcharters. They mainly apply to program maintenance.

- Standardized and complete documentation
- Accurate and up-to-date documentation which is always synchronized to actual coding
- Charting and lists providing a valuable debugging aid. (COBOL DIAGRAMMER, for example, can produce 174 error diagnostics—more than most COBOL compilers!)
- Faster documentation with less resources

Another claimed advantage is that the free availability of accurate flowcharts is a valuable training aid. Trainee programmers can learn the logic of a well-structured program written by an experienced programmer. Similarly, management can evaluate the work of the junior programmer during his training period. (With properly applied standards, both these should be possible with hand-drawn flowcharts.)

With these advantages, the installation can realize a number of important benefits:

- More efficient use of programmers by relieving them of clerical tasks
- Reduction in secretarial and other clerical costs
- Faster program testing
- Clear and concise documentation for management evaluation (quality and quantity control)
- Efficient and effective maintenance, and thus lower maintenance costs

Certainly, many of these benefits have been realized by many installations using source-level detailed flowcharts.

But what are the disadvantages?

Documentation Too Bulky: The argument here is that the charts produced are bulky documents. This means that it tends to be harder to locate a desired point with copious page turning. This is a rather dubious disadvantage—if we accept that flowcharts to a detailed level are a prerequisite to program maintenance. (How bulky is bulky remains a very subjective point! FLOSORCE, for example, produces some four pages of flowchart to two and one-half to three pages of program listing. Is this bulky?) There is certainly evidence that it is the *source program* which is consulted in the first instance when a change is to be made. The flowchart is consulted generally as a last resort. A program listing has to be well annotated and constructed to be used as input to a flowcharter; then why can't this be used instead for a flowchart? If this *is* the case, then a detailed flowchart (manual or machine produced) could be considered an expensive luxury. The simple fact is that any complex program is difficult to follow in coded form. There is always the problem of "what is the impact of the maintenance debugging change made?" In this instance, the flowchart *and* the cross-reference lists can be very valuable indeed. Note that from the programmer's point of view the *approach* to altering a program is different for locating/correcting operational bugs as opposed to requirement changes.

Logic Errors Transmitted to Flowchart: One approach to the precoding flowchart is that the design chart provides an independent check on the program coding. Here again we come to the distinction between design and post-implementation maintenance. By the time a program becomes operational it is to be hoped that logic errors have been debugged. The primary requirement for maintenance documentation is that the flowcharts accurately reflect the source program coding. (The converse is sometimes true—time is spent debugging part of a flowchart when the coding is, in fact, correct!) A flowchart prepared before coding is a valuable aid to design. It enables a problem to be defined clearly before a detailed solution is attempted. Some installations have found that the manual preparation of precoding, design flowcharts is the best solution. Some go further and say that a well-planned program, with meaningful data names, etc., and the judicious use of comments, diminishes the need for detailed flowcharts. But it is dubious whether such program construction will completely obviate the need for a detailed flowchart.

Chapin, in a very thorough analysis of flowchart packages,* notes that many packages conform to the ANSI Standard as regards flow and symbol shape, but "on most other points, nonconformance was the rule."

The selection of the right package is vital to the development and implementation of program documentation. It is unsatisfactory to have one set of rules for software-produced flowcharts and one for manually produced flowcharts. If a package is used, it should form an integral part of the installation's documentation standards.

It is certainly the case that a program documentation package makes for standardization in the sense of uniformity of format and completeness. The documentation standards are easier to enforce because there is less effort on the part of the programmer to produce the documentation. Care must be taken, however, that the installation does not become complacent about setting up and enforcing additional standards. For example, three installations who adopted a flowcharter (working at a detailed level) reported that the

---

*N. Chapin, Flowchart Packages and the ANSI Standard, *Datamation,* Volume 18, Number 9, September 1972, pp. 48-53.

Software Documentation Aids 171

programmers tended to become lax in the precoding design stage. A flowcharter operating on a source program uses, of course, the programmer's statements. There is certainly scope to improve program documentation (even with a flowcharter) by good program construction and the standardized use of meaningful data or procedure names.

OTHER DOCUMENTATION PACKAGES

Many types of software packages, in addition to language assemblers and compilers, produce useful documentation. For example, many file management and retrieval packages produce listings of file data content and format which reflect the *current* status of the data. Program library packages are an aid to development documentation. One of the biggest problems in developing a system is the definition and documentation of all types of data.

The clerical effort in defining and maintaining the data descriptions (e.g., the forms shown in Chapter 4) can be considerable. Without adequate controls there can be redundant and repetitive statements of data descriptions. For example, data definitions can be written and rewritten

- In source documents and related procedure manuals
- As part of the computer program which processes the source data
- As part of the computer files which carry the source data to subsequent programs
- As part of the programs which maintain a master file
- As part of the program which produces the output reports

In addition to the initial definition of the data during development, there is also maintenance of these definitions after implementation.

One package which has attempted to help in this area is LEXICON, developed by Arthur Andersen & Company. The facilities offered by LEXICON can be divided into two groups. The first is the automated Data Dictionary which describes the data to be processed. The second is the program generation and information processing facilities. The latter includes the Input Processor (which automatically generates validation and control programs) and a Data Extractor and Report Writer. (File processing can be achieved via PL/1, COBOL, or BAL—written source programs using the Data Dictionary.) It is the Data Dictionary functions that concern us here. The Data Dictionary enables the characteristics of each element of data (at its lowest level) to be defined and held on an automated dictionary. Further, the contents of data records, files, and reports can be defined in terms of the basic data elements defined in the automated dictionary. This dictionary can then be used by subsequent programs. One data element may appear in a number of files or reports, but need only be defined once by the user. Similarly, one file may be used in a number of programs but need only be defined once. A schematic of the LEXICON system (all facilities) is shown in Figure 9.8.

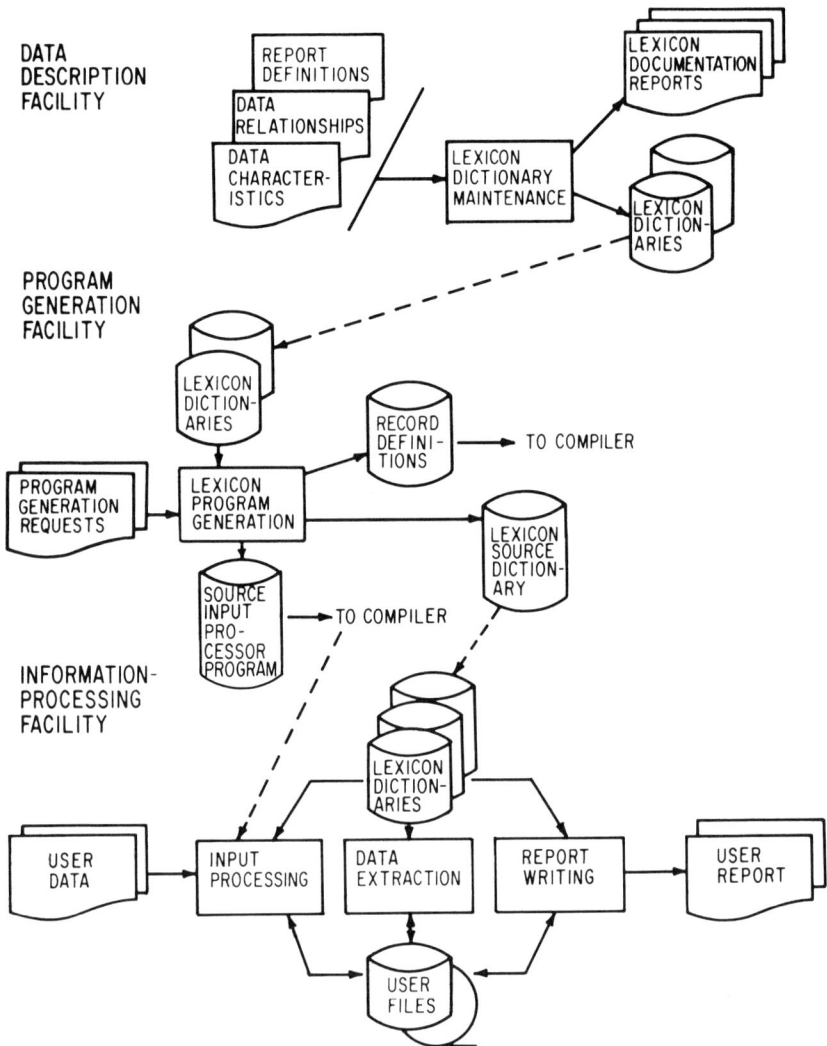

FIGURE 9.8 Example of Automated Data Administration—LEXICON Facilities. Courtesy of Arthur Andersen & Co.

Software Documentation Aids

There is a hierarchy of definitions, from the lowest data element to file:

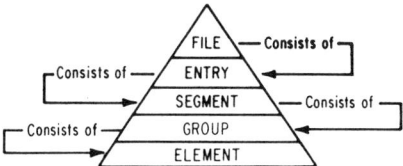

A Data Dictionary Language (DDL) is provided to maintain the items in the data dictionary. (An "item" is any defined system, program file, entry, segment, or element.) The facilities include:

- Setting up new data items and deleting old ones
- Establishing and maintaining owner-member relationships between data items (e.g., that an entry comprises certain elements, that a program uses certain files)
- Inserting, modifying, and removing characteristic descriptions of a data item

Figure 9.9 shows an example of a data definition of a new data element. Figures 9.10 and 9.11 illustrate the types of reports which can be produced for data administration purposes:

Element Glossary—listing of all elements
Element Catalog—detailed description of selected element(s)
Segment Catalog—detailed description of a selected segment

(Note that the selected segment description does not detail all the characteristics of an element.)

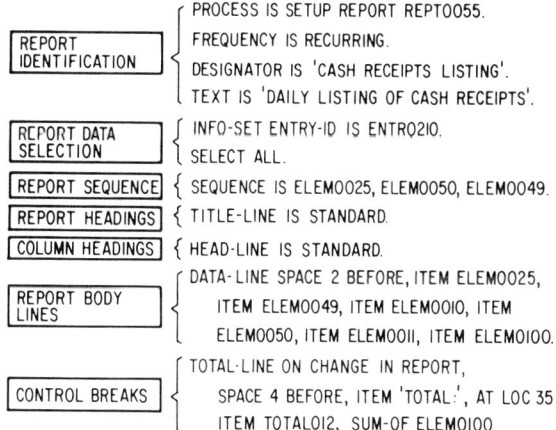

FIGURE 9.9 Example of Automated Data Administration—Report Definition in LEXICON. Courtesy of Arthur Andersen & Co.

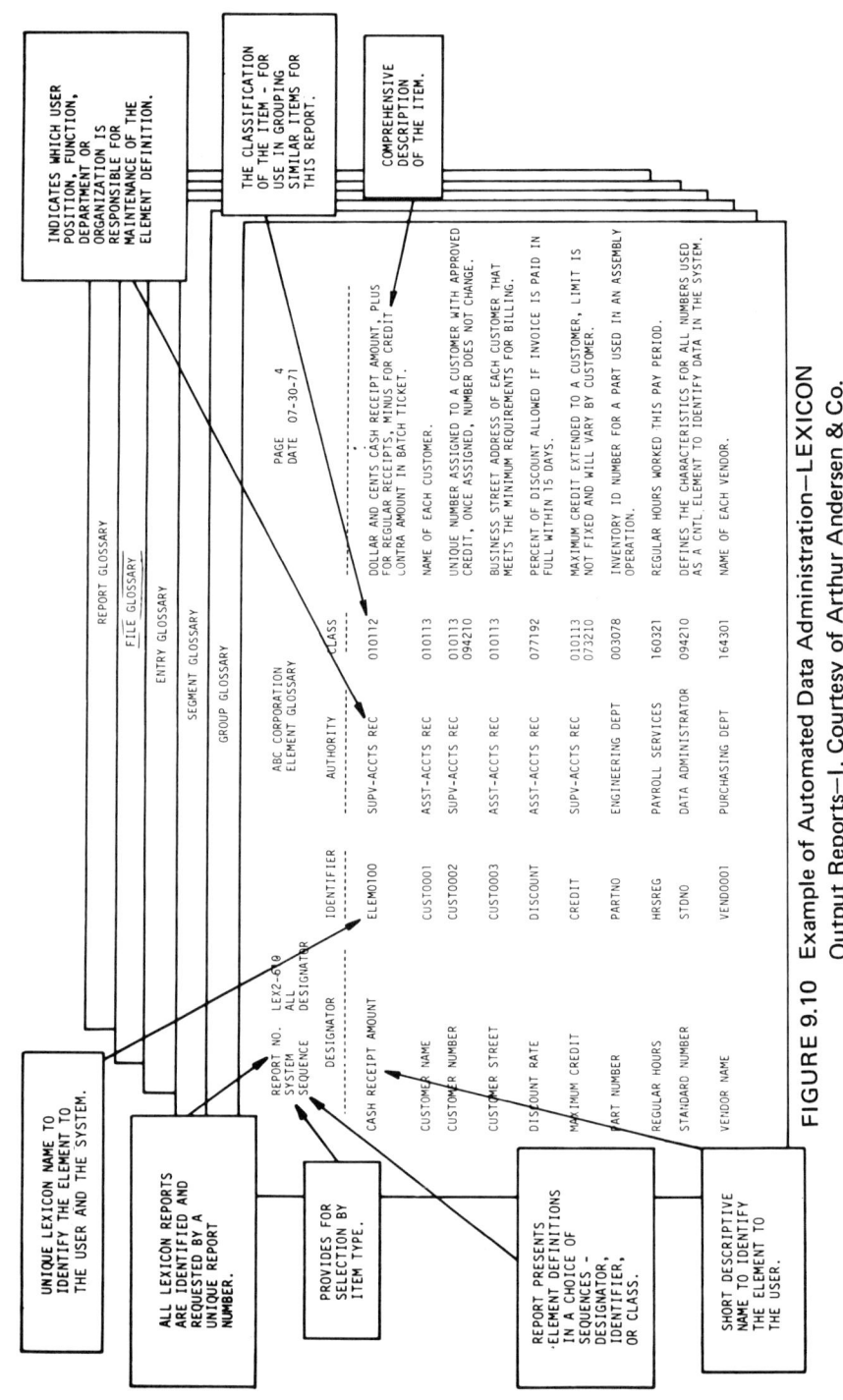

FIGURE 9.10 Example of Automated Data Administration—LEXICON Output Reports—I. Courtesy of Arthur Andersen & Co.

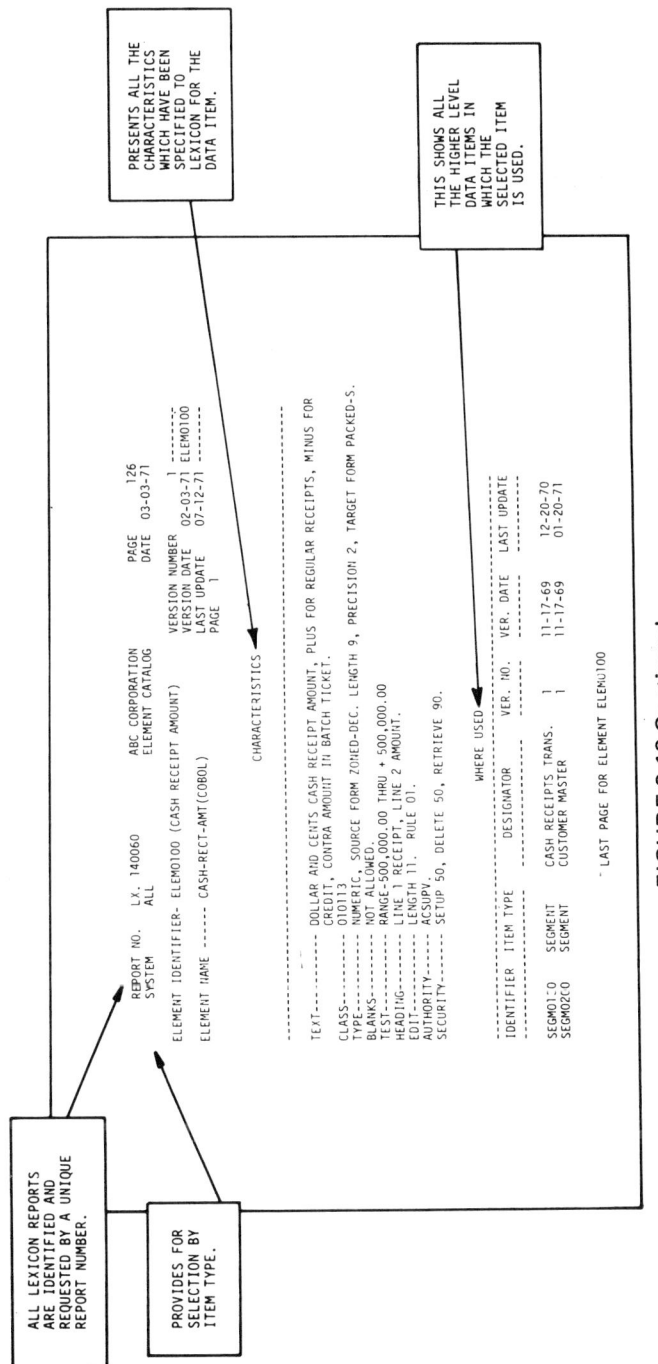

FIGURE 9.10 Continued

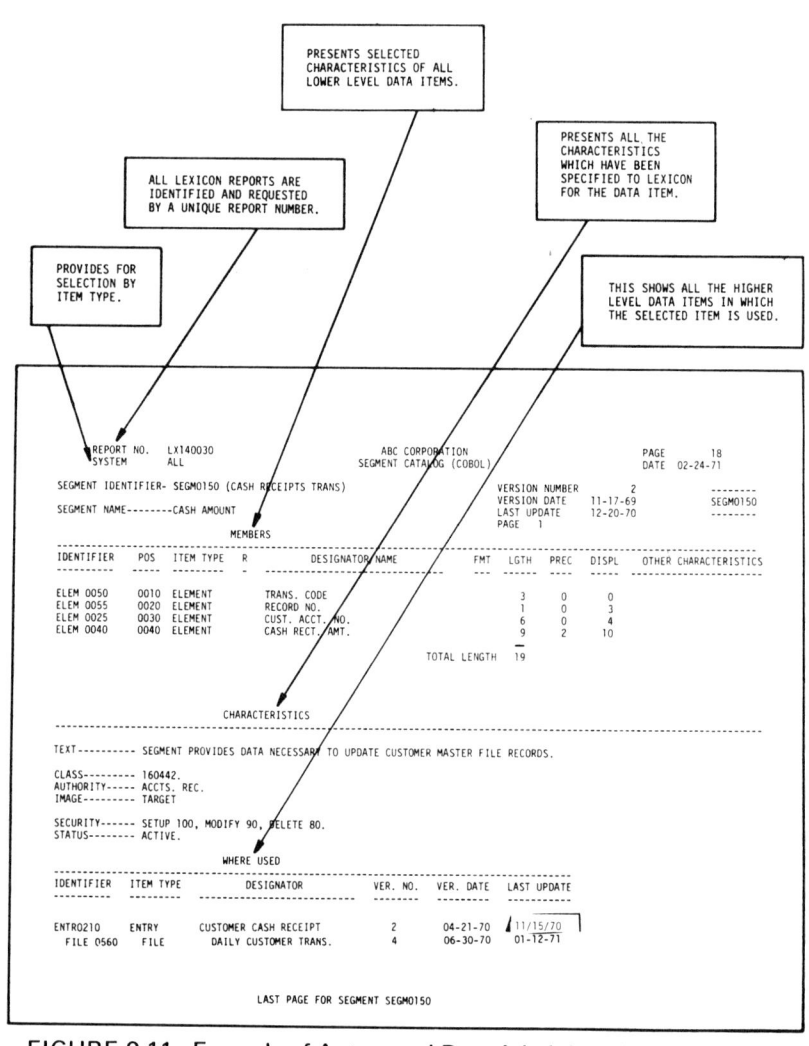

FIGURE 9.11 Example of Automated Data Administration—LEXICON Output Reports—II. Courtesy of Arthur Andersen & Co.

Software Documentation Aids 177

LEXICON is an interesting attempt to come to grips with the problem of data documentation. It is, essentially, automating the data descriptions as described on page 64.

Operations documentation is sometimes neglected, with all the standards effort being put into systems and programming development documentation. One example of an automated approach to operations documentation is GRIM (Generated Run Instruction Manual) developed by Macro Services Corporation of Boston, Mass. This package was initially developed for internal use in 1965 (IBM 1401) and subsequently redesigned around COBOL and operating systems. It is not now commercially available, but it does illustrate the possibilities of producing operations documentation automatically.

GRIM is more than just a software package. To quote the Users Reference Manual, GRIM is a

> ... solution to the problem of collecting information from systems analysts and programmers, then presenting the information to computer operations personnel in a clear, consistent format. GRIM is designed to encourage "style-free" run documentation and to help develop intelligent computer operating procedures. It is organized toward specialization and delegation of work connected with creating and maintaining good run instructions.

The latter is an important point. The preparation, use, and maintenance of computer run instructions can involve many people. Standards are vital for both documentation and procedures.

GRIM identifies files and forms within three levels:
- ACCOUNT (user to be charged)
- SYSTEM (a group of programs which are, or could be, executed in a single uninterrupted job stream)
- JOB (a program execution step within a SYSTEM)

Thus, one or more JOBs define a SYSTEM and one or more SYSTEMs are associated with an ACCOUNT. The package developers recognize that operator decisions regarding job flow are important in running a system. (If an operator has to make job-flow decisions at all, he makes them at the inter-SYSTEM level rather than at the inter-JOB level.) Let us consider a simple example. Ten programs are to be run on different cycles: daily, weekly, monthly, and annually:

Cycle:	DAILY	WEEKLY	MONTHLY	ANNUALLY
	Prog/1	Prog/1	Prog/6	Prog/10
	Prog/5	Prog/2	Prog/7	
		Prog/3	Prog/8	
		Prog/4	Prog/9	

As further complications, Prog/4 is to be run as a middle part of the monthly cycle in months with five work weeks, and the monthly cycle has to be rerun every year just before the annual cycle. Under GRIM, the following SYSTEMS are defined:

SYSTEM

1	2	3	4	5
DAILY	WEEKLY	NORMAL MONTHLY	5-WEEK MONTHLY	ANNUAL
Prog/1	Prog/1	Prog/6	Prog/6	Prog/6
Prog/5	Prog/2	Prog/7	Prog/7	Prog/7
	Prog/3	Prog/8	Prog/4	Prog/8
	Prog/4	Prog/9	Prog/8	Prog/9
			Prog/9	Prog/10

Each of these five SYSTEMS is an independent, self-contained entity which can be referenced easily for scheduling purposes. The operator decision normally following Prog/7 is eliminated by putting the alternative job flows in separate predetermined paths. An example schedule would be:

Date	*To be run*
December 30	System 1
31	1
January 1	—
2	1, 4
3	1, 2, 5
etc.	

Note that this cataloguing would be used for frequent production runs, and could be phased in gradually for all applications. It is not worthwhile for one-off or very infrequent runs.

The inputs to the GRIM system are shown, in summary, in Figure 9.12. The printed reports produced are:

- File Equate Cross-Reference
- Detail Run Instructions
- System Flowchart
- System Operating Summary
- Physical Tape Labels

The File Equate Cross-Reference report lists details of all files by account. Examples of the Detail Run Instructions, System Flowchart, and System Operating Summary are shown in Figures 9.13, 9.14, and 9.15 respectively.

Software Documentation Aids 179

G1 *Operator Instructions* (used to describe a job step)
   Key: account/system/job/step
   Job Description: functional description, author/approval, release date, run time, operating system, memory required, bound code (e.g., printer-bound, cpu-bound, punch-bound, etc.), revision status.
   Input/Output Specification: symbol (identifier), device type and address, Sysno, input origin/output destination, footnotes, EOJ file status, revision status.
   Printer Identification: symbol (identifier), device address, Sysno, destination, footnote, paper (form) type, control tape usage, line spacing, revision status.
   Alignment: description of forms alignment procedure, revision status.
   Footnotes: comments and special instructions.
G2 *Additional Comments* (used as overflow from G1)
   Key: account/system/job/step
   Comments and revision status
G3 *File Equate* (used to allocate files to Accounts and to describe a file)
   Key: account
   File Equate: symbol (identifier), file name, retention requirements, cycle, mode, revision status.
G4 *Account and System Names* (identifies systems to accounts, and names them)
   Key: account
   Title of User
   Account Name: name, revision status.
   System Name: system code, name, revision status.
G5 *Request* (used to request documentation from GRIM and provide tape library control data)

FIGURE 9.12 Sample Operating Instructions Documenter—GRIM Inputs

GRIM ensures standardization and discipline, and does force development personnel to submit complete computer operations documentation. The penalty is the "conversion" effort required to accept GRIM, i.e., documenting existing systems. This can require considerable manual cataloguing and form completion. This is not a problem in, say, using a program flowcharter because existing programs can, with only minor additions or changes, be processed quite simply.

```
                    G E N E R A T E D   R U N   I N S T R U C T I O N   M A N U A L              01/06/71                    PAGE   1

RESEARCH AND DEVELOPMENT                                                                                            ACCOUNT R925
TIME UTILIZATION (WEEKLY CYCLE)        EMPLOYEE NO. ORDER                                                           SYSTEM     3
TIME UTILIZATION CARDS TO DISK                                                                                      STEP      01
STEP 01   JOB 1601          PROGRAMMER 010                                                                          JOB     1601

          UNIT  SYSNO   NO  FILE/FORM DESCRIPTION           DISPOSITION           RETENTION           NOTE         REVISED
          ----  -----   --  --------------------            -----------           ---------           ----         -------
INPUT---
 (01) CARD 00C  SYSC09      021=TUS CARD DATA FILE          FROM
                                                             CONTROL                                   01*

OUTPUT---
 (02) DISK 291  SYS012      WRK=WORK-FILE                   TO
                                                             STEP 02/1602         SCRATCH AT EOJ

PRINTER        00E  SYS011   041=INV-CC-TU-DATA              CONTROL              STANDARD TAPE
                                                                                  6-LPI 1-PLY WIDE

         *NOTE 01 DATE CARD PRECEDES DATA. SEE ADD'L COMMENTS FOR DETAILS.

         ****************       ADDITIONAL COMMENTS      ********************
                                DATE CARD SPECIFICATIONS       * *
                 COLUMN 1 = '0'
                 COLUMN 2-7 = START DATE. FORMAT= MODYYR. MUST BE A THURSDAY.
                     THRU DATE IS OPTIONAL (CCL 8-13, MODYYR)...SHOULD
                     ONLY BE USED AT YEAR'S END WHEN LAST WEEK WILL BE
                     LESS THAN 7 DAYS.
                                                               * *
                 CONSOLE MESSAGES.........
                     SINCE THE PROGRAM INTERNALLY CALCULATES THE THRU DATE
                     (A WEDNESDAY) AND IT WAS IMPOSSIBLE TO CHECK OUT
                     EVERY WEEK DURING TEST STAGE, THE START AND THRU DATES
                     ARE DISPLAYED ON CONSOLE FOR A DOUBLE CHECK.
                     THE PUNCHED START DATE AND THE CALCULATED THRU
                     DATE. THESE DATES MUST BE CORRECT OR ELSE ENTIRE
                     CYCLE WOULD HAVE TO BE RERUN. HOPEFULLY A
                     RESPONSE OF A CAPITAL 'YES' WILL BE GIVEN.
                     NOTIFY PROGRAMMER AT ONCE IF DATES APPEAR
                     INCORRECT. CUT OFF IS ON A WEDNESDAY OR LAST
                     DAY OF YEAR.

                 RECORD COUNTS WILL ALSO APPEAR.
```

FIGURE 9.13 Example of Automated Operations Documentation—GRIM Detail Run Instructions. Courtesy of Marco Services Corporation.

```
                                                                              ACCOUNT R925
                     ACCOUNT R925    SYSTEM 4           01/06/71              SYSTEM     4
                                                                              STEP      03
                                                                              JOB     1641

181 IN           182 IN        183 IN        184 IN        181 OUT

......           ......        ......        ......        ......
 WRK  .           . 051  .      . WRK  .      . WRK  .      . 052   .
 SYS005 .         . SYS006 .    . SYS007 .    . SYS008 .    . SYS005 .
........          ........      ........      ........      ........
  1                  1             1             1             1
--------------------1            ++++++++++++
                                 +           +
                                 +  JOB 1641 +
                                 +  STEP 03  +
                                 +           +
                                 ++++++++++++

                                                 **NOTE   MULTIPLE SYSTEM ASSIGNMENTS ON 181


WRK=WRK-FL      051=F1625/R        052=F1641/S
```

FIGURE 9.14 Example of System Flowchart. Courtesy of Macro Services Corporation   (FOR PAGE 182)

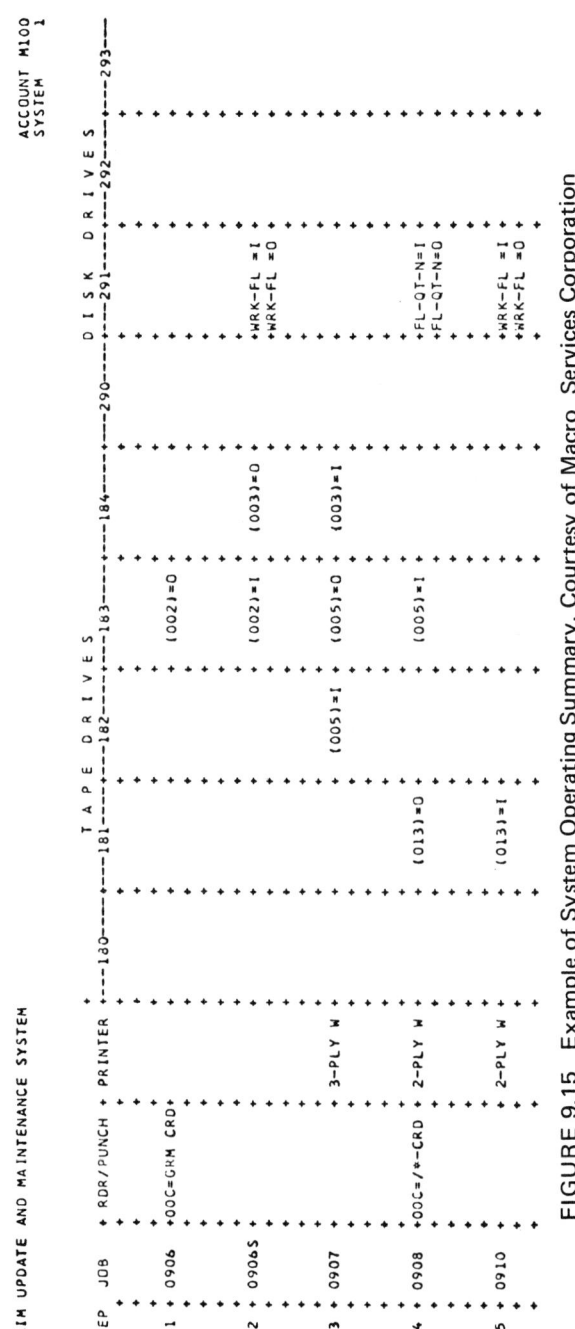

FIGURE 9.15 Example of System Operating Summary. Courtesy of Macro Services Corporation

CHAPTER 10

Documentation of Software Packages

A software package is defined here as one or more programs specifically constructed for general release; i.e., it is designed with more than one user in mind. Figure 10.1 gives a general list of types of software packages. The range varies from the operating system (closest to the machine) to the complete application package consisting of the program(s) to do a specific job. A common characteristic of a software package is that it is constructed to accept variable data (parameters) to specialize it for a particular task.

The impact of packaged software on the documentation standards of a company can be considerable. Three example instances of the development and use of software are given below.

Internal Library Facilities: This is typical of large companies with decentralized data processing installations or a large number of project teams, each with its own programming function. Generalized programs can be prepared in any of the decentralized functions (or a centralized software development function) and placed in a central Software Library. Documentation standards must be laid down for the program descriptions in the library and the detailed specifications of program usage.

Bought-in Software: All computer installations use software packages which originate from outside the company. The majority of the software so used emanates from the computer manufacturer, and includes the operating system, languages, and basic utilities. However, more and more companies are purchasing a greater range of software from other sources, such as specialist software houses, user trade associations, and other computer users. It is important to note the difference between own-produced documentation and imported documentation. A primary rule for instituting any standards is that they must be enforceable, and unauthorized exceptions must be limited to an absolute minimum. In other words, exceptions must be defined and not admitted by default. External software is subject to change as are internally produced pro-

- Operating Systems
  - input/output functions
  - multiprogramming control
  - interrupt processing
  - administration and accounting functions
  - work control
- Utilities
  - sorts
  - transcriptions
  - operations housekeeping (file set-up, dumping, etc.)
- Languages and Programmer Aids
  - medium/high-level language assembly and high-level compilers
  - debugging aids
  - automatic documentors
  - special language processors (decision table preprocessors, etc.)
- Generalized File Processors
  - programs used to create, report, manipulate, and maintain files
- Application Programs
  - complete programs and suites of programs performing specific jobs, both commercial and scientific

FIGURE 10.1 Types of Software

grams. Procedures must thus be incorporated for the updating of software documentation.*

Exported Software: An increasing number of commercial computer users are making their programs available to other organizations. Some of the programs are truly generalized packages as defined previously, and some are specific application packages. The standard program documentation as described in Chapter 5 is rarely sufficient for external users. Generally, further descriptive matter and "instructions for use" must be prepared.

The discussion above applies to the many organizations who use software and occasionally produce it as a by-product. Any specialized software house requires methods and documentation standards as much as commercial users. Indeed, one of the methods used by the author and his colleagues in recommending a software package is to evaluate the software house. Part of this

---

*There is also the situation where the writing of application programs is subcontracted to a programming house. In this instance, the client company has control over the method and quality of the final program documentation. There is little case for having one set of standards for own-documentation and one for externally produced documentation. The client company program documentation standards should be incorporated into the project contract.

Documentation of Software Packages

evaluation is reviewing the standards used. The absence of good standards must call the professionalism of the company into question.

Software Documentation—The Major Differences

How do the standards for documenting software packages differ from those required for specific application programs? To answer this question we must examine the basic objectives of program documentation.

The primary objective of the documentation described in Chapter 5 for own-produced specific programs can be defined as:

> To describe the construction of a program, and the testing procedure, so that the program can be effectively maintained.

The ancillary objectives are to provide a means of controlling the quality and quantity of work produced. The program manual cannot stand alone: The relationship between the programs is shown on the Systems Flowchart; the operating instructions define how the programs are to be run.

Software documentation has to enable one to answer the following questions about the package:

- What does it do?
- Do we want to use it?
- Can we use it?
- How do we use it?
- What do we do if it changes?

As a general rule, therefore, software documentation must concentrate on *how to use the program.* Maintenance is performed by the originator and there is thus *less emphasis on documenting, in detail, how the program works.*

The exact scope of the documentation standards depends on the installation and its involvement in software usage and development. This chapter gives *guidelines* for setting standards to cover software documentation.

Documentation Standards—Using Software

The checklist given below suggests possible areas for applying standards to the control of documentation of bought-in software.

1. *Copy Control and Maintenance:* It is important to minimize the number of software reference manuals within practical limits of usage. The greater the number of copies in circulation the greater the maintenance effort—and the need for control. A master copy should be maintained by the library function.

Maintenance control can be exercised by circulating amendments according to a simple indexing system. For example, all copies can be identified by a unique reference number as follows. The format of the reference number is: TTMMSS

    TT = manual type (by subject)
    MM = manual number (serial number within subject)
    SS = manual set number

(An additional prefix can be used to denote software supplier if more than one major supplier is used).

Example manual type codes are:

- 01 General Information
- 02 Hardware
- 03 General Programming
- 04 Disc Operating System—Languages
- 05 Disc Operating System—Control, Service, and Utilities
- 06 Operating Systems and Time Sharing
- 07 Application Programs

The manual number is allocated serially within manual type. The set numbers are used to identify the location of a group of manuals. Example set codes are:

- 01   Master Set—held in the central documentation library
- 02-04 Programming Reference Set—copies held in the programming action for reference
- 05-07 Operations Sets—sets of certain manuals held in the computer room and off-line area
- 08-   Programming Sets—sets of certain manuals held by individual programmers

The responsibility for circulating amendments and updating the manuals must be clearly stated in the standards manual.

2. *Documentation References:* Obviously, the major advantage of using software is that the programs are prewritten, tested, and *documented.* The production of a Program Manual in the normal form is thus unnecessary and alternatives must be specified. Standards must be laid down for how the use of software is to be recorded in the program documentation. For example, the presence of standard subroutines in a program should be clearly stated in the program.

A standard subroutine description can include:

- Subroutine name
- Purpose of subroutine
- Call method
- Parameter description

Documentation of Software Packages

- Length of subroutine
- List of enclosed subroutines
- Programmed halts

(Subroutines forming an integral part of the operating system, e.g., which perform standard input/output functions, need not be catalogued.)

A specification sheet should be included for each stand-alone program used. A description of the facilities used and the relevant parameters should be stated. Preprinted forms can be used for frequently used routines.

Documentation Standards—Internal Library Functions

Many large companies have established an internal, central library function which acts as a "pool" of available software. Details of subroutines and programs which are of a general nature and could be of use in other programming projects are submitted to the central library. The documentation submitted is usually some form of Program Abstract. The purpose of this document is to answer the first three questions in the list on page 185. An example table of contents for a Program Abstract is shown in Figure 10.2. Note that for a subroutine or a relatively simple program, a description of the parameters (how to use the software) can be added. There are two ways of dealing with the detailed documentation. The first is to require the Program Manual, together with detailed instructions for use, to be submitted to the library. The alternative is to leave the Program Manual with originator and to include a reference in the Program Abstract: "for further information, contact . . . " etc.

Documentation Standards—Documenting Generalized Software

Software can be developed in many situations. If it is produced for internal use only, then a Program Abstract and Program Manual may be sufficient. If the program(s) has many optional facilities and requires various combinations of parameters then some form of user instruction or reference manual is required. This is especially important if the program(s) is to be used remotely. If the package is to be offered outside the organization, then some form of sales-oriented literature will have to be produced. The amount of detail released on the actual construction of the program is usually limited.

A three-level system of documentation which is generally applicable is:

- General Description
- User Guide
- User Reference Manual

The General Description is the equivalent of the internal Program Abstract.

PROGRAM ABSTRACT

1. Identification

    1.1 Descriptive Title
    1.2 Reference Number
    1.3 Program Number/Name
    1.4 Originator
    1.5 Date of Writing/Issue

2. Capabilities and Facilities

    2.1 Purpose and Use
    2.2 Limitations
    2.3 Facilities Used

3. Method

    3.1 Summary of Method
    3.2 Parameters Required
    3.3 Timing

4. General Comments

FIGURE 10.2 Sample Table of Contents—Program Abstract for Software Documentation Library

The basic objective of this document is to enable the reader to answer the questions:

- What is it?
- Can we use it?
- Should we use it—is it worth following up?

Many such General Descriptions are far too sales oriented. A glossy sales description certainly serves a useful function—but not to the exclusion of technical sense.

The User Guide and the User Reference Manual serve two very different functions and will be used differently. The User Guide is a teaching document which gives a broad picture of how the package works, the facilities available, and how it can be used. The User Reference Manual is an encyclopedia or dictionary of how to use the package. The major difference is that the User Guide is read from cover to cover while the User Reference Manual is used for selective reference.

The exact content and format of the manuals depends on the scope and complexity of the subject software. However, some guidelines for preparing these manuals are given below.

User Guide: The objectives of this manual must be very carefully set and the manual constructed accordingly. Typical objectives are to provide a general description of the package, its facilities, and ways in which these facilities can be used. The manual should be constructed logically, going from the general to the specific. Liberal use should be made of examples, and at least one complete job should be shown. Complex technical material should be placed separate from the general text, as in an appendix. Very specialized facilities, or those which are rarely used, should be placed in a separate chapter.

User Reference Manual: The sequence of material should be for ease of reference. For example, facilities can be grouped by type, and alphabetically within type. If there are many facilities or parameter entries which are subject to change, one item should be described to a page. (The title should be shown clearly on the upper right-hand side of a right-hand page or on the upper left-hand side of a left-hand page.) Wherever possible a standard format should be used in describing facilities. For example, for a parameter

- Title
- Purpose
- Description
- Format
- Rules for use
- Limitations or exceptions
- Example

Where combinations of options are possible, simple tables should be used.

PART FOUR

CONTROL
OF
DOCUMENTATION

CHAPTER 11

Development Documentation and Project Control

As discussed in Chapter 2, this book is concerned with development documentation, rather than with control documentation (i.e., that documentation produced solely for project control purposes). It was mentioned, however, that standardized development documentation can be used as an aid in project control. This is achieved by establishing formal checkpoints during a development project and by monitoring progress and quality of work at these points by an appraisal of documentation. This chapter discusses the establishment of formal checkpoints with the use of development documentation.

PROJECT PHASES AND TASKS

A data processing project can be segmented into a number of distinct phases, which in turn may be further subdivided into tasks. Generally any project may be considered as comprising three basic phases: Project Initiation, Project Fulfillment, and Project Conclusion. A complete list of tasks within these phases is shown in Figure 11.1. The segmentation of a project as shown in the figure provides management with a capability of monitoring smaller units of activity.

The conclusion of each phase or task may be considered as a project checkpoint. A project checkpoint is therefore established at each point in a project where there is a "turnover" of work from one task to another. For example, the turnover of a Systems Specification to the programming function would require a checkpoint, as would the turnover of programs with associated documentation to the operating function.

Specific documentation requirements, as well as other requirements, can be defined as marking the completion of a task. The purpose of a checkpoint at the completion of each task is to verify that the work performed so far has been completed satisfactorily and according to established standards. Work does not progress onto the next task unless the work output from the previous task, as reflected in the documentation, is approved in terms of quality (workability and accuracy), completeness, and legibility.

Of course, the output from many tasks is a defined product which must also be reviewed, e.g., the review of a program in terms of the quality of its output, running speed and ease of operation. However, in this chapter, we are primarily concerned with the documentation aspect of project checkpoints. Further, the actual grouping of tasks for any one project and the review criteria at any one

```
                   PROJECT CONTROL POINTS

      Project Initiation

            1.  Project Selection
            2.  Project Authorization
            3.  Project Planning
            4.  Personnel Assignment
            5.  Estimating
            6.  Scheduling
            7.  Budgeting

      Project Fulfillment

            8.  System Study-1st Phase
            9.  System Study-Completion
           10.  System Analysis Completion
           11.  System Design-Data Base Specification
           12.  System Design Completion
           13.  Programming-Coding Completion
           14.  Programming-Third Machine Test
           15.  Programming-75% of Program Test Budget
           16.  System Test Plan Completion
           17.  System Test-Intermediate Review
           18.  System Test Completion
           19.  Volume Test Plan Completion


      Project Conclusion

           20.  Pre-Conversion Preparation Completion
           21.  Post-Implementation Audit
```

FIGURE 11.1 Typical Project Control Points

Development Documentation and Project Control 195

checkpoint will depend on the characteristics of a project. This is discussed in Chapter 13 when the considerations for establishing documentation standards for a particular environment are reviewed.

DOCUMENTATION CHECKPOINTS

The development documentation required at each task is discussed below. This documentation is based on the levels and types of documentation as described in Part II of this book.

Phase 1—Project Initiation

Task 1–Project Selection. Project Selection requires that the project objectives be clearly stated and the project is properly defined and its scope established. The User Request must be completed.

Task 2–Project Authorization. When the user and data processing are ready to proceed, the project objectives are reviewed and accepted. The System Proposal must be completed.

Task 3–Project Planning. The Project Plan includes a detailed task outline and an analysis of required skills. The Analytical Report and Design Requirements Statements are prepared.

Task 4–Personnel Assignment. The personnel required for the project are assigned in this phase. No new development documentation is prepared.

Task 5–Estimating. Analytical documentation and list of project tasks are reviewed in detail; standards are applied for the estimation of time required to complete the project. No new development documentation is prepared.

Task 6–Scheduling. Task estimates are reviewed to develop a total project schedule. No new development documentation is prepared.

Task 7–Budgeting. Tasks and time are listed; standard rates are applied to develop a complete picture of project costs. No new development documentation is prepared.

Phase 2—Project Fulfillment

Task 1–First Stage of System Study. The user's initial reaction to the Project Plan is elicited and possible problem areas reviewed. No new development documentation is prepared.

Task 2–System Study Completion. The proposed system is reviewed with the user; exceptions and expansions in the scope of the project are identified. All analytical documentation (User Request, Analytical Report,

Design Requirements Statement) is reviewed and approved, and the Systems Summary is prepared.

Task 3—System Analysis Completion. Design alternatives and systems requirements are reviewed and design estimates made. Documentation prepared to date is reviewed and accepted. The Systems Specification (file, transaction, output, and processing and system test plan) is prepared.

Task 4—Data Base Design Completion. Specifications for files, transactions, outputs and related reports are reviewed, checked against the System Summary, and discussed with and approved by the user.

Task 5—System Design. All Systems Specifications are reviewed and additional Program Specifications are prepared, if necessary. Specifications for files, input/outputs, reports, controls, processing requirements are prepared and reviewed. Readiness for programming to begin is ascertained.

Task 6—Coding. Logic flow specifications and the program test plan are prepared. Coding is reviewed to insure that it is faithful to the logic design. The program test plan, test data, and instructive output specifications are prepared and reviewed.

Task 7—First Stage of Program Testing. A review of the status of a program is made after the third test. At this point the Programming Specification is reviewed and checked against the initial output. No new development documentation is prepared.

Task 8—Final Stage of Program Testing. The Program Test Plan is checked to insure that it has been followed. Program test results are also checked against the Program Specification to determine whether results are satisfactory.

Task 9—Systems Test Plan Completion. Upon completion of program testing, the Systems Test Plan is reviewed. At the same time, preliminary operating instructions are reviewed and the completion of program testing validated.

Task 10—Interim Stage of Systems Testing. The number of program changes required, running time, program interface, errors, and test results are reviewed and checked against the Systems Test Plan to determine whether results are satisfactory.

Task 11—System Test Completion. The results of the systems test are checked against the Systems Specification. Changes already made and documentation changes required are reviewed, and user acceptance obtained.

Task 12—Volume Test Plan. All user aids (data input, output, collection, preparation, and control instructions), and data processing (system and program) operating instructions are reviewed prior to scheduling a volume test.

Phase 3—Project Conclusion

Task 1—Preconversion Check. Results of the volume test are reviewed to determine adequacy of documentation and readiness for conversion.

Task 2—Postimplementation Audit. The anticipated system benefits are compared with actual benefits to determine if the system has fulfilled requirements. Needed improvements are identified and documentation changed accordingly.

SUMMARY

1. Standardized documentation, in conjunction with an established system of checkpoints, is a major aid to effective project control.

2. A development project may be divided into three major phases

- Project Initiation
- Project Fulfillment
- Project Conclusion

which may be further subdivided into a number of tasks as shown in Figure 11.1.

3. At the completion of each task a review is made of any documentation prepared during that task.

4. The review of documentation against the prescribed standards should cover

- Workability
- Accuracy
- Legibility
- Completeness

5. Work does not proceed to the subsequent tasks until the review described in item 4 above is satisfactory.

6. Suggested tasks and checkpoints have been discussed.

CHAPTER 12

The Documentation Library and Documentation Maintenance

The term "documentation library" as used in this chapter, relates to a centralized function responsible for the control, retention, storage and distribution of master documentation files. The exact functions and responsibilities of a documentation library will depend on the particular characteristics and requirements of any one company. Some general aspects of the contents and organization of a library are given below.

DOCUMENTATION LIBRARY—ORGANIZATION AND RESPONSIBILITIES

The position of the documentation library within an organization will depend on local conditions. However, in any company but the smallest with little data processing activity, the documentation library must be recognized as a specific independent function. The resources expended on the library will depend on many factors such as

- Scope of data processing activities
- Frequency of reference to contents
- Whether data processing functions are centralized or decentralized
- Internal structure of the data processing department
- Project types

Depending on the degree of sophistication required of the library, it may have responsibilities for some or all of the following:

 1. Review of development documentation to insure adherence to standards and appropriate authorization of exceptions.
 2. Registration and storage of acceptable documentation.
 3. Revisions handling.
 4. Notification and distribution to interested parties.

The Documentation Library and Documentation Maintenance

At the lowest level of usage, the documentation library may be simply existing for the control, storage, retention, and distribution of master development documents, with a part-time librarian. In this case the library would probably contain all final systems development documentation. However, a documentation library may also serve as a control function related to the programming or operations facilities. Thus, it may also act as a control point for software information handling. For example, in a company with a large or decentralized programming capability, summary specifications of all programs produced are filed with the documentation library. In the library the specifications are indexed (say by application, type of program, and originator) and copies circulated to programming personnel.

Similarly, the documentation library may be linked to the operations function. In a large installation where many different applications are run, the availability of a program or suite of programs to run may be indicated by the presence or absence of the operations documentation, or a clarification code filed against the operations documentation. The documentation library may also be used to file and update master copies of manufacturer's literature. In some cases, updating software literature for languages and utilities can represent a major task. The library, while maintaining a master set, can also be given the responsibility for distributing manufacturer's material to local working copies. This has the added advantage of having one reception point for all manufacturer's literature.

Thus, as can be seen from the above discussion, the documentation library should initially not only be considered as serving a storage function; it may be used as a central point of control with any other data processing function.

Contents and Procedures

The basic classifications for documentation are

- System
- Program
- Operations
- Users

Each of the above documentation elements may be grouped into a folder identified by a project or task number. Within each folder may be

- A file log and checklist
- Revision notices
- Cross-reference index or indexes
- Distribution list
- Development documentation

Note that this information must be included for all projects, even if the project has been suspended, thus forming a master documentation file. This file is up to date and complete even though various functional groups may maintain duplicate files pertinent to their own needs. A brief description of the folder content listed above is given below.

The file log records the revisions made and the status of the project, e.g., operational under revision, suspended or obsolete, etc. A checklist is a useful method of ensuring the completion of the documentation in the folder. For each folder type, a standard list of contents should be shown (with space for listing optional additions). Against this list should be space for recording that an item is included, or referencing its location if it has been omitted; examples are shown in Figure 12.1 (*a*)-(*d*). Revision notices should contain

- Project identification and date of revision
- Revision originator authorization
- Brief summary and scope of revision
- List of attachments detailing the revision

A suggested method of processing revisions is as follows. The librarian should log the appropriate section of a file as soon as it is known that there is a revision in hand. Formal notice of the revision, with appropriate authorization, should be sent to the library where the change is entered into the file log and the required amendments made to the documentation. The cross-reference index is then inspected to determine if all appropriate secondary appearances of the information have been covered by the distribution list. The revision is then circulated as per the distribution list.

The cross-reference index(es) lists all folders or files in which a document is duplicated, thus giving an easy means of keeping track of documentation for maintenance purposes.

The actual development documentation should have been prepared in accordance with the laid-down standards. The documents are filed in numerical sequence within the folder.

Within the library, therefore, each documentation element of a project is represented by a folder containing complete information. A subject-reference index may be maintained to permit the rapid location of the individual folders. Note that, in certain instances, information may appear in more than one folder; repetition of the information, rather than the use of cross-references, allows each folder to be used separately and facilitates the maintenance and control of distribution. The documentation relating to general-purpose programs or files used by more than one program should be stored in the originating project/task file. However, it is often useful for an additional copy of this documentation to be filed separately under a general-purpose documentation category.

	SYSTEM FOLDER
	DOCUMENT CHECKLIST

Project/Task Number _____ Date _____

Prepared by _____ Approved by _____

Document Name	Included	Document Used as Replacement	Associated Reference Material	Source
SYSTEM NAME				
1. Project/Task Statement (User Request)				
2. Systems Proposal				
3. Analytical Report (name) Attachments: (name & number)				
4. Design Requirements Statement				
5. System Summary				
6. File Specifications: (file name & nos.)				
7. Transaction Specs.				
8. Output Specs.				
9. Segment Processing Specs: (Segment names & nos.)				
10. System Test Plan				

FIGURE 12.1 (a) System Folder Document Checklist; (b) Program Folder Document Checklist; (c) Operations Folder Document Checklist; (d) File History Form—Revision Page

PROGRAM FOLDER
DOCUMENT CHECKLIST

Project/Task Number _____ Date _____

Prepared by _____ Approved by _____

PROGRAM NAME		PROGRAM NUMBER		
Document Name	Included	Document Used as Replacement	Associated Document Reference	Source
11. Programming Specification				
12. Transaction Specification				
13. Instructive Output Specification				
14. Internal Flow Specification				
15. Programming Parameters				
16. Program Test Plan				

FIGURE 12.1 (*b*)

OPERATIONS FOLDER				
DOCUMENT CHECKLIST				

Page ____ of ____
Project/Task Number _____ Date _____
Prepared by _____ Approved by _____

SYSTEM NAME

Document Name	Included	Document Used as Replacement	Associated Document Reference	Source
17. Program Test Instructions				
18. System Setup Instructions				
19. System/Program Operating Instructions				
20. Input Collection and Preparation Instructions				
21. Input Control Instructions				
22. Output Review and Distribution Instructions				
23. Output Control Instructions				

FIGURE 12.1 (c)

Date	Section	Chapter	Page	Reviser	Approval Initials	Purpose	Description

FILE HISTORY FORM

REVISION PAGE

FIGURE 12.1 (*d*)

Within this general framework for the library, specific procedures must be specified for

- Method of review to insure that documentation is prepared in accordance with the standards
- Registering (indexing and storing) acceptable documentation
- Recording and distribution of revised information and project status
- Record of loans/returns from the library

DOCUMENTATION SECURITY

Documentation security is an important factor in the design and implementation of library control standards. Insuring the security of documentation can be considered under a number of headings. The first is unauthorized disclosure of company confidential material to an outside party. A company may have spent many thousands of dollars developing a new program or system which could be a valuable acquisition to a competitor. A Systems Proposal of interim system documentation may contain confidential information about the company's activities. Disclosure of the documentation of a proprietary software package may be an infringement of the purchase/leasing agreement and reasonable care must be exercised in guarding such information. (As an example, the author was recruiting senior programmers and no less than two applicants came to the interview with program documentation of their projects together with the latest reports produced by these programs. Both included what must have been company confidential data. When asked if they could leave the documentation and reports, the applicants said "Yes, of course." So much for *their* employers security!) As a duty to both employer and employees, a statement must be issued which clearly defines the status of documentation. This should be published in the company data processing standards manual. It should be checked with the personnel and legal departments. An *example* is shown in Figure 12.2. Basic controls should also be exercised on taking any documentation outside company premises.

Four simple rules for document security are:

1. Use the "need to know" criterion for access to documentation.
2. No staff permitted to remove documentation from the premises without a record being made (and, preferably, a master copy being left).
3. Number all copies and keep records of use.
4. Keep strict control of access to photocopying equipment. (For "classified" material, consider the use of paper which cannot be photocopied.)

The second area for controls lies in minimizing the impact from the loss or damage of documentation. This is mainly a problem with interim or working documentation since multiple copies of the formal documentation (Systems

---

NOTICE

The Documentation Standards Manual is the official guide to the documentation of all systems and programs at the Associated Conglomerated Group, Inc. The information contained herein is proprietary. The Manual is the copyrighted property of Associated Conglomerated Group, Inc.

The holder of this manual may not divulge any of its contents to an outside party without prior permission. The Manual must be surrendered if the holder's employment is terminated for any reason.

Computer personnel are advised that all computer programs and associated material prepared by the Associated Conglomerated Group, Inc. (the Corporation) are the property of the Corporation who owns the copyright therein. Without the written consent of the Corporation, given by contract or otherwise, no document or associated material concerned with the design development or implementation of its computer programs may be copied reprinted or reproduced in any material form, either wholly or in part, nor may its contents, or any method or technique available therefrom, be disclosed, either wholly or in part, to any other person whatsoever.

Computer programs and associated material available to the Corporation but not prepared by them may nonetheless be the property of the Corporation, who may also have control of the copyright, and personnel are advised to assume that the above regulations apply to such programs and materials.

FIGURE 12.2 Sample Security Notice

Specification, etc.) are produced. The rule is that if there is only *one* copy of an important document, a security copy is made and stored in a remote location or keep the master in a fireproof safe.

DOCUMENTATION MAINTENANCE

The key to the successful use of documentation is that it must be maintained—it must be current and represent the exact requirements and methodology of a system. Thus, any standardization of documentation must specify the authority, control, and techniques for documentation maintenance.

Authority and Control

The placement of authority for insuring that systems and operating changes are correctly documented depends on the project development "team" structure. However, in most instances, overall responsibilities for documentation are maintained by the technical project personnel. The actual mechanics of distributing and recording amendments are the responsibilities of a documentation library as described previously in this chapter.

Thus, for a major systems change, a suggested procedure for documentation updating is as follows:

1. Project leader obtains master copy from systems documentation library.
2. Project leader reviews master documentation and notes areas (sections) where revision is necessary.
3. Project personnel process the required changes and draft documentation revision(s).
4. Project leader reviews work, documentation and obtains revision authority from appropriate parties.
5. Submit revision notice(s), plus attachments(s) to library.
6. Documentation library processes revisions.

Techniques

The actual techniques for revising the documentation will depend on the nature of the changes and the structure of the documentation. Within the documentation standards, explicit rules must be given for amendments. Some general considerations are given below. Documentation amendment procedures should make provision for the following types of changes.

1. Changes which can be made directly on existing documentation without making it illegible or unintelligible.
2. Additions which amplify, clarify, or augment existing documentation without making obsolete the present contents.
3. Changes which are a whole or partial replacement of existing documentation.

SUMMARY

1. The basic responsibilities of the documentation library are the control, retention, storage, and distribution of master documentation files.
2. The position of the documentation library in the organizational structure is dependent on many conditions. However, for all but the small data processing installations, consideration should be given to establishing the documentation library as a specific independent function.

3. The conditions which influence the establishment of a documentation library have been discussed, and additional functions of the library in the programming and operations areas were suggested.

4. The contents of the library were discussed in terms of a "folder" comprising documentation housekeeping information and the actual development documentation itself. Critical procedures for processing these folders in the library were outlined.

5. Documentation maintenance is a major area in which rigid standards should be specified and *enforced*.

6. The documentation library can be used to control documentation maintenance distributions. Procedures should be established for maintenance techniques and amendment originator/library/recipient communication.

CHAPTER **13**

Development of Documentation Standards

Thus far in this book, we have reviewed the requirements for a standard system of documentation, identified the main types of documents and described a basic level of document content. This chapter discusses the problems facing a company which has decided to prepare definitive documentation standards.

As discussed in Chapter 2, there is no one universal documentation system which is valid for all environments. How then can a company produce its own individual documentation standards? If we accept that computer-aided information processing has been with us for a quarter of a century, there is obviously no basis for any company starting at "ground zero." The experience gained in the industry in only the last five years should be a sufficient basis for embarking on a documentation standards program without repeating the same groundwork covered previously many hundreds of times. Thus, the development of documentation standards should to a large extent be a process of *adaptation* rather than *origination*. The information presented in Part II of this book should provide an adequate technical starting point for the production of documentation standards for a particular company.

The development of company documentation standards may be only a subsidiary project to the production of a comprehensive set of company data processing standards. Such standards would include methodology for all data processing tasks, and possibly performance standards for personnel and equipment. The requirements for developing company methods and performance standards are described in *Management Standards for Data Processing* by Dick H. Brandon (Van Nostrand, Princeton, N. J., 1963). This chapter considers only the development of documentation standards rather than complete company data processing standards. But, as discussed previously, this exercise in itself can lead to a certain amount of standardization in methodology, since the end product of a task has been clearly defined.

Irrespective of the scope of the standards program, to achieve any worthwhile output will require *management backing*; a belief by management that standards *are* necessary, that the expending of resources *will* lead to a product which will enhance the company's data processing effort. Besides the commitment of resources to a "nonproductive" function, management must recognize that their backing is essential for standards enforcement. They must also be prepared to accept that time scales for some projects will be extended (compared to similar work performed previously) to compensate for the learning period of the new standards. Similarly, time scales may be extended to make allowances for more rigid documentation requirements; e.g., the current average of 5 percent of project time spent on documentation may be increased to 20 percent after the standards are implemented.

Thus, bearing in mind this major emphasis on the importance of management backing, we may now consider the outputs from, and tasks in, a documentation standards development program.

The output of the standards development program should be

- A Manual of Documentation Standards
- A maintenance and support program
- A training and implementation scheme

The tasks which must be performed to achieve the above output may be grouped into three phases

- Preparatory tasks
- Development tasks
- Postimplementation tasks—audit, maintenance, and support

These tasks are discussed in detail below.

PREPARATORY TASKS

A documentation standards development project may be compared with a systems development project. It must be subject to the same controls, planning, and resource allocation. Further, a standards development project will require analysis of the current environment, projections of future requirements, design of a product, development of maintenance functions, audit of finished product, and so on. Thus, the preparatory tasks in a standards development project may be likened to the project initiation phase in a systems development project.

The three major preparatory tasks are

- Establish organization of the project and allocation of resources
- Define scope of standards program
- Define organization of the Manual

and are discussed below.

Development of Documentation Standards

Project Organization and Resource Allocation

The key to a successful standards project is usually the initial planning. The planning serves three aims

- To provide a master plan for project development
- To assure precise understanding of task assignments and responsibilities
- To establish a control system for the project to monitor quality and progress

The ways and means by which these three aims are met depends, of course, on the size, organization, and attitude of a particular company. However, some methods which have been found by experience to work well are discussed below.

Of equal weight to the prerequisite of management backing is the complementary requirement that the personnel actively concerned with the project consider it as a first- or second-priority task. Without management backing, the "working priority" of the standards project may be relegated to a fifth- or sixth-priority rating behind all productive project work. For large companies, an independent function of "Standards Development" may be created. This would comprise a staff working full time on standards coordination and development. Any other alternative approach to the separate standards function will lead to problems. A common case is the assignment of the various areas for standardization to the relevant technical specialists. Without a strong coordination function for consolidation of the various outputs, the standards manual degenerates into a collection of informal papers. These may be written in different styles, in various levels of detail, in a multitude of formats and so on.

A simple approach to developing standards is the Review Committee/Working Committee approach. The Review Committee functions as the policy decision making body; it also serves as review function for final output. For continuity therefore, it should comprise the same permanent members. The composition of the committee will depend on the local company structure. For example, in a company with a number of completely decentralized data processing functions, the Review Committee would comprise all divisional data processing managers. Thus, the first task is to organize the Review Committee; that is, define its function and composition.

The Working Committee is responsible for the actual preparation of draft material. Since, as we shall see later, the manual will be divided into sections, each section dealing with different functional areas (programming, systems, operating, etc.), the composition of the Working Committee will be flexible. Thus, the second task is the organization of a Working Committee. Initially, the general items of reference must be established and its method of working defined. As the scope and contents of the standards manual are agreed, the assignment of responsibilities for the Working Committee is made as members are seconded to the committee.

After the "charts" have been formulated, liason procedures between the committees and their members must be defined including procedures for scheduling meetings, recording and distributing results, and review methods. After the standards manual has been released, the Review Committee should function in the auditing of the standards for effectiveness and in the review of new or revised material.

At this stage in the project there will probably be at least a rough draft of the table of contents of the standards manual. An initial arrangement can therefore be made for the allocation of personnel in the "Standards Development Group" (if applicable) required to develop each section in the manual.

Project Scope

The first act of the Review Committee is to define the scope of the standards development program, if this has not been specified precisely by higher management.

That is to

- Define the levels and type of material to be included in the standards program
- Identify overlapping between current operating procedures and proposed standards

Of major importance is the definition of the limits of the standards project: Is the project to cover methodology standards, performance standards, and documentation standards? Similarly, what general approach is to be used in a decentralized company in the area of "local" standards? An example of the latter is where one company comprises a number of decentralized data processing development functions, each function having a different project mix and working environment. The standards manual may specify mandatory standards for all "divisions" but a procedure would probably be necessary for the inclusion of local standards peculiar to each division.

It should now be possible to define a firm outline table of contents for the manual and to assign the responsibility and authority for the development of each section in the manual.

Finally, the relationship between the standards project and other procedures and policies must be clearly established and a method of coordination agreed. Most companies, for example, issue management directions on policy. These "company instructions" may or may not have precedence over the standards manual; after the issue of the standards manual all statements of data processing organization and policy may be issued as an amendment to the manual, rather than by the issue of a company instruction.

Organization of the Manual

Having defined the general scope of the manual, the actual content may now be planned in terms of the logical order of the content and the physical format of the manual. As an indication of the layout of a documentation standards manual, a sample table of contents is given in Figure 13.1. The actual sequence of the material will, of course, depend on the particular environment of one company. (More will be said about content later in this chapter.)

In addition to defining the logical order of content, the physical format of the manual should be determined in terms of

- Structure of manual
- Indexing and page numbering system
- Positioning and referencing of illustrations
- Page layout and identification block
- Distribution requirements and procedures
- Methods of reproduction

A commonly used structure requires a breakdown to section, chapter, and subject. This gives a referencing system of SCs, where S = section number, C = chapter number, and s = subject number. For ease of amendment and identification, pages should be numbered within each subject.

Similarly, illustrations (referred to as Exhibits or Attachments) should be numbered within subjects. Thus, the basic unit of work is the subject.

Within each subject, the treatment given to the material will depend on the working environment. One approach is to make the presentation of material below subject level informal. Beyond defining that an ordered system of indentation of headings is to be used to break up the text and that paragraphs giving individual rules are to be numbered, no other format standards may be imposed.

On the other hand, in a large or complex manual rules may be defined for the presentation of material. For example; each subject may begin with two standard headings: Purpose (of the subject) and References (to related subjects). The remainder of the subject is developed, within a prescribed paragraph layout and numbering system, as the material dictates. An example of format and layout rules for a presentation which is generally applicable is given below.

Example Rules

1. The manual will be divided into

    - Sections
    - Chapters
    - Subjects

```
        DATA PROCESSING STANDARDS
          AND PROCEDURES MANUAL

          Table of Contents
          Documentation Section

10.0 Documentation Standards

10.1 Documentation Requirements
     10.1.1 Documentation Library
     10.1.2 Project/task document file
     10.1.3 Procedures and responsibilities
     10.1.4 Documentation conventions

10.2 Systems Analysis and Design Documentation
     10.2.1 Preliminary studies and proposals
     10.2.2 General system description
     10.2.3 Input/Output description
     10.2.4 Detailed system description
     10.2.5 System testing

10.3 Programming Documentation
     10.3.1 General program description
     10.3.2 Input/output description
     10.3.3 Detailed program description
     10.3.4 Program testing

10.4 Operations Documentation
     10.4.1 Test operations
     10.4.2 Job operation
     10.4.3 Input management
     10.4.4 Output management

10.5 Reference Documentation
     10.5.1 User's Guide
     10.5.2 Technical Guide
```

FIGURE 13.1 Sample Table of Contents for Documentation from a DP Standards Manual

Development of Documentation Standards 215

2. The numbering system to be used is SCs, where S = section, C = chapter, and s = subject. Pages will be numbered within subjects and referenced as SCs-p, where p is the page number.

3. The first page of each subject will contain an identification block thus

SECTION	
CHAPTER	
SUBJECT	Date of Issue:

4. Continuation pages must have the page numbers only in the form SCs-p, in the upper right-hand corner of the page.

5. Illustrations must be numbered within subject in the form SCs-e and referred to in the text as Exhibits. All exhibits should be grouped in sequence at the end of a subject.

6. Exhibits should be identified by the caption ["Subject SCs Exhibit e. page P."] on the bottom right-hand corner of the page.

7. References to an exhibit contained in the same subject should be by "see Exhibit e" or "as shown in Exhibit e," etc. References to an exhibit in another subject should be by "see Exhibit SCs-e" or "as shown in Exhibit SCs-e," etc.

8. Immediately beneath the identification block on the first page of a subject should be a brief summary of contents as shown in the example in Figure 13.2.

9. Each subject will be broken down into a number of paragraphs according to logical content. Each paragraph will be identified by a heading typed in capitals and underlined, and a paragraph number (see Figure 13.2).

10. The first two paragraphs in each subject will be "1. PURPOSE" and "2. REFERENCES." Paragraph 1 is a brief, one- or two-sentence, description of the content of the subject. Paragraph 2 will contain applicable references to other subjects or other material (e.g., company instructions or programmer's reference manuals).

11. If a further breakdown is required within a paragraph, such as in a list of items, each item must be identified by a lower-case alphabetic character.

12. The writing style will depend on the type of material presented. Specific mandatory standards must be written in an authoritarian style, breaking up the material into a list of precise statements as described in 11 above. Where general guidelines are given, narrative text presented in an instructional style may be used.

In addition to the above rules, general notes may be provided as the job progresses on such subjects as

- Standard spelling where alternatives are available
- Use of capital letters for job titles and forms, etc.

- Use of imperative and conditional expressions, and standard tenses (e.g., rules for use of "must," "should," and "will")

By this stage, therefore, the content, scope, and layout of the manual will have been determined. Work may thus begin on the development tasks.

```
                    FORMAT OF STANDARDS MANUAL


          SECTION
              Documentation Standards        1      4        1
                                          section chapter subject page
          CHAPTER
              Documentation Requirements

          SUBJECT
              Documentation Conventions


                                                        Paragraph

          Purpose                                           1
          References                                        2
          Identification Cover Page                         3
          Table of Contents                                 4
          Narrative Format                                  5
          Flowcharting Format                               6
          Table and Exhibit Formats                         7
          Glossaries                                        8



          1.  PURPOSE:  This subject defines the rules governing format for
          the routinely used elements of documentation described in other
          subjects in this Section of the Manual.

          2.  REFERENCES:

          3.  IDENTIFICATION COVER PAGE:  This page serves as the title
          page for each element of documentation, describing the document
          and specifying the desired coordination, review and approval
          cycle.
```

FIGURE 13.2 Sample Layout of Standards Manual

Development of Documentation Standards

217

DEVELOPMENT TASKS

Within the policy, scope, contents, and format definition previously agreed, development work may now commence in detail. The standards development process may be subdivided into twelve tasks as summarized in Figure 13.3. The first four tasks may be grouped together for explanatory purposes as "initial development tasks." Because the exact allocation of these tasks and the work involved is so dependent on the local environment, they are summarized briefly in list form in Figure 13.4.

We may now review the work involved in developing the actual documentation standards.

The research task is necessary to

- Provide the groundwork for development of each standard
- Determine the formal and informal practices now in effect
- Gather data for comparison of the various approaches or possible solutions
- Establish priority of needs and probability for successful implementation

In Chapter 3, a brief examination was made of the major factors influencing the type, level of content, and distribution of documentation in any working environment. It was shown that the documentation system employed would vary not only from company to company, but also from project to project within any one company. This is illustrated by the chart shown in Figure 13.5. This chart shows for each project type and by frequency of use, the relative importance of each of the control elements, i.e., quality, time, and resources, where "X" indicates most important. A further breakdown by project control points is shown in Figure 13.6. As can be seen from these examples, it is of primary importance to establish documentation standards for all types of projects. It is, of course, impracticable and undesirable to establish one mandatory level for documentation since the chosen level would either be inadequate for a "long-term development project" and too complex for a "maintenance rescue project."

One method of catering to this varied project mix is to set standards for the "long-term development project" and qualify the requirements for documentation for each other project type.

Thus, having established the project types to be covered in the manual, detailed "data gathering" and research can take place. Principally, research should include the following areas:

- Review present methods for achieving desired results
- Establish the needs and criteria that the standard must satisfy
- Investigate the various methods and procedures that can fill the needs
- Review any informal standard or method that is being used currently
- Define accountable exceptions to the standard that must be considered
- Document all available information

STANDARDS DEVELOPMENT TASKS

Task

- I. Develop Schedule
- II. Define Policies and Procedures
- III. Select Subject Sequence
- VI. Cross Reference Index
- V. Research
- VI. Subject Definition
- VII. Review with Working Committee
- VIII. First Draft Preparation
- IX. Steering Committee Coordination
- X. Final Draft Preparation
- XI. Implementation Definition
- XII. Distribution

FIGURE 13.3 Standards Development Tasks

\	Summary of Initial Development Tasks	\
Task	Purpose	Task Assignments
I. Develope Schedule	1. To plan and project manpower requirements and assignments 2. To provide control points for management review. 3. To coordinate the standards effort. 4. To anticipate and tentatively schedule the implementation of sets of standards	1. Review work to be performed in detail. 2. Determine resources required and available. 3. Establish time schedule.
II. Define Policies and Procedures	1. To verify that standards will comply with management policy and other existing procedures, departmental and divisional. 2. To resolve conflicts and eliminate duplication of effort. 3. To verify that the standards effort complies with the existing management controls.	1. Review and define external policies which may affect the technical standards. 2. Identify current internal department policies and procedures. 3. Identify and review informal procedures and practices which may affect standards development. 4. Classify all unresolved or conflicting procedures in effect. 5. Resolve all above conflicts. 6. Prepare final definition of the relationship between technical standards and all other procedures

FIGURE 13.4 Summary of Initial Development Tasks

Initial Development Tasks (cont.)		
Task	Purpose	Task Assignments
III. Select Subject Sequence	1. To provide the framework for the development of a comprehensive standard package, section by section. 2. To eliminate repetition of tasks.	1. Determine priority of development. 2. Select desired approach for subject development. 3. Determine sequence of development to eliminate overlap.
IV. Cross-Reference Index	1. To assure that standards are developed in logical groups within the limitations or restrictions of the current procedures. 2. To verify that the standards will be integrated within the manual.	1. Develop a cross-reference technique, including document format. 2. Establish the relationships of the various standards and procedures now in effect. 3. List each procedure or policy that references or affects the standards, by subject matter.

FIGURE 13.4 Continued

ANALYSIS OF TYPICAL CONTROL POINTS BY PROJECT TYPE

Control Points	Long-Term Development	Short-Term Development	Maintenance Modification	Maintenance Rescue
1. Project Selection	X		X	
2. Project Authorization	X	X		
3. Planning	X			
4. Personnel Assignment	X			
5. Estimating	X			
6. Scheduling	X	X	X	X
7. Budgeting	X		X	
8. System Study – First Stage	X			
9. System Study – Completion	X			
10. System Analysis Completion	X			
11. System Design – Data Base	X			
12. System Design – Completion	X	X		
13. Programming – Coding Completion	X	X	X	
14. Program Testing – First Stage	X	X		
15. Program Testing – Final Stage	X	X	X	X
16. System Test Plan Completion	X			
17. System Test – Interim Stage	X			
18. System Test – Completion	X	X	X	X
19. Volume Test Plan Completion	X	X		
Project Conclusion				
20. Pre-Conversion Prep. Completion	X	X		
21. Post-Implementation Audit	X	X	X	X

FIGURE 13.5 Analysis of Typical Control Points by Project Type

	Project Life and Nature				Frequency of Use		
Control Element \ Project Type	Developmental Long Term	Developmental Short Term	Maintenance Modification	Sustaining Projects and Maintenance Rescue	Recurring Runs	On-Demand Runs	One-Time Runs
Quality	Constraint	Control Element	Constraint	Control Element			
Correctness	X	X	X	X	X	X	X
Turnover-Documentation	X	X	X		X	X	
Development Doc. (historical)	X		X		X	X	
Efficiency of System/Program	X				Dependent on run time		
Time	Flexible Element	Constraint	Flexible Element	Constraint	Start Time Only		Key Item
Resources	Control Element	Flexible Element	Control Element	Flexible Element			Total Cost Control
D. P. Staff	X		X				
Equipment	X		X				
User Staff	X						

FIGURE 13.6 Analysis of Control Elements by Project Type

Development of Documentation Standards

Based on this research, a definition of the method of presentation and content of each subject may be made in a working level document.

This document can then be presented to the Working Committee. The working document should present

- Logical flow for subject presentation
- The standard(s) to be incorporated
- The scope or technical range of the standard
- The relationship to external policies and procedures that are affected
- Enforcement policy and methods (including documentation control points)

Working Committee Review and Draft Preparation

The Working Committee reviews the working document and validates the accuracy and viability of each of the proposed standards. The output is thus a finalized working document for standards development from which a draft will be prepared for submission to the Review Committee. In the review, special attention should be paid to

- Weakness or omissions in the prepared standards
- Exceptions because of special conditions
- Accuracy of technical data to be included in the final standard

Acting on the comments and discussions in the Working Committee a first draft is prepared for the Review Committee. Ideally, many of the technical points should have been validated or rejected by the Working Committee. Thus, the Review Committee should function primarily as a final quality control check, reviewing policy aspects of the prepared standards and ensuring management support for the implementation of the standards.

To enable a comprehensive review to be made, the draft should be prepared by block of subjects, forming at least one self-contained unit of information. All reference material must be prepared, including special forms and/or exhibits. To present the Review Committee with a complete overall picture of the standards, it is generally best to prepare the generalized or summary sections first and then progress to the specific standards for individual functions or documents. This can prevent much wasted time in processing Review Committee comments on the information which is to be presented before and after the specific subject(s) currently under review.

The comments made by the Review Committee should be evaluated by the Working Committee and a comprehensive critique of the findings and recommendations of the committee prepared. The proposed standards and the critique are then reviewed with the Review Committee and final revisions and modifications agreed.

Final Draft Preparation, Implementation Definition, and Distribution

After each Review Committee meeting, the first draft is updated with the agreed revisions and amendments, and the final version of each section prepared.

Concurrently with the standards development tasks, an implementation plan should be defined. In detail, this plan should include

- Identification of the methods required for the implementation of individual standards
- Assignment of responsibilities for implementation tasks
- Development of an implementation schedule

Part of the implementation plan should cover the prepared distribution of the standards, i.e.,

- The timing of the release of each section (or the complete manual)
- Distribution criteria by level of personnel affected by the standards
- A distribution check-off list (e.g., copy numbering scheme for new material and amendment distribution)

POST-IMPLEMENTATION TASKS

The standards project does not end with the issue of the manual for usage. Procedures must be formulated to review and maintain the standards. The first requirement is a good, day-to-day feedback procedure through which all users of the standards (systems analysts, programmers, operators, etc.) are encouraged to comment on the working of the standards and to suggest enhancements. The procedure for this feedback of comments should be clearly stated at the front of the manual. All comments should be considered from time to time by the Review Committee. A further procedure is needed to promulgate new and revised standards agreed by the Review Committee.

A formal review should be carried out after the standards have been in use for an appropriate period of time, for example, after two or three systems have been completely documented and implemented. All staff are consulted as to the efficiency and effectiveness of the standards and a report prepared for the Review Committee, who will review the report and implement the appropriate changes. From time to time thereafter, further reviews are carried out in addition to the general feedback procedures.

SUMMARY

1. This chapter has presented some rules and guidelines for the preparation of documentation standards. However, it was stated a documentation standards project is usually a subject of a data processing standards program, including at least methods standards, and possibly performance standards.

2. Documentation standards development should be primarily a process of adaption rather than origination.

3. The documentation standards development program can only succeed with full management backing.

4. The output from the standards development program should be

- A Manual of Documentation Standards
- A maintenance and support program
- A training and implementation scheme

5. The development work may be divided into three distinct phases:

- Preparatory
- Development
- Post implementation

6. Each of the tasks within these three phases was broken down and discussed.

APPENDIXES

APPENDIX A

Indexed Glossary of Forms

This appendix presents a checklist of documentation in the form of an indexed glossary. Each entry shows

Document: the document name.

Reference: the major reference in the book by page number.

Prepared by

Assisted by   an example job function.

Approved by

Note, however, that the project leader is assumed to approve all documentation in addition to the functions shown.

Document	Reference	Prepared by *Systems Folder*	Assisted by	Approved by
1. User Request	19	Systems Analyst/Proponent	Proponent/Systems Analyst	Proponent
2. Systems Proposal	19		Proponent	
3. Analytical Reports	27	Project Leader/Senior Systems Analyst	Proponent	Proponent and appropriate DP management
4. Design Requirements Statement	30	Project Leader and Systems Analyst	Job/System Analysts	Proponent and DP Technical Specialists
5. Systems Summary	54	Systems Analyst	Programming Function	Programming Function
6. File Specifications	64	Systems Analyst	Programming Function	Programming Function/Proponent
7. Transaction (input) Specifications	75	Systems Analyst	Programming Function	Programming Function/Proponent
8. Output Specifications	80	Systems Analyst	Proponent	Programming Function/Proponent
9. Segment (Processing) Specification	64	Systems Analyst	Programming Function	Programming Function/Proponent
10. Systems Test Plan	88	Systems Analyst		Project Leader/Proponent
11. Programming Specifications	85	Systems Analyst		Programming Function

Document	Reference	Prepared by	Assisted by	Approved by
		Program Folders (In Program Number Sequence)		
12. Programming Description	96	Systems Analyst		Programming Function
13. Data Specification	98	As for file, input and output specs		Systems Analyst or Lead Programmer
14. Program Logic Specification	98	Programmer		Lead Programmer
15. Listings	98	Programmer		
16. Program Test Plan	100	Programmer		Systems Analyst or Lead Programmer
		Operation Folder		
17. Program Test Instructions (In Program Number Sequence)	105	Programmer		Operations Function
18. Program Operating Instructions (In Program Number Sequence)	110	Systems Analyst and Programmers		Operations Function
19. Input Collection and Preparation Instruction	109	Systems Analyst		Point of Preparation or Collection and DP Operation

231

Document	Reference	Prepared by	Assisted by	Approved by
		Operation Folder		
20. Input Control Instructions	112	Systems Analyst		Point of Preparation or Collection and DP Operation
21. Output Review and Distribution Instruction	112	Systems Analyst		Operations Functions
22. Output Control Instructions	112	Systems Analyst		Customer or Appropriate Directorate Responsible for Subject Matter Area
		Interim Systems Documentation		
23. Organization Charts	35	Systems Analyst		All relevant customers (users)
24. Functional/Document Chart	40			
25. Data Analysis Chart/Matrix	47			
26. System Description	48			

APPENDIX B

System Documentation Example-Composite Descriptive Forms*

This appendix describes a technique which uses one basic form to specify all information about a file, an input, or an output report. (Note that an "output" file retained in the system is described on a file form.) There is, of course, the sheer practicality of designing a form of usable physical size. However, experience has shown that if more space is needed, continuation sheets can be used quite successfully, provided additional sheets are appended and cross-referenced to the form.

The principle of this technique is to produce one description which can be used by users, programming, and operations. Note that this requires that the users have some knowledge and experience of computer systems. The report descriptions are *not* intended to replace report samples which a user will review for approval; rather, they should be used to support the samples.

Each of the forms

- Input Description Form
- File Description Form
- Report Form

is reviewed below by

- Presenting a sample of the form and describing the basic content of the form
- Describing each of the entries in detail
- Discussing special points of usage

---

*This technique is based on material drawn from the Manual of Data Processing Standards of Standard Telephones and Cables Limited, gratefully used by permission.

INPUT OR FILE

Input Origin			
Record Name	⑤		
From (Title/Dept)	⑥		
Frequency	⑦		
Take-on volumes (average/peak)	⑧		
Normal volumes (average/peak)	⑨		
Record size (average/max)	⑩		
Input Medium/Device	⑪		
Conversion method	⑫		
Code	⑬		

File Size		
Number of Records	Take-on	Normal
Ave		
Peak		
Record Size Ave		
Peak		
% Hit Rate		
% Change		
% Growth		

Position	Correlation	Level	Field Code Names
⑲	⑱	⑳	㉑

File Sequence	
Key Fields Major	
Minor	⑭

Cycling & Security Procedures
⑮

Programs using File			
Program No.	R_W	Program No.	R_W
		⑯	

File Description	
Prepared by ⑰	Approved by

FIGURE B-1 Sample Input Description Form

DESCRIPTION FORM

File Storage Details	
Medium	
Number of volumes	
Device model no.	
Number of drives	
Blocking factor	

Identification	
File No.	①
File Title	②
Page No.	of
Brief Description	③
Date	④

FIELD DESCRIPTION

Format & Size	Bytes Words	Occur	V	Ldg Zero	Sign	Further Description (including details of validity checks to be applied on input).
㉒	㉓	㉔	㉕	㉖	㉗	㉘

FIGURE B-1 Continued

INPUT DESCRIPTION FORM

Sample and Basic Content

The form is shown in Figure B-1. Note that the same printed form is used for both input and file description. When used as an Input Description Form the boxes "File Storage Details" and "File Size" are not used. The form specifies:

- Identification Data
- Field Content Data
- Statistical Information
- Retention and Security Requirements
- Input Preparation Requirements

The circled entries are shown for explanatory purposes only. The basic content of the form is described below.

Circled Nos. in Figure B-1	Entries
1 to 4	Basic identification
5 to 13	Descriptions of the origination and preparation of the input, and record size, frequency, and volume data. Each input type is assigned a record name (5), and entries 6 to 13 in a vertical column are completed for each input type.
14 and 15	The sequence of the input (if any) and the retention requirements for original documents and media.
16	A list of those programs which use the prime input.
17	Housekeeping entries recording by signature the persons who have prepared and approved the form.
18 to 28	These columns are used to identify each data element (e.g., record and field) existing in an input. Entries must be made according to a COBOL-type level structure where level 01 corresponds to a record. If more than one type of record exists in an input, each record type should be shown. Record descriptions should be separated by a bold horizontal line.

Detailed Entries

Figure B-2 describes the individual entries. The circled numbers on Figure B-1 are cross-referenced to the entry list in Figure B-2.

CIRCLED ENTRIES ON FIGURE B-1	
1 A local code which is a unique number assigned to the input.	12 The means by which the input is converted to a machine-sensible form.
2 A brief English language title of the input.	13 The code (e.g., card or paper punching code) of the input medium.
3 A brief description of the input in non-technical terms.	14 Where the input is required to be in a particular sequence the sort key fields must be specified in this box. In other cases the word "RANDOM" must be specified.
4 The date on which the Input Description Form was completed.	
5 The record name identifying each record name.	15 The retention time and manner of authorization for disposal of the source documents (if any) or coded input media.
6 The source of the record type, specified by either title of person or department originating the input. Names of persons must not be used.	
	16 The numbers of all programs using the input.
7 The frequency at which the record type is processed (e.g., daily or weekly).	17 The signatures of systems designer and/or job analyst.
8 The volume of input records that must initially be processed during the conversion process to the new system.	18 This column may be used for correlation purposes, e.g., to indicate the untimate use of the data.
	19 The position of the start of the data element in a record specified by column number or character.
9 The estimated volume of input records during actual system running. It is the number of records per day, week or period, etc. as specified under "Frequency."	20 The level number as described on page 76.
	21 The COBOL (or other preferred language) name for the date element should be entered in this column. The name should not be more than 8 characters.
10 The size of the record specifying the maximum and, for variable length records, average record size.	
11 The medium used for the input, e.g., paper tape, encoded document, transmission keyboard, must be entered here.	22 A code is entered in this column to indicate the format and size of the data item. The codes used are:

FIGURE B-2 Summary of Contents of Input Description Form

CIRCLED ENTRIES ON FIGURE B-1

(22)
- A — alphanumeric (characters)
- B — binary (bits)
- C — packed decimal (digits)
- D — decimal (digits)
- E — long precision floating point (double words)
- F — short precision floating point (words)
- P — PICTURE

The code is followed by a number in brackets indicating the number of digits or characters. Decimal or binary codes may be followed by two numbers separated by a period: the second number indicates the number of digits following the assumed decimal or binary point. Examples of the codes are:

- A (25) — a 25 character alphnumeric field
- B (32) — a 32 bit binary number
- C (8.2) — a 10 digit packed dec decimal number including 2 digits to the right of the decimal point
- D (5) — a 5 digit unpacked decimal number

The code P is used for data whose format cannot easily be described with the codes above. Following the P any valid COBOL or LP1 picture may be written enclosed in quotation marks.

23. This field is not applicable for prime input descriptions.

24. This column must be completed for any data field which may occur more than once. The maximum number of occurences is entered.

25. The letter 'V' is entered in this column if the number of occurences is variable.

26. Presence of leading zeros exist in the input field.

27. A code should be entered to indicate the existence and position of an operational sign. A suggested code is:
    - L — sign in left hand digit position
    - LO — sign as overpunch in left hand digit position
    - R — sign as right hand digit position
    - RO — sign as overpunch in right hand digit position
    - NS — not signed

28. Any other relevant information may be written in this column.

FIGURE B-2 Continued

Appendix B 239

Comments

The Input Description form may be supplemented by sample layouts. When designing cards and documents for input to the computer system it must always be remembered that one of the aims of the computer-based data processing is to eliminate tedious clerical procedures. Layouts should always be designed first for ease of user completion, secondly for ease of punching, and last for ease of computer processing.

The layout of input medium should be drawn on card layouts or file layout forms supplied by the manufacturer.

FILE DESCRIPTION FORM

Sample and Basic Content

The form is shown in Figure B-3. When used as a File Description Form the "Input Origin" box is not used. The form is the definitive description of a file and shows:

- Identification Data
- Field Content Data
- Statistical Information (sizes, hit rates, volumes, etc.)
- File Storage Device Characteristics
- Cycling and Security Requirements

The basic content of the form is described below:

Circled Nos. in Figure B-3	Entries
1 to 4	Basic identification entries
5 to 9	Definition of the file storage device to be used.
10 to 15	File size and hit-rate statistics, and file sequence.
16	Cycling and security requirements for the file.
17	List of programs which use the file.
18	Housekeeping entries, recording by signature the persons who have prepared and approved the form.
19 to 29	These columns are used to identify each data element (e.g., record and field) in a file. Entries must be made according to a COBOL-type level structure where level 01 corresponds to a record. If more than one type of record exists in a file, each record type should be shown. Record descriptions should be separated by a bold horizontal line.

INPUT OR FILE

Input Origin			
Record Name			
From (Title/Dept)			
Frequency			
Take-on volumes (average/peak)			
Normal volumes (average/peak)			
Record size (average/max)			
Input Medium/Device			
Conversion method			
Code			

File Size

Number of Records		Take-on	Normal
	Ave	⑩	
	Peak		
Record Size	Ave	⑪	
	Peak		
% Hit Rate		⑫	
% Change		⑬	
% Growth		⑭	

File Sequence

Key Fields	Major	⑮
	Minor	

Cycling & Security Procedures

⑯

Programs using File

Program No.	R_W	Program No.	R_W
		⑰	

File Description

Prepared by ⑱ Approved by

Position	Correlation	Level	Field Code Names
⑲	⑳		㉒

FIGURE B-3 Sample File Description Form

DESCRIPTION FORM

File Storage Details	
Medium	⑤
Number of volumes	⑥
Device model no.	⑦
Number of drives	⑧
Blocking factor	⑨

Identification	
File No.	①
File Title	②
Page No.	of
Brief Description	③
Date	④

FIELD DESCRIPTION

Format & Size	Bytes Words	Occur	V	Ldg Zero	Sign	Further Description (including details of validity checks to be applied on input).
㉓	㉔	㉕	㉖	㉗	㉘	㉙

FIGURE B-3 Continued

241

Detailed Entries

Figure B-4 describes the individual entries. The circled numbers on Figure B-3 are cross-referenced to the entry list in Figure B-4.

CIRCLED ENTRIES ON FIGURE B-3	
1 A unique file identification number assigned to the file.	13 This is the rate of change of indicative information on the file over a specified period of time. For example, "20% per month" indicates that 20% of the records are amended by applying new indicative information in a month.
2 A brief English language title of the file	
3 A brief description of the file in non-technical terms.	
4 The date on which the File Description Form was completed.	
5 The file storage medium, e.g., disc or tape.	14 This is the net growth rate of the file (total number of records added – number of replaced deletions) as a percentage of total number of records over a specified period of time.
6 This is the estimated number of volumes (discs or tapes) used to hold the file. Where the file size	
7 is variable, minimum and maximum figures should be given.	15 Where the file is required to be in a particular sequence, the sort key fields must be specified in this box. In other cases, 'RANDOM' should be specified. Where the file may be held in more than one sequence, the sequence required for each program should be specified.
7 The device model number on which the file is to be held.	
8 The number of drives that must be allocated to the file when it is held on-line.	
9 The blocking factor for the file when stored on the stated device.	16 The cycling procedure and security requirements for this file.
10 The number of records in the file under average and peak conditions. The number of records at file take-on (i.e., file conversion) and at normal run time must be stated.	17 A list of all programs using the file, stating whether it is read and/or written.
	18 The signature of systems designer and/or job analyst.
11 The record size defined in characters or words. Fixed length record sizes must be entered under 'MAX' and an 'F' must be written under 'AVE'.	19 This column may be used for correlation purposes, e.g., to indicate the ultimate use of the data.
12 The percentage of records in the file that are matched by input records during run. This should be shown by record type within program.	20 The position of the start of the data element in a record specified by character position.
	21 This is the level number in text.

FIGURE B-4 Summary of Contents of File Description Form

Appendix B 243

Comments

In addition to the specification of the file on the File Description Form, a detailed layout of the file must be shown on a File Layout Form. Suitable forms for this purpose are provided by the computer manufacturers. The

CIRCLED ENTRIES ON FIGURE B-3	
22 The COBOL (or other preferred language) name for the data element should be entered in this column. The name should not be more than 8 characters.	The code P is used for data whose format cannot easily be described with the codes above. Following the P any valid COBOL or PL1 picture may be written enclosed in quotation marks.

23 A code is entered in this column to indicate the format and size of the data item. The codes used are:
  A – alphanumeric (characters)
  B – binary (bits)
  C – packed decimal (digits)
  D – decimal (digits)
  E – long precision floating point (double words)
  F – short precision floating point (words)
  P – PICTURE
 	
The code is followed by a number in brackets indicating the number of digits or characters. Decimal or binary codes may be followed by two numbers separated by a period; the second number indicates the number of digits following the assumed decimal or binary point. Examples of the codes are:
  A (25) – a 25 character alphanumeric field
  B (32) – a 32 bit binary number
  C (8.2) – a 10 digit packed decimal number including 2 digits to the right of the decimal point
  D (5) – a 5 digit unpacked decimal number
	24 In cases where the number of bytes (IBM 360) or words (ICT 1900) to be occupied by the data field is not clear from the 'Format and Size' entry, the size in words or bytes should be stated here.
	
	25 This column must be completed for any data field which may occur more than once. The maximum number of occurances is entered.
	
	26 The letter 'V' is entered in this column if the number of occurences is varaible.
	
	27 The presence of leading zeros in the field.
	
	28 A code should be entered here to indicate the existence and position of an operational sign. A suggested code is:
	  A (25) – a 25 character alphanumeric field
	  B (32) – a 32 bit binary number
	  C (8.2) – a 10 digit packed decimal number including 2 digits to the right of the decimal point
	  D (5) – a 5 digit unpacked decimal number
	
	29 Any other relevant information may be written in this column.

FIGURE B-4 Continued

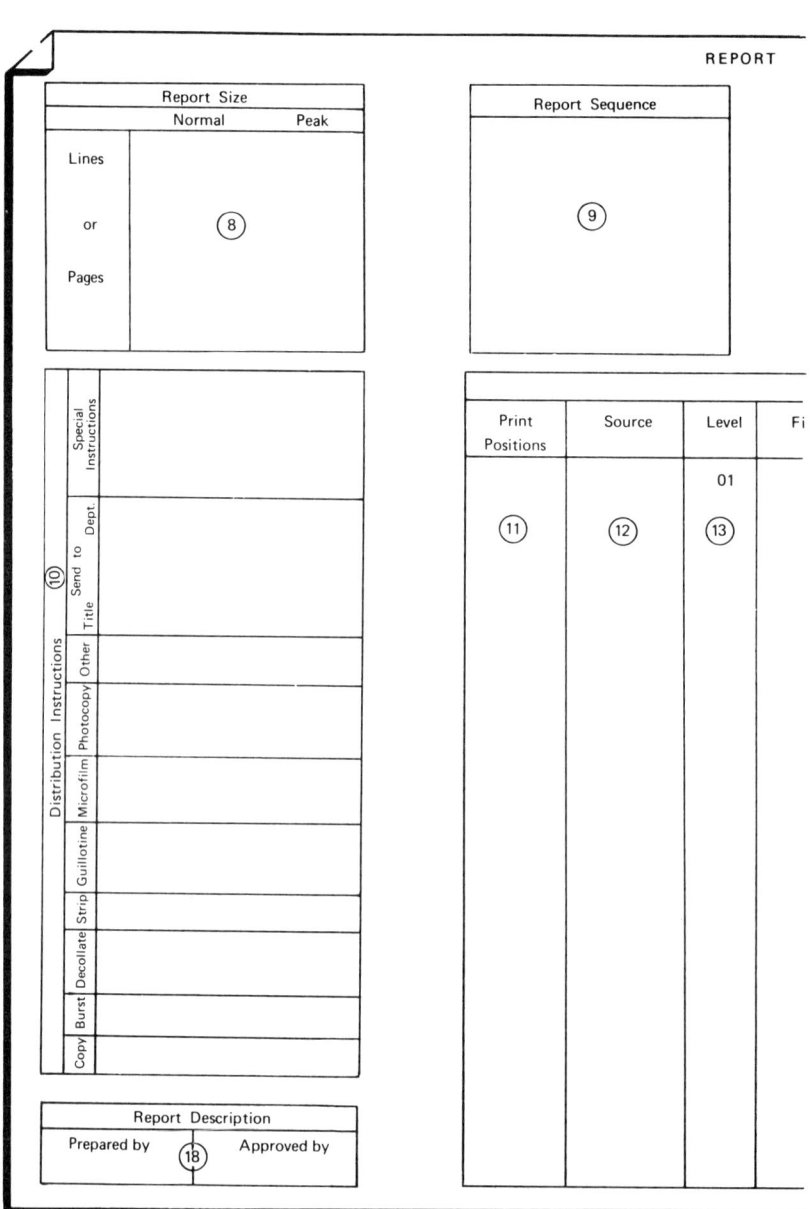

FIGURE B-5 Sample Report Description Form

DESCRIPTION FORM

Format Information	
Staty · Type	⑦
Format Tape No.	⑥
Page Numbering System	⑤

Identification	
Report No.	①
Title	②
Page No.	of
Brief Description	③
Date	④

FIELD DESCRIPTION

eld Code Names	Format & Size	Editing Requirements	Further Description
⑭	⑮	⑯	⑰

FIGURE B-5 Continued

layout must include labels, tape marks, and any special software data fields, such as block length records, as well as all the data fields. Where a file is held on a direct-access device, a File Map should be prepared to define the layout of the file on a device, e.g., the start/end limits of the file, the index areas, and the overflow areas.

REPORT FORM

Samples and Basic Content

All reports produced in a system are defined by means of a

- Report Description Form (Figure B-5)
- Report Layout
- Report Production Form (Figure B-7)

The Report Description Form defines the relevant data elements, distribution data, report sequence, and size. The Report Layout is an example of the printed form. The Report Production Form specifies the conditions under which records (lines) are printed, spacing between lines, and so on. These documents will be the basis for the communication of information about the report to the users, programmers, and operations personnel.

Each report produced in a system must be defined by means of a *Report Description Form,* as shown in Figure B-5. The report comprises

- Identification Data
- Field Content Data
- Distribution Instructions
- Report Size and Sequence Information

The main part of the form is a Field Description (circled numbers 11 to 17, Figure B-5). These columns are used to identify each data element existing in a report. Entries must be made according to a COBOL-type level structure where level 01 corresponds to a record. If more than one record type exists in an output, each record type should be shown. Record descriptions should be separated by a bold horizontal line.

Figure B-6 gives brief notes on individual entries on the form.

A detailed layout of each report must be drawn on a *Report Layout* sheet as supplied by the manufacturer. If the report is to be printed on preprinted stationery, a sample of the form should be attached to the layout sheet and the preprinted portion pasted over the layout sheet. Information which results from processing should be indicated by Xs written in the appropriate print position. The maximum field sizes for variable data should be shown.

Appendix B 247

Constant information, such as headings, fixed signs, etc., should be printed neatly in the required print positions.

A *Report Production Form* as shown in Figure B-7 must be completed for each report. For each record (i.e., line) defined by a level 01 entry on the Report Description Form, this schedule specifies the conditions governing the production of the record and the vertical spacing required before printing it.

CIRCLED ENTRIES ON FIGURE B-5

1	A unique report identification number.
2	A brief English language title of the report.
3	A brief description of the report in non-technical terms.
4	The date on which the Report Description Form was prepared.
5	The page numbering method required on the report.
6,7	The stationery type and format tape numbers as defined by local standards.
8	The anticipated size of the report in lines and/or pages.
9	The sequence in which the records are printed.
10	Distribution instructions should be entered here.
11	This column is used to specify where on the line the data is to be printed.
12	The source of the data should be stated here. The entry should show whether the data field is taken directly from an input or a file, or is the result of calculation. The name of the file or input and record should be stated. For example, F-SC121M MFSTK INV indicates that the data comes direct from the record called MFSTKINV on file SC 121 M.
13	The COBOL (or other preferred language) name for the data element should be entered in this column. The name should not be more than 8 characters.
14	This the level number as previous in text.
15	A code is entered in this column to indicate the format and size of the data item. The codes used are:
	A – alphanumeric (characters)
	B – binary (bits)
	C – packed decimal (digits)

D – decimal (digits)

E – long precision floating point (double words)

F – short precision floating point (words)

The code is followed by a number in brackets indicating the number of digits or characters. Decimal or binary codes may be followed by two numbers separated by a period; the second number indicates the number of digits following the assumed decimal or binary point. Examples of the codes are:

A (25) – a 25 character alphanumeric field

B (32) – a 32 bit binary number

C (8.2) – a 10 digit packed decimal number including 2 digits to the right of the decimal point

D (5) – a digit unpacked decimal number

The code P is used for data whose format cannot easily be described with the codes above. Following the P any valid COBOL or PL1 picture may be written enclosed in quotation marks.

16 The systems disigner must specify the editing requirements in detail. Items to be specified may include:

zero suppresion,

insertion of punctuation symbols,

insertion of currency symbols, and

cheque protection characters.

17 This column is used for any other information.

18 The signature of the systems designer and/or job analyst.

FIGURE B-6 Summary of Contents of Report Description Form

Record Name	Conditions governing the production of this report line.	Spacing before this line	
		Normal	H.O.F.

Form header:
REPORT PRODUCTION FORM
Form Prepared by............................ Report Number....................
Date.............................

FIGURE B-7 Sample Report Production Form

Useful References

Alexander, G. "Control of Program Changes." *Data Management.* December 1968, pp. 35-36.

ANSI. *American National Standard X3.5-1970 Flowchart Symbols and Their Usage in Information Processing.* New York: American National Standards Institute, 1971.

Brandon, D. *Management Standards for Data Processing.* New York: Van Nostrand, 1963.

Brandon, D., and Gray, M. *Project Control Standards.* Philadelphia: Auerbach, 1970.

Chapin, N. "Program Documentation: The Valuable Burden." *Software Age,* vol. 2, no. 4, May 1968, pp. 24-26, 28-30.

———. "Perspective on Flowcharting Packages." *Computers and Automation,* vol. 20, no. 3, March 1971, pp. 16-19, 26.

———. *Flowcharts,* Philadelphia: Auerbach, 1971.

———. "Flowchart Packages and the ANSI Standard." *Datamation,* vol. 18, no. 9, September 1972, pp. 48-53.

Computer Management. "Standards for Project Control," vol. 6, no. 2, p. 66.

EDP Analyser. "The Programmer Operations Interface," vol. 9, no. 4, April 1971, pp. 1-14.

EDP Analyser. "That Maintenance 'Iceberg'," vol. 10, no. 19, October 1972, pp. 1-14.

Foulds, G. "How to Automate the Essential Flowchart." *Computer Weekly,* February 17, 1972, p. 6.

Harris, G. M. "FLOWRITE—a Computer-Generated Flowchart Technique of the NCR Century." *Computer Bulletin,* vol. 12, no. 8, December 1968, pp. 293-300

Howarth, R.J., and Lim, A.L. "An Approach to Program Documentation." *Computer Bulletin,* vol. 13, no. 8, August 1969, pp. 291-295.

Jones, G.E. "The Impact of Standards." *Computers and Automation,* vol. 18, no. 5, May 1969, pp. 38-39.

Katzenelson, J. "Documentation and the Management of a Software Project— A Case Study." *Software, Practise and Experience,* April-June 1971, pp. 147-157.

Lenher, J. *Flowcharting: An Introductory Text and Workbook.* Philadelphia: Auerbach, 1971.

London, K. *Decision Tables.* Philadelphia: Auerbach, 1972.

Maynard, J. "The Value of Software Aids." *Computer Management,* August 1972, pp. 32 and 34.

Menkus, B. "Defining Adequate Systems Documentation." *Journal of Systems Management,* vol. 21, no. 12, December 1970, pp. 16-21.

Michener, J. L. "The Flowchart Programming Language System," *Simulation,* vol. 16, no. 1, January 1971, pp. 42-44.

Morris, D. (et al.) "Flowcoder." *Computer Journal,* vol. 14, no. 3, August 1971, pp. 221-223.

Navalta, G. M. "Adapting the Use of Documentation." *Journal of Systems Management,* vol. 22, no. 5, May 1971, pp. 39-41.

Riggs, B. "Computer Systems Maintenance." *Datamation,* November 1969, pp. 227, 231-232.

Roberts, K. V. "The Readability of Computer Programs." *The Computer Bulletin,* vol. 19, no. 4, March 1967, pp. 17-24.

Stamper, R. "Computer Aids in Systems Analysis." *Computer Weekly International,* no. 14, July 12, 1971, p. 18.

Van Duyn, J. *Documentation Manual.* Philadelphia: Auerbach, 1972.

Welke, L. (Ed.). *How to Buy Proprietary Software Products.* International Computer Programs, Inc., Indianapolis, Ind.: 1970.

Wigg, J. D. "COBOL Coding Standards." *Computer Bulletin,* vol. 15, no. 7, July 1971, pp. 249-252.

Index

Analytical documentation 6-7
  description 21-31
  scope 19-21
Analytical report
  alternative to systems proposal 20-21
  checkpoint 195
  contents 27-29
Checkpoints 193-197
Communication
  inter-task/phase, importance 2
  paths 10
  programming 95
  with users 5
Conditional logic
  basic methods for recording 122-134
  relevance 121-122
Data analysis charts/matrices 47-48, 49-50
Data documenters 171-177
Decisions tables 127-128
  advantages 132-133
  programming 133-134
  systems specification standards 140, 145-147
Design requirements statement
  checkpoint 195
  contents 30-31
  preparation 27

purpose 21, 27
Documentation
  control (definition) 1
  development (definition) 1
  factors determining usage 10
  preparation 14
  project control 193-197
  purposes 1-6
  types 6-8
  see also Library; Maintenance; Standards
File specifications 64
  contents 67-75
  use of file description forms 239-246
Flowcharts
  complex logic 123-124
  detail (by software aids) 149-158
  high-level (by software aids) 166
  operation instructions 108, 178
  pros and cons of automatically produced 169-171
  standards for programming 134-140
  system 56-61
Function/document flowcharts 40-47
Historical reference 4

Input specifications: *see* Transaction specifications
Instructional reference   5
Job functions   12-13, 52
Library
  organization and responsibilities   198-205
  security   205-206
Maintenance
  documentation   4, 206-207
  staff turnover   2
Management aids   8
  contents   115-117
  scope   114-115
Management summaries   115
Narrative   121-123
Operations documentation   7
  contents   105-112
  scope   105
Operations documenters   177-182
Organization charts   35-40
Output specifications
  contents   81-85
  definition   80
  report form use   246-248
Processing specifications   85-87
Program documentation   7
  alternative approaches   101-104
  scope   94
  traditional approach   96-101
Program documenters   149
  examples   149-158
  pros and cons of flowcharters   168-171
  reference lists   158, 161-166
Program manual
  alternatives   101-104
  contents   96-101
  general purpose software   103-104, 187
Program specifications: *see* Processing specifications

Program test instructions   105
Programming
  steps   95
  decision tables   133-134
  see also Program documentation
Project
  characteristics and documentation   11-12, 217
  checkpoints   193, 195-197
  control   3, 5, 193-197
  investigation and analysis   32-34
  phases and tasks   14, 193-195
  programming tasks   95
  standards development   211-213
Quality control   3
  see also Checkpoints
Reference manuals   115-116
Security   205-206
Segment specification   64, 85
Software
  development and use   183-185
  documentation   185-189
  documentation aids (definition)   148
  documentation library functions   187
  impact on program documentation   102-103
  impact on standards   13-14
Standards
  corporate environment   12
  developmental tasks   210-225
  logic representation   122, 134
  management commitment   10-11, 209-210
  manual   213-217
  technical environment   13-14
  universiality   209
System description   48-49
System documentation   7
System life   11

Index

contents 50-93
interim 32-50
scope 32
System operating instructions 106-112
Systems proposal
  checkpoint 195
  contents 23-27
  preparation 20
  purpose 19, 22
System specification
  checkpoints 196
  composite description forms 92
  input to programming 94
  presentation 53
  problems 51-53
  scope 50-51
  summary of contents 51
  systems summary 54-64

see also File specifications; Transaction specifications; Output specifications; Processing specifications; Systems test plan
Systems test plan 88-92, 196
Training manuals 116
Transaction specifications 75-80
  input description form 233, 236-239
User aids 8
  contents 115-117
  scope 114
User operating instructions 117
User request
  checkpoints 195
  contents 22
  preparation 20-21
  purpose 19

QA
76
L574
1974

MAR 25 1974